SHAKESPEARE'S CHRISTIANITY

Shakespeare's Christianity

Catholic-Protestant Presence in *Julius Caesar, Hamlet,* and *Macbeth*

Beatrice Batson, Editor

© 2006 by Baylor University Press
Waco, Texas 76798
All Rights Reserved. No part of this publication may be reproduced, stored in a retrieval system, or transmitted, in any form or by any means, electronic, mechanical, photocopying, recording or otherwise, without the prior permission in writing of Baylor University Press.

Scripture quotations are from the New Revised Standard Version Bible, copyright 1989, Division of Christian Education of the National Council of the Churches of Christ in the United States of America. Used by permission. All rights reserved.

Book Design by Helen Lasseter
Cover Design by David Alcorn, Alcorn Publication Design

Chapter 2 originally appeared as chapter 23 in *The Bible in English*, edited by David Daniell (New Haven: Yale University Press, 2003). Reprinted by permission of Yale University Press.
Chapter 5 originally appeared in *Christianity and Literature* 52.3 (2003): 307–24. Used by permission.
Chapter 7 originally appeared in *Cahiers Élisabéthains* 64 (2003): 19–28. Used by permission.

Library of Congress Cataloging-in-Publication Data

Shakespeare's Christianity : Catholic and Protestant presence in Julius Caesar, Hamlet, and Macbeth / Beatrice Batson, editor.
   p. cm.
 Includes bibliographical references (p.).
 ISBN 978-1-932792-36-2 (pbk. : alk. paper)
 1. Shakespeare, William, 1564-1616--Religion. 2. Shakespeare, William, 1564-1616. Julius Caesar. 3. Shakespeare, William, 1564-1616. Hamlet. 4. Shakespeare, William, 1564-1616. Macbeth. 5. Catholic Church--In literature. 6. Protestantism and literature--History--16th century. 7. Protestantism and literature--History--17th century. I. Batson, E. Beatrice.

PR3011.S49 2006
822.3'3--dc22
                            2006027494

For the staff of
Archives and Special Collections
at Wheaton College

Contents

Acknowledgments		ix
Preface		xi
1	Meta-drama in *Hamlet* and *Macbeth* Peter Milward, SJ	1
2	Explorers of the Revelation: Spenser and Shakespeare David Daniell	19
3	The Problem of Self-Love in Shakespeare's Tragedies and in Renaissance and Reformation Theology Robert Lanier Reid	35
4	"I Could Not Say 'Amen'": Prayer and Providence in *Macbeth* Robert S. Miola	57
5	*Hamlet* and Protestant Aural Theater Grace Tiffany	73
6	Providence in *Julius Caesar* John W. Mahon	91
7	Cobbling Souls in Shakespeare's *Julius Caesar* Maurice Hunt	111
Notes		131
Bibliography		159
Contributors		175

Acknowledgments

As editor of the essays, I wish to express personal thanks to all Shakespearean scholars who contributed to this volume. I also wish to thank David Malone, Head of Special Collections, David Osielski and Keith Call, both members of the staff of Special Collections who worked long and diligently before and during the 2003 Shakespeare Institute when these essays, with one exception, were first presented. Special gratitude goes to Keith Call for his immeasurable help as editorial assistant and for assuming additional responsibilities in preparing the papers for publication.

Sincere gratitude goes to Yale University Press for permitting us to include one chapter, "Explorers of the Revelation," from David Daniell's book, *The Bible in English* (New Haven: Yale University Press, 2003). The chapter appears in this volume as the author wrote it and as Yale editors edited it. Although Maurice Hunt and Grace Tiffany gave their papers first as lectures at the 2003 Shakespeare Institute, both scholars sent them to journals for publication before we prepared this manuscript. Therefore, we offer our thanks to the editors of *Cahiers Élisabéthains* for kindly giving us permission to include Maurice Hunt's essay, "Cobbling Souls in Shakespeare's *Julius Caesar*," which first appeared in *Cahiers Élisabéthains* 64 (2003): 19–28. We also express our deepest gratitude to coeditors of *Christianity and Literature* for granting permission to publish Grace Tiffany's paper, "*Hamlet* and Protestant Aural Theater" in *Christianity and Literature* 52.3 (2003): 307–24.

I should surely like to acknowledge the debt I owe to various editors of Baylor University Press for their invaluable help and for their patience with my many queries. I also express my appreciation for their discerning suggestions.

Preface

The study of the Christian dimension of Shakespeare's plays has had a long history, so the issue is not whether there is a Christian aspect to his works, but how this feature functions in the thought and language of the dramas. As early as the eighteenth century both Catholic and Protestant writers have expressed their points of view, and for several decades the subject of Shakespeare's embodiment of Protestant and Catholic doctrine, rituals and motifs has been at the heart of a hotbed of scholarly interest, especially with a distinct focus on Shakespeare's personal belief. Was he Catholic or Protestant? Readers interested in this book are well aware of the scores of books and essays that have come from the press, declaring definite influences of both Catholicism and Protestantism.

This volume enters the discussion and/or controversy of Catholic-Protestant presence in Shakespeare. The book has not as its focus the question of whether Shakespeare's personal beliefs were either Catholic or Protestant but rather addresses the presence and function of Protestant and Catholic thinking in three of Shakespeare's tragedies. By the term "presence," we mean doctrines, sacred ritual, tradition, biblical primacy, or conviction on various topics, such as prayer, free will, predestination, intercessory prayer, providence, images, faith, and other subjects. Included also are the religious struggles and conflicts of the Elizabethan era. Receiving, therefore, special scrutiny in this volume are allusions to the presence of both Catholicism and Protestantism. This does not include at all any attempt to prove whether Shakespeare was a Protestant or Catholic in his personal beliefs. It seems clear, as David Daniell states, that Shakespeare's plays declare allegiance to neither faith to the exclusion of the other. The three selected tragedies for this study are *Julius Caesar, Macbeth* and *Hamlet*. To be sure, other dramas might well have depicted more clearly and more intensely religious thinking or religious characters, especially dramas like *Measure for Measure* with its emphasis on justice and mercy, *Henry VIII*, which dramatically addresses the religious battle between Catholics and Protestants, and even *Twelfth Night* with its various epiphanies. Yet, the three chosen tragedies show distinct dissimilarities in tone, subject and thought, as well as in their depiction of a Catholic or Protestant presence. On occasion, allusions to both Catholicism and Protestantism will occur. One drama may abound in Catholic references, another in Protestant.

That the writers in this volume will provoke disagreement is incontrovertible; that each author will see some evidence of a Catholic or Protestant presence (or both) is undoubtedly equally true. Whatever the findings of the authors on the selected dramas may be, it is unquestionably true that the various allusions to Christian teaching indicate a dramatist interested in religious issues.

Peter Milward focuses on what he calls "Meta-drama in *Hamlet* and *Macbeth*." He sees the word as similar to Aristotle's use of it in the sense of what comes "after physics," or "by way of a deeper penetration into the causes of the things discussed in physics, or the philosophy of nature." There is also a meta-drama that is implicit in words and actions which spectators observe on the stage even though this may not be apparent either to the audience, the reader, or the scholar. The well-known "to be or not to be" in Hamlet's soliloquy, in Milward's judgment, belongs not simply to a prince in eleventh-century Denmark, but also to "Shakespeare and his fellow Catholics in Elizabethan England." These words underscore his strong conviction that Shakespeare was a Catholic in his personal belief and felt the suffering of persecuted Catholics.

He next turns to the drama beyond the drama in *Macbeth* and concludes that the play unfolds the Christian mystery of the passion, death and resurrection of Christ. In his words this "companion play to *Hamlet*" also demonstrates the reenactment of the Christian mystery in the existing conditions, especially the flight of persecuted Catholics, of Elizabethan and Jacobean England.

Following Milward's study is an opposite viewpoint. David Daniell's chapter "Explorers of the Revelation: Spenser and Shakespeare," from his book *The Bible in English* is practically a complete reversal of the previous position. Both Spenser and Shakespeare wrote at a time of daunting religious and cultural differences; yet, Daniell's position on the two authors' religious orientation is unmistakably clear: they were Protestant. When he discusses Spenser's poetry, he spends a large section on the Protestant characteristics of various poems, and with regret states that "critics of *The Shepherd's Calender* have been squeamish in understanding that Spenser was a fully Protestant writer."

In his study of Shakespeare, Daniell recognizes a dramatist who is both "learned and thoughtful" and one whose drama and poetry embrace "multiplicity of sources, interests—and of levels of reading"; that Shakespeare also knew the Bible is obvious from his many quotations from less familiar sections. In his judgment, both *Julius Caesar* and *Hamlet*, written close together in 1599 and 1600, are in part Calvinist plays. Never does Daniell deny the religious struggle and its horrible consequences, but he strongly believes that for all of his life, Shakespeare lived in a nation that was officially Protestant, and Protestant teaching was a large influence on Shakespeare's thinking and writing.

The focus of Robert Reid's essay is on the questions of how Shakespeare conceives of self-love and how to determine what appeared to be the predominant ideas about self-love among the Renaissance thinkers, whether of Catholic or Protestant sympathy. He also wants to discover the directions toward which Shakespeare leans in portraying varied forms of self-love. Are his leanings toward a Catholic or Protestant persuasion? The answer is difficult for Reid.

Seeing primarily two forms of self-love—perverse and positive—Reid turns to reputable Renaissance and Reformation thinkers, as well as to authors of the past; he looks to Augustine and simply concludes that the author discusses both perverse and positive forms. In *The City of God*, and *De genesi ad litteram*, he recognizes the perverse form, but in *De doctrina Christiana* and *De Trinitate*, his focus is on the "essential goodness of Creation and of the human soul." Shakespeare's mature works show the influence of "diverse intellectual traditions."

Reid next considers only the positive form of self-love, placing here the names of Aristotle, Aquinas and La Primaudaye. Buttressing his position with a strong analysis of the writings of the three scholars, Reid concludes that each of these stresses that self-love, including love for one's body, is "natural and vital to ethical well-being." For him, Shakespeare's characters who are most capable of expressing positive self-love are the "generous-spirited and wittily ironic protagonists . . . refined by the sufferings and joys they share with friends and lovers." The complexity of the subject of self-love or Shakespeare's handling of the characters does not suggest a systematic preference for one religious faith over the other. Reid's position thus far is that self-love can be best understood by a broad understanding of human nature which, as the paper clearly indicates, is built on Aristotle's *Nicomachean Ethics*, Aquinas's *Summa Theologiae*, and La Primaudaye's *The French Academie*; yet, to come to a firm and clear decision regarding Shakespeare's specific orientation toward Protestant or Catholic belief remains an arduous task that calls for further study.

To scrutinize another angle of Catholic-Protestant presence, Robert Miola in "I Could not Say 'Amen': Prayer and Providence in *Macbeth*," shows an inclination toward Catholic presence in the tragedy, but he never ignores Protestant thinking wherever he discovers it. In the extraordinary moment when Macbeth cannot say "Amen," Shakespeare takes us into the heart of the protagonist's tragedy: he has most need of blessing and is unable to say "Amen." Thus, there is urgent need for blessing but at the same time, Macbeth has an incapacity for praying. On the essential necessity and nature of prayer both Catholics and Protestants agree, yet both accused the other of lip-labor, says Miola. The word "Amen" also became a crucial point of controversy in the Harding-Jewel debates on the vernacular.

Miola recognizes that later in the play Macbeth holds contempt for the gospel and prayer; consequently, the beginning of his moral deterioration, and the drama then takes the reader on a journey into the heart and soul of the damned. The journey reveals how Shakespeare in writing this drama of damnation purposefully "evokes and engages contemporary theology, particularly the disputes about divine foreknowledge, human responsibility, the nature of grace and the freedom of the human will." Some Protestant critics, who respond to the driving propulsion of the evil there represented, have a tendency to coopt Macbeth into Protestant predestination schematics, but Miola strongly contends that Shakespeare clearly adopts a Catholic view of the action and theology of free will by emphasizing "the initial inevitability of the crime, the sheer gratuitousness (as Augustine sees it) of the evil freely chosen."

Early in her paper, "*Hamlet* and Protestant Aural Theater," Grace Tiffany takes a decisive position. While recognizing that for decades many critics have argued either that "Protestantism or Catholicism inform the general Christian ethos of *Hamlet*," she declares that her "purpose is not to argue that *Hamlet* is a Catholic or Protestant play," but rather to argue the influence on *Hamlet* of what David Daniell calls Shakespeare's "Protestant inheritance." That inheritance embraces the fact that Shakespeare lived in a nation that was aggressively and officially Protestant, the most popular pastors of the era were Protestant, with sermons frequently Calvinistic in their thrust, and in Shakespeare's lifetime 142 editions of the Geneva Bible were printed. Thus, it will be no surprise that Tiffany emphasizes "echoes of Protestant moral views" in *Hamlet*.

She does, however, choose a specific aspect of Protestant thought which Jonas Barish calls "anti-theatrical prejudice." Tiffany's concern is with what many Reformers implicitly or explicitly championed—a "virtue-inspiring aural theater." She uncovers how and why a discussion of aural elements in *Hamlet* is significant and shows how the play echoes "the Protestant emphasis on the moral authority of true things said and heard."

John Mahon carries further the subject of one of the disputes of contemporary theology and has a slightly different emphasis from Miola. Choosing the subject of providence in his study "Providence in *Julius Caesar*," Mahon states that Protestants and Catholics basically agree on the role of providence, but that, although the presence of both is undeniable in *Julius Caesar*, Shakespeare does not show his specific stance. Whether Catholic or Protestant, thinkers who are persuaded that God moves history toward a final goal will see the workings of providence. Also, Mahon suggests that further evidence of providence may be seen in "the action of the play [as it] moves Rome closer to the time when it will host the birth of Jesus and support (even, ironically, through its efforts at suppression) the growth of the Jesus movement into the Christian church." The presence of wild weather, omens, auguries, dreams and at least one ghostly visitation also support the role of providence. Divine providence advances primarily through two characters: Mahon reasons that if Augustus was "God's agent in establishing the best conditions for the birth of God's son, then God's agents in *Julius Caesar*, the characters who advance God's providential design by making Augustus 'sol sir o' the world' . . . are most especially, Cassius and Antony."

It seems appropriate to include as the final paper one that uses neither the Catholic nor Protestant label to discuss the Christian dimension of *Julius Caesar*. Not even admitting that there is a Catholic or Protestant presence—as did John Mahon, who insisted on the presence of both in his study of *Julius Caesar*—Maurice Hunt in "Cobbling Souls in Shakespeare's *Julius Caesar*" writes only of Christian allusions or values or subtexts. (The fact that he does not discuss the "Catholic/Protestant Presence" definitely does not mean that Hunt has failed to give thought to the subject. One has only to glance at his book *Shakespeare's Religious Allusiveness* to see clearly how in his thorough study of several plays he reveals ways in which Shakespeare integrates Reformation and Roman Catholic motifs and thought-systems.)

What Hunt declares early in his essay clarifies the route he will go: "I want to do more here than simply confirm what many commentators . . . have previously noted: that Christian values inform Shakespeare's depiction of a famous moment in Rome's history" and "I shall be suggesting that Shakespeare's association of Caesar and Christ is at times a positive rather than a uniformly parodic relationship, and I do so by starting with some unexplained overtones in minor characters' play-opening dialogue . . . concerned with 'cobbling souls.'" The opening dialogue among two tribunes and two plebeians gives birth to the phrase "cobbling souls" that becomes a dramatic motif throughout the play, which Hunt suggests has a sacred or metaphysical level. Some of the most subtle discoveries in his study come when he develops "soul" in contexts consonant with the play's Christian allusions, and in those "consisting of the usage of the word 'soul' in the dramatist's plays and poems antedating *Julius Caesar.*"

The essays included in this volume show a variety of approaches and differences of opinion on the overarching subject. Almost all of the authors see a Catholic or Protestant presence; most essayists think that Shakespeare depicts both positions in a given play, and others see either a decidedly Protestant or Catholic thrust. An occasional writer portrays Shakespeare as one who, in his personal beliefs, lived and died a Catholic *or* Protestant. For some of the essayists, Shakespeare as author provides insight into his culture (with the Catholic-Protestant struggle constituting a larger part of that culture). What is obvious is that not one fails to believe that the dramatist of the three tragedies is a consummate artist whose works reveal a Christian dimension.

Chapter 1

Meta-drama in *Hamlet* and *Macbeth*

Peter Milward, SJ

To begin with, what, I may be asked, is the meaning of "meta-drama"? It is not a word to be found in the massive *Oxford English Dictionary*, nor in its four-volume supplement, nor in any of the other dictionaries I have consulted. Yet on further investigation I find it has been used as long ago as 1971, in the title of a book by James L. Calderwood, *Shakespearean Metadrama* (without a hyphen), though on more careful inspection of his book, insofar as I understand his precise meaning, I find it altogether different from mine.[1] The meaning I intend to give this word—which I have come to use without any dependence on Calderwood—is much simpler, I contend, than his, being based not on any critical theory but on the nature of the compound word itself (which I prefer to spell with a hyphen). We all know the meaning of "metaphysics" as first used by Aristotle in the sense of what comes "after physics," by way of a deeper penetration into the causes of the things discussed in physics, or the philosophy of nature. This is the meaning that I wish to apply to drama, which is literally the action (including the words) that we see and hear on the stage. It is my contention that there is also a "meta-drama" which is implicit in the words and actions but which are not necessarily apparent either to the audience or even to scholarly commentators.

In particular, what I now wish to speak about is the meta-drama in the dramatic work of William Shakespeare, with special reference to his two great tragedies *Hamlet* and *Macbeth*. This is indeed a quality

I find in all his plays, and I maintain it is precisely that which makes Shakespeare stand out above all his peers as a dramatist of genius. By contrast, I wonder whether there is such a thing as meta-drama in the work of Marlowe or Ben Jonson, of Sheridan or Shaw, or even of T. S. Eliot. Yet I have to add, with regret, that it is a quality largely overlooked by scholars, including James Calderwood, who prefer to concentrate their attention on the merely dramatic aspects of Shakespeare's plays. For the most part, they seem to be content with passing recognition of the enigmatic genius of the great dramatist, without so much as asking themselves in what precisely his enigma or his genius consists. They are like Matthew Arnold, that idolater of the Bard, for whom Shakespeare simply smiles and remains still, "out-topping knowledge" (*l.* 3)[2]—which is his poetic excuse for ignorance. Such men prefer to shrug their scholarly shoulders and murmur that genius is not to be explained—it just *is*. Rather, they prefer to direct their attention to what we can know by means of scientific scholarship concerning the dramatist and his plays on the level of phenomena or outward appearances. They fail to look with the eyes of the mind, as Shakespeare himself insists, to "that within which passeth show" (1.2.85), still less to "thoughts beyond the reaches of our souls" (1.4.56). They are afraid to venture beyond what I have called "the horizon of Hamlet."[3]

Let us consider the play *Hamlet* for more detailed thinking on its being Shakespeare's dramatic turning point between his preceding comedies and histories, which belong to the passing Elizabethan age, and his great tragedies and romances, which usher in the new Jacobean age. First, it seems to me no accident that for the subject and title of this great drama Shakespeare took the name of his only son Hamnet, who died in 1596 at the age of eleven, and whose memory reappears in such characters as Prince Arthur in *King John*, Macduff's unnamed son in *Macbeth*, and Prince Mamillius in *The Winter's Tale*. Then, his father John died in 1601 at a time when the dramatist was probably already immersed in the composition of his drama, which might well be alternatively entitled "Fathers and Sons" since there is old Fortinbras, the father and young Fortinbras, the son; Polonius, the father, and Laertes, the son, as well as Hamlet's father's Ghost and Hamlet the son.

Secondly, this is a play which comes on the heels of comedies with such titles as *Much Ado About Nothing*, *As You Like It* and *Twelfth Night, or What You Will* (assuming, as I do, that this last-mentioned play comes in chronology immediately before *Hamlet*). What strangely nonchalant titles they are![4] It is as if the dramatist does not care about such trifles as titles for those plays, as if he has tossed them off on the spur of the moment! Of course, they have their charm, their interest, their fascination, treating as they do the follies of romantic love. But in contrast to the subsequent tragedies we might say of them what Claudius says of Hamlet after his staged interview with Ophelia, "Love! His affections do not that way tend," but "There's something in his soul / O'er which his melancholy sits on brood" (3.1.173–74).

Claudius was far more perceptive of reality than the tedious old fool Polonius, who could see no further than the seemingly rejected love of Hamlet for Ophelia—as if Hamlet had ever been really in love with her. But even Claudius was not perceptive enough, for he could only see, like most critics, within the prescribed limits of the play. After all, there is far more to Hamlet than what is seen of him within the limits of his play, and far more to his melancholy than he himself can understand. In any case, we have to realize that Hamlet is not really Hamlet: he is not himself, whether as a Danish prince of the eleventh century or as an English prince of the sixteenth-century Renaissance. As T. S. Eliot has correctly observed, if without fully understanding his own observation, what Hamlet lacks in all his words and actions is an "objective correlative."[5] In simpler words, Hamlet does not fit into his own play: he is just a shadow not of himself but of his creator. He is a dramatic projection of the dramatist.

I am not saying that Hamlet is entirely Shakespeare. The dramatist is not to be identified with any of his characters, not even with Prospero, but he is present in them all, even in villains like Iago, who says of himself (as it were echoing the mind of Shakespeare), "I am nothing if not critical" (*Othello* 2.1.119). What I am saying is that where Hamlet leaves off, where he comes to the horizon, the limits, the boundaries of his conscious self, there Shakespeare takes over. Only, I would add that Shakespeare is more present in Hamlet, in this respect, than in almost any other of his characters for the following reason: there are few if any characters who look so insistently beyond the limits not just of this play but of human life. Take, for instance, that most enigmatic of Hamlet's speeches, "To be, or not to be" (3.1.56).[6] It is enigmatic because it seems to have so little to do with anything either preceding it or following it in the play. It can so easily be cut, and it would make no difference to the action of the play—except that those who come to a performance of the play expecting this speech would be disappointed if it were omitted. All is impersonal, all is abstract and objective, since all has been lifted out of the book of Job. It is as if the book Hamlet has been reading on entering the lobby is the Bible, and the prince is merely meditating on what he has just read. But it is not only out of the book of Job. Hamlet has evidently been reading Shakespeare's sonnet, which begins with the words, "Tir'd with all these, for restful death I cry" (66.1) echoing Job's lament, "Why is light given to him that is in misery, and life unto the bitter in soul?" (Job 3:20). But it is not Hamlet who is really speaking. It is Shakespeare applying the words of Job to his own bitter life in the circumstances of his own age, the Elizabethan age which is even then creeping to its inglorious end.

This speech of Hamlet is a question, the question of "To be, or not to be?" (3.1.57). It is a question defined by Hamlet himself in terms of the practical dilemma, whether to go on suffering "the slings and arrows of outrageous fortune," (3.1.58–59) or to do something drastic about them—either by killing the queen or by blowing up the houses of Parliament, as certain followers of the Earl of Essex were ready to do.[7] His speech is a question, and all his words and actions from his first appearance in the play are marked with such a question—which is what makes it, above all other plays, a "problem play." And the original question, from which the play as a whole takes its point of departure, is symbolized by the ghost. He—or perhaps "it"—is the very incarnation of a question. Its very form might be presented as a question mark hovering in the air, in much the same manner as when, with the smoke from his hookah, the caterpillar asks Alice the overwhelming question, "Who are you?" The very mention of the ghost by Horatio sets up question after question in the mind of Hamlet (1.2). It is the same when the ghost actually appears to Hamlet on the castle battlements at midnight, prompting the frantic questions, "What does this mean?" and "Say, why is this? Wherefore? What should we do?" (1.4). Still the ghost says nothing. It merely beckons, and that is what it effectively does throughout the play. It beckons not only to Hamlet but to every spectator and every reader. For in it, and in Hamlet, Shakespeare is speaking to the hearts of his audience. Nor is it unlikely that, as Nicholas Rowe said of him, Shakespeare himself played the part of the ghost as "the top of his performance."[8]

The appearance of the ghost from the very beginning of *Hamlet* has two main functions in the subsequent course of the play. First, there is its revelation to the young Hamlet that his father was murdered while resting in the garden and that the murderer was Hamlet's uncle, now king and married to his mother, the current queen. And there is its consequent appeal for revenge. This appeal, however, raises two further problems in Hamlet's mind. One is how to take revenge on Claudius, considering (in the latter's own words), "There's such divinity doth hedge a king, / That treason can but peep to what it would, / Acts little of his will" (4.5.123–25). The other, once the ghost has disappeared, is how to make sure that what the ghost has told him is true, since, as he reflects, "The spirit that I have seen/ May be the devil, and the devil hath power / To assume a pleasing shape" (2.2.591–93). So by way of solving these two problems, Hamlet first resolves "to put an antic disposition on" (1.5.172), in order to mislead his mighty opposite for the better effecting of his purpose—though this only serves to attract the attention of others to himself and to raise their further question as to what Claudius calls "the head and source" of Hamlet's "distemper" (2.2.55). As for the second problem, Hamlet finds a providential means of solving it with the arrival of a group of players, whom he can ask to perform a play that resembles the ghost's description of his father's murder—and then he can observe the reaction of Claudius, whether or not he will betray his "occulted guilt" (3.2.85).

Such is the situation in which the dramatist leads the action of this drama to the performances of not one but two plays within the play in act 3. First, there is the play of Hamlet and Ophelia, staged by Polonius for the benefit of Claudius in order to find out whether Hamlet's distemper has been caused by Ophelia's supposed rejection of his love. In other words, the two conspirators wish to know the mind or consciousness of Hamlet behind the strange words and deeds of his "antic disposition." Secondly, there is the play "The Murder of Gonzago," or what Hamlet calls "The Mouse-trap," staged with the players onstage and the king with his court in the audience, while Hamlet and Horatio observe the king's reaction to the play. Here one may distinguish two levels of drama, one being that of the players for the entertainment of the audience, and the other that of players and audience together for the instruction of Hamlet and his friend. Thus the two "mighty opposites" (5.2.62), the king and the prince, are engaged in an elaborate spying match on each other. But the object of their spying is something hidden in the other's mind—in the conscience of the king and the consciousness of the prince (if one may distinguish two meanings in the one word). From Hamlet's point of view, is Claudius really the murderer of his father? And from Claudius's point of view, how much does Hamlet know about his father's murder? In this way, one may say, the play leads up to something beyond the mere drama of action, something in the hearts of the respective agents that may be called meta-dramatic.

What is this something in terms of the play? As a result of the play within the play staged by Polonius for Claudius, we have the opening soliloquy of "To be, or not to be," which tells them nothing about the true mind of Hamlet—or rather, nothing Polonius and Claudius were expecting to hear from him. On the other hand, it tells us much about Shakespeare, as we have noticed by comparing it with his private sonnet, "Tir'd with all these, for restful death I cry" (66.1). It also tells us much about his attitude to the age in which he was living—which is very much at odds with what has been termed "the Elizabethan myth." For what is rarely noticed by the innumerable commentators on the play is that Hamlet's problem belongs not to a prince in eleventh-century Denmark, still less to a student in twentieth-century Paris, but to Shakespeare and his fellow Catholics in Elizabethan England. He and they were facing just such a dilemma, whether to go on enduring "the slings and arrows" of a persecution they were facing from day to day, month to month, year to year, ever since they could remember in the reign of Queen Elizabeth, or to take arms against this "sea of troubles" by joining in some such desperate "enterprise"[9] as the Armada of 1588, the Essex Rebellion of 1601, or the Gunpowder Plot of 1605—which, in fact, only made their situation worse.

Within the terms of the drama, this all-important speech of Hamlet is paradoxically of no importance. It is seemingly pointless, inserted (one might conjecture) as a purple patch to gratify the self-esteem of a Burbage, and as such it is committed to memory by generations of English schoolboys and schoolgirls—for whom, as for Macbeth, it is "full of sound and fury, signifying nothing" (5.5). Rather, its real importance lies beyond the play. It lies on the level of meta-drama, in the mind of the dramatist and in the situation of Elizabethan Catholics. This is a meaning which the dramatist cannot state openly, for fear of some "suborned informer" (Sonnet 125, line 13) in his audience. The most he can say is, with Hamlet from the outset, "But break, my heart, for I must hold my tongue!" (1.2.159). He is himself, like Hamlet, and like all recusants, surrounded by spies, among whom, we know, were not a few fellow dramatists like Anthony Munday and Christopher Marlowe, and perhaps even Ben Jonson,[10] who certainly turned informer after the Gunpowder Plot of 1605 to save his own skin.

Secondly, as a result of the other play within the play that is staged by Hamlet as a means of spying on the conscience of the king (2.2.606), we have the other impressive soliloquy of Claudius, which may well be called the most religious speech in all the plays of Shakespeare. How strange, one might think, that so religious a speech should have been put into the mouth of a villain! But for the dramatist, Claudius is not a mere villain according to the rigid conventions of melodrama. He is a human being, who is not only a sinner but also free to repent of his sin. Hamlet's little play has, moreover, revealed the "occulted guilt" of Claudius not only to the prince but also to the king himself, and now he is on the point of repenting of his sin—with the grace of God.[11] Now he is kneeling at prayer as a sinful man in the presence of God—a situation that occurs all too rarely in Shakespeare's plays. He is recalling the sin of Cain, with "the primal eldest curse upon't, / A brother's murder" (3.3.37–38), and he is also recalling the repentance of David as expressed in the famous penitential Psalm 51, "Wash me, and I shall be whiter than snow." Everything in his speech is recognizably biblical in its expression and soundly theological in its thought. He well knows that the prayer of repentance alone will be of no help to him, unless he also has what is technically termed "a firm purpose of amendment." He asks, as it were echoing a central meditation in the Spiritual Exercises of St. Ignatius (that on "The Three Classes of Men"), "may one be pardon'd and retain the offence?"[12] His conscience has indeed been caught by Hamlet, according to the prince's express intention to "catch the conscience of the king" (2.2.41–42)—but in a manner and to an extent of which Hamlet never dreamed.[13] Yet alas, this catching of the king's conscience, at first so seemingly successful, ends in failure, as Claudius rises from prayer without having been able to repent—or rather, unwilling to make a firm purpose of amendment.

In yet another respect, however, also unintended by Hamlet, his little play has been successful beyond his dreams. He may have failed to catch the conscience of the king, as we know from the outcome of the king's soliloquy, but at least he succeeds in catching the conscience of the queen in the following scene. Here is no soliloquy. The queen seems to be lacking in that interiority of conscience which is so clearly manifested by Claudius—not in spite of but because of his sinfulness. She has to be goaded into self-reflection by her self-righteous son, who himself lacks the conscience which she goes on to manifest. As a result of his accusations, as with a personified voice of conscience, she exclaims, "O Hamlet, speak no more! / Thou turn'st mine eyes into my very soul, / And there I see such black and grained spots / As will not leave their tinct" (3.4.88–91). And so, unlike Claudius, Gertrude does repent, and she also goes on to keep her firm purpose of amendment, so far as we can see it in what remains of the play. Regardless, what is interesting about both this and the preceding scene is the way they both move from drama, and from a double mini-drama, by way of a kind of melodrama in the crazed mind of Hamlet, to a meta-drama of religious conversion in the seeming villains, so as to put them paradoxically, if only temporarily, in the position of hero and heroine—while

Hamlet, who seems to have no conscience, plays the role of villain. Thus it may be said that, for all the seeming secularity of the play, and for all the insistence of modern critics on the "secularity" of Shakespeare, here right at the heart and center of his dramatic career, and at the heart and center of his great drama *Hamlet*, there is a religious meaning which looks at once to the heart of the Bible, with its appeal for repentance, and to the heart of the religious problem in Elizabethan England.[14]

There, I leave further development of the meta-drama in *Hamlet* in order to make room for discussion on what I regard as the companion play of *Macbeth*. It is not that I have sufficiently dealt with all the meta-dramatic elements in the former play, which is indeed so full of them that they can hardly be covered even in a lengthy paper.[15] From a purely religious point of view, which is more than just biblical, *Hamlet* is rich in homiletic material of all kinds, reflecting almost every aspect of the religious situation in a deeply religious age—as I have attempted to show at more length in a book entitled *Shakespeare's Religious Background*.[16] It is all too often maintained, even by Christian scholars like Roland Frye in his too influential study *Shakespeare and Christian Doctrine*,[17] that all this homiletic material merely serves a secular, dramatic purpose. Such a contention may perhaps be valid insofar as the play is interpreted on the level of drama, and then it becomes tautologous. But it is when we pass from drama to meta-drama that the roles of secular and religious are strangely reversed, and then, to borrow the words of Lear, "handy-dandy" (4.6.158), where is the world, and where is religion? It is then that the outwardly secular values of the mighty opposites, Hamlet and Claudius, with Ophelia and Gertrude behind them, fade into nonentity, and the religious value of conscience, soon to be replaced by that of providence, comes to the fore. What is more, I insist, the dramatist is speaking not just of distant events in distant lands and ages, but of his own age and nation, even to the hearts of his Elizabethan audience—as he tells them in the words of Hamlet to his mother, "Let me wring your heart . . . / If it be made of penetrable stuff" (3.4.35–36). It is also, I would add, what he is speaking to the hearts of every audience, if only they have ears to hear.

But now, turning to *Macbeth*, why, it may be asked, have I called it a companion play to *Hamlet*? Is it not commonly counted as the last of the "four great tragedies," as *Hamlet* is indisputably the first? And are not they separated from each other by a gap of some five years? Indeed, I will answer, yes it is, and no it is not. If we follow the customary methods of dating Shakespeare's plays, observed in most critical editions, we have to admit this separation of *Hamlet* and *Macbeth*, applying to them what the poet says to his friend in Sonnet 36, line 1, "Let me confess that we two must be twain." On the other hand, once we forget about such methods and matters of text and composition, and turn to the plays themselves and their respective heroes, we cannot fail seeing how close they are to each other, as if the dramatist composed them in one and the same burst of inspiration.

Needless to say, Hamlet is more hero than villain in his play—though he does turn villain for a time, while his enemy Claudius is trying to repent of his sin. It may even be doubted whether or not he remains villain to the end, considering how coldly and with set purpose he sends the relatively unoffending Rosencrantz and Guildenstern to their certain deaths in England, "not shriving time allowed" (5.2.47). But Macbeth is certainly the villain of his play, from the moment he yields to the temptations of the witches and then of his wife, thereafter going from crime to crime, with not a sign of repentance—as contrasted with the previous Thane of Cawdor, whose title he has taken over. Yet it is perhaps because he is so certainly the villain, even more than either Claudius or Hamlet, that he is more religious than they are. So it may be said that the drama of *Macbeth* is as a whole more religious, and more meta-dramatic, than the drama of *Hamlet*. At the same time, it has to be added, if *Macbeth* is meta-dramatic, it is so in a very different way from *Hamlet*. Neither in Macbeth himself, nor in his lady, nor in any other character in the play of *Macbeth*, do we find any trace of the conscience which is so abundantly illustrated in the play *Hamlet*. Macbeth's sense of what he has done in the murder first of Duncan, then of Banquo, then of Lady Macduff and her children, is hardly to be called "guilt." He himself hardly knows the meaning of either "guilt" or "conscience." Rather, it is to be called "horror," as in his own approach to the deed (*Macbeth* 2.1) and in Macduff's horrified reaction to what has been done (2.3). So there is no room for repentance, either in Macbeth himself or in his lady. And so, from one viewpoint, the play might well be described, like Marlowe's *Faustus*, as a morality play of damnation.[18]

From yet another viewpoint, the play might also be described as a biblical play, following in the tradition of the mystery plays of the Middle Ages, which continued in Coventry right up to the 1570s, and which had their climax in the succession of scenes representing the passion of Christ.[19] As with *Hamlet*, so long as one keeps one's attention fixed on the old Scottish story dramatized on the stage, *Macbeth* is indeed a secular story, and scholars may focus their minds on its secularity, and even sexuality, to their hearts' content, while insofar as they recognize its undeniably religious overtones, they may interpret them as serving to underline the resolutely secular purpose of the play. But such a way of approaching and interpreting the play *Macbeth* might well be described in the hero's own words as "cabin'd, cribb'd, confin'd" (3.4.24), restricted as it is to the merely outward appearances of plot and character, and to the seeming world of a play set in eleventh-century Scotland. It is what those same scholars assert concerning the religious interpretation of the plays, that it is "reductive," reducing the meaning of the dramatist to what can be seen and heard on the stage, with reference to this transitory world. Rather, once we look beyond the Scottish drama to the implicit meta-drama, we expand our minds and hearts with the mind and heart of the dramatist. We share in his Christian vision, if (as St. Paul says) "in a glass darkly" (1 Cor 13:12), as he looks from his imaginary character of Macbeth and his no less imaginary Scotland to the central Christian mystery of the passion, death and resurrection of Jesus Christ—not as it took place in Palestine some fifteen centuries before but as it was still being reenacted in Elizabethan and Jacobean England. In this way, we may see the true universality of Shakespeare, looking from one place and one time to all places and all times. And it is his Catholic faith that makes him so.

Where, then, in *Macbeth* do we come upon echoes of the gospel story of Christ's passion? For those who have eyes to see and ears to hear, they are everywhere scattered in the play. Already from the opening description of Macbeth's performance on the field of battle, in the words of the bleeding sergeant, we are introduced to him as one set to "memorize another Golgotha" (1.2.41), and so he does, not just in the battle but in his subsequent murder of "the gracious Duncan" (3.1.66). For the time being he seems to be a loyal subject to his king, but his loyalty is soon undermined (or betrayed) by the witches, when they greet him with "All hail!"—the very word used by Judas on his betrayal of Christ in the garden of Gethsemane (Matt 26:49).[20] Thus Macbeth in turn becomes Judas to his lord and master Duncan. There is also something satanic about him when he calls on the stars to hide their fires (1.4). We may further recall the comment of St. John concerning Judas on his leaving of the supper-room, "Satan entered into him" (John 13:27). It was then, moreover, that Jesus said to Judas, "That thou doest, do quickly!"—and similarly, when Macbeth has left the supper-room, he begins his famous soliloquy, as though it were echoing the thoughts of Judas, "If it were done when 'tis done, then 'twere well / It were done quickly" (1.7.1–2). In this soliloquy he goes on to emphasize the meekness of Duncan and his virtues that have made him—far more than history shows him to have been—"clear in his great office" (1.7.18). Subsequently, he describes "the gracious Duncan" in the moment of his death, "His silver skin lac'd with his golden blood" (2.3.113), as if recalling the words of St. Peter on "the precious blood" of Christ being of more value than "gold or silver" (1 Pet 1:18-19). And so, if Macbeth is Judas, inspired in his deeds by Satan, Duncan may correspondingly be seen as Christ: not in any "allegorizing" or "theologizing" sense as ridiculed by secularizing critics like Roland Frye, but in the evident intention of the dramatist.[21]

Even so, I have drawn attention to only a few of the biblical echoes that are crammed into the narrow space of this short play, and I have to apologize for not examining more of them owing to their overwhelming multitude—which I have already set forth in detail in a book entitled *Biblical Influences in Shakespeare's Great Tragedies*. I have drawn attention to those which cluster around the passion and death of Duncan, which are to be found mainly in the first two acts—and they are, for that reason, the most memorable acts of the play. I will now briefly dwell further on the two other memorable soliloquies of Macbeth, where his characterization comes closest to that of Hamlet: in his "dagger" soliloquy and his "tomorrow" soliloquy.

Between himself and the king's bedchamber there are only the stone steps for Macbeth to climb. But now he sees something else in the way, a dagger in the air before him. He tries to seize it by the handle, but it eludes his grasp. It is not only in the air, but of the air. It is, he fears, "a fatal vision," sent perhaps by the witches. Or is it perhaps "a false creation / Proceeding from the heat-oppressed brain"? Can he trust his eyes? Or must he distrust his other senses? Again he looks at the dagger and finds on its blades "gouts of blood." This is a word unique to Shakespeare and his contemporaries, an English form of the French *gouttes* for drops, maybe suggested to him at this point—though to few of his commentators—by the Latin *guattae sanguinis* for the sweat of blood during the agony of Jesus in the Garden as narrated by Luke (22:44). One can also connect the scene with the entry of Jesus into Jerusalem on the eve of his passion, when Jesus defends the welcoming children against the censorious Pharisees: "If these [children] should hold their peace, the stones would cry out" (Luke 19:40). Macbeth utters his fear that "[t]he very stones prate of my whereabout" (2.1.59).

In this speech Macbeth is indeed in a biblical mood. He is such a pious murderer! From the book of Job, too, comes his description of the murderer that "abhors the light" and "in the night is as a thief" (24:13-14); also his mention that the witness of heaven and earth shall rise up against him, "The heaven shall declare his wickedness, and the earth shall rise up against him" (20:27). Finally, the summons of the bell, a signal arranged between himself and Lady Macbeth, he hears as a funeral knell for Duncan calling him "to heaven or to hell" (2.1.65), and thus putting himself in mind of the last judgment and the "four last things." As a murderer, Macbeth is so pious, but alas, he applies all his piety to his victim, not to himself. Secondly, consider his "tomorrow" speech in act 5.

It seems Macbeth has become lost in reverie. Then he quite forgets the person of Lady Macbeth and the news he has just heard. All his thoughts, like those of Hamlet in that other great soliloquy, are preoccupied with "the vanity of human wishes" and "the misery of all mankind." So from "hereafter" he turns to "tomorrow," and again "tomorrow," and yet again "tomorrow," with each "tomorrow" as the singular subject of the verb "creeps." He thinks only of time, slowly passing "in this petty pace from day to day," and eventually "to the last syllable of recorded time." He has no time for the present, which he abjured in abjuring "the life to come" (1.7.7). He can only think of the future, as the days pass before him in unending succession, like the apparitions of kings, stretching out "to the crack of doom"—to the sounding of the last trumpet. Yet with the passing of time, tomorrow becomes yesterday, and then, he reflects, "all our yesterdays have lighted fools / The way to dusty death."

All this weary reflection on human life as bound up with time—how biblical it all is! In Genesis, in the punishment of Adam as he is sent out of Eden into the wilderness of the outer world, we hear the sentence of death passed on him, "Thou art dust, and to dust shalt thou return" (3:19). In Psalm 22 we read of "the dust of death." Above all, Macbeth's words are deeply influenced by Psalm 90, "Thou turnest man to destruction" (*v.* 3) and "A thousand years in thy sight are as yesterday when it is past" (*v.* 4). Here his mind rejoins that of Hamlet, who is no less influenced by the book of Job. Thus, when Macbeth exclaims, "Out, out, brief candle!" with reference to man's life in this world, he recalls the words of Job concerning the wicked, "The light of the wicked shall be quenched . . . and his candle shall be put out with him." Also from Job comes his comparison of life to "a walking shadow," as when Job says, "We are but of yesterday and are ignorant, for our days on earth are but a shadow" (8:9). Not that the comparison is peculiar to Job. It is quite commonplace in the Old Testament, not least in the Psalms. Also from Psalm 90 comes the idea of life as "a tale / Told by an idiot," in the words, "We bring our years to an end, as it were a tale that is told." As G. K. Chesterton humorously remarks of this speech, "A murderer might grow cheerful, if he were able to utter his misery in those words about life being a thing full of sound and fury, signifying nothing."[22]

But here Macbeth, like Jacques, is only sucking melancholy out of selected passages from the Old Testament, whose wisdom provides him with ample scope for skepticism, pessimism, even nihilism. But his is, alas, a one-track mind, "full of sound and fury / signifying nothing." At the same time, paradoxically, he is nothing if not biblical—whereas his commentators, who will not recognize his indebtedness (or that of Shakespeare) to the Bible, are less than nothing!

Space forbids me to indulge in leisurely expatiation, and I must hasten to that other meta-dramatic aspect of *Macbeth* which points not only to the passion and death of Christ as recorded in the Gospels— and as similarly recalled in the other Jacobean tragedies of *Othello* and *King Lear*—but also to the religious situation in Shakespeare's England. Shakespeare scholars have long since recognized in *Macbeth* a rich vein of reference to the Gunpowder Plot of 1605, with the trials of the conspirators and chiefly of the Jesuit Father Henry Garnet in March of 1606—which were amply recorded in the official pamphlet on *The Whole Proceedings against the late Most Barbarous Traitors* (1606). This vein of reference is most evident in act 2, in the comic speech of the drunken Porter,[23] imagining himself as "porter of hell-gate," with his allusions to "a farmer" and "an equivocator" (2.3)—which point to Father Garnet, one of whose aliases happened to be Farmer, and whose trial centered on his use of the Jesuit theory and practice of equivocation.[24] Then there is the horrified speech of Macduff, whose words on discovering the murder of Duncan echo those of Sir Edward Coke in his speech for the prosecution of the plotters: "Considering the monstrousness and continual horror of this so desperate a cause . . . neither hath the eye of man seen, nor the ear of man heard the like things to these. . . . This offence is without any name sufficient to express it." Only, what few scholars realize is the great difference between the murder of Duncan as perpetrated by Macbeth, and the Gunpowder Plot which never came to the point of perpetration.[25] Even in those days there were those who regarded it, not without reason, as a plot by Sir Robert Cecil to cast discredit on the Catholics, in the same way his father Lord Burghley had been responsible for many similar "plots" on the life of Queen Elizabeth. Rather, if we would understand the true topical meaning implied in the horrified words of Macduff, "O horror, horror, horror! . . . Confusion now hath made his masterpiece! / Most sacrilegious murder hath broke ope / The Lord's anointed temple, and stole thence / The life o' the building!" (2.3.72–75), we have to look into "the dark backward and abysm of time" (*The Tempest* 1.2.50) and recall that series of real sacrileges that had taken place within the living memory of the older members of Shakespeare's audience. I mean the wholesale desecration of the monasteries and shrines of England by Thomas Cromwell and his henchmen, under the orders of Henry VIII, in the years 1536–1540. Shakespeare himself must have often seen and brooded on one such monastery of nuns, Wroxhall Priory in the Forest of Arden, where two of the nuns in pre-Reformation times had borne his surname and one of them had provided him with the Christian name of his pious heroine in *Measure for Measure*.[26] He also went on to record his nostalgic impressions of the ruins in his Sonnet 73, as "Bare ruin'd choirs, where late the sweet birds sang" (73.4).

All that had happened, it is true, in far-off days, and only the ruins remained as sad reminders of the past. But there is much in the Jacobean plays of Shakespeare in which he seems to be casting his mind back from the troubles of his Elizabethan fellow Catholics to those of their forefathers in the reign of Henry VIII, when those troubles had their beginning—till he actually comes to collaborate in a final play on the history of that reign.[27] Still, there is one crucial scene in act 4 of *Macbeth*, in which Malcolm and Macduff are engaged in a long conversation. It not only vividly recalls the problems of Elizabethan Catholics, but it is strangely prolonged by the dramatist out of all proportion to the prevailing brevity of the play. It shows the extreme caution Malcolm has to observe in dealing with Macduff, who for all he knows may be a spy for Macbeth, as he has experienced not infrequently in the past. Such, too, was the caution that had to be observed regularly by Catholic recusants in Elizabethan England, and no doubt by Shakespeare himself in view of the above-mentioned suborn'd informers— men who had been in the spy system devised by Lord Burghley with Sir Francis Walsingham.

A similar caution we find in the previous scene between Lennox and an unnamed lord, in which again Lennox has to be on his guard lest his words be reported to the tyrant. All he can say is, "My former speeches have but hit your thoughts, / Which can interpret further. Only, I say, / Things have been strangely borne" (*Macbeth* 3.6.1–3). Such, too, was the atmosphere of fear among Catholics in Elizabethan England, an atmosphere that has been accurately reproduced by the dramatist. If, however, I am asked for demonstrative proof that Shakespeare definitely had those Catholics in mind, his very situation in Jacobean England, not least in the immediate aftermath of the Gunpowder Plot, made it impossible for him, or for me, to provide such proof. There can be no precise proof to satisfy the resolutely agnostic mind. Only, when we consider these many bits and pieces of proof together are they found to add up to what John Henry Newman calls, in his *Grammar of Assent*, "a convergence of independent probabilities" which amounts to a certain conclusion.

Such in brief is my thesis on the presence of meta-drama, or what may alternatively be called the "drama beyond drama," in the two great tragedies of Shakespeare, *Hamlet* and *Macbeth*. There is in these two plays, even more than in his other plays, "something in his soul / O'er which his melancholy sits on brood" (*Hamlet* 3.1.173–74). It is something that occurs to Shakespeare's mind partly from his reading of the Bible, colored by the dramatic tradition of the Middle Ages which was still alive in his early years, notably the morality and mystery plays, and partly from his sympathetic awareness of the religious troubles of his time, as experienced above all by his fellow Catholics. Here I dare to say "fellow Catholics"—with much the same feeling as when Paulina defends the "good queen" in *The Winter's Tale* (2.3), and when Emilia insists on the innocence of Desdemona in *Othello* (5.2)—considering all the evidence that has come to light in recent years that Shakespeare received a Catholic formation not only at home in Stratford but also in recusant Lancashire, while I would go even further in maintaining that he remained a Catholic throughout his dramatic career, if only in sympathy, and if with some fluctuation. For this essay I have limited my discussion to only two of the great tragedies to which I have devoted a whole monograph entitled *Shakespeare's Meta-drama—Hamlet and Macbeth* (2003).[28] In this respect, I regard the four great tragedies as standing remarkably close together, so as almost to constitute one dramatic masterpiece. Only, I would qualify and explain my grouping, as opposed to that of most scholars from the time of A. C. Bradley onwards, by maintaining that *Hamlet* and *Macbeth* are to be paired as Elizabethan tragedies—for all the seeming reference in the latter to the Gunpowder Plot—while *Othello* and *King Lear* are contrastingly Jacobean.

Chapter 2

Explorers of the Revelation: Spenser and Shakespeare

David Daniell

Edmund Spenser was considered by his contemporaries in the 1580s and 1590s to be the greatest English poet, valued in later ages, by Milton himself, for example. 'Epithalamium' is one of the most beautiful love-poems in the language, celebrating his midsummer marriage in southern Ireland in 1594. He was a skilled lyricist and sonneteer, to rank with Shakespeare and Sidney.

Spenser's great unfinished allegory *The Faerie Queene* (only six books and a fragment, out of the proposed twelve, were published) makes the first high English epic, with only Milton's *Paradise Lost* greater. In it, Spenser set out to show, in an original stanzaic form and high language, Aristotle's 'twelve moral virtues' as understood through the British narratives of late medieval and Renaissance romance.

The eighteenth-century Augustan writers admired Spenser's colourful imagery and narrative splendour. *The Faerie Queene* was to them a supreme poem of the imagination, though distasteful in allegory and form. Spenser was supremely important to the English Romantic writers as 'the poets' poet' of dreams, beauty and sensuous appeal. He was the immediate model for Keats, first showing him early in his youth those 'Charm'd magic casements, opening on the foam / Of perilous

• From chapter 23 in David Daniell's *The Bible in English: Its History and Its Influences* (New Haven: Yale University Press, 2003), 376–88. This chapter appears in its original form courtesy of Yale University Press.

seas, in faery lands forlorn.'[1] Wordsworth, in Book III of *The Prelude*, recalled at Cambridge reading 'Sweet Spenser, moving through his clouded heaven / With the moon's beauty and the moon's soft pace, / I call'd him Brother, Englishman and Friend'.[2] Now *The Faerie Queene* is less read. The advocacy of C. S. Lewis in the mid-twentieth century, strong on both sides of the Atlantic, showing Spenser to be both fiercely didactic and movingly appealing, has faded, sadly. Spenser, second only to Shakespeare as the poet of that time, like him has much to teach about how to live, morally and spiritually, and about the high shapes of art. Even enthusiasts among twentieth-century academic appreciators, however, found one part of Spenser's mind so strange, even distasteful, as to be something from which commentary had to save him. It is always acknowledged that his models were of many kinds: he combined classical and Christian humanist culture, from Aristotle to Ariosto. His Christian dependence not only on humanism but, as a Calvinist, on the English Bible, however, has been something, it seems, hardly to be mentioned. This is to misrepresent.

Spenser was at Cambridge in the early 1570s, a period when there was great interest in that University in making a new English poetry. After university, he went into the service of the Bishop of Rochester, who had been Master of Pembroke, Spenser's college. From there he moved to the service of the powerful Earl of Leicester, making friends with the earl's nephew Sir Philip Sidney. In 1579 he published twelve eclogues, admired by Sidney, under the title *The Shepherd's Calendar*. In 1580, he became secretary to Lord Grey de Wilton, the Lord Deputy of Ireland. In that country Spenser spent most of the rest of his life, though publishing much fine poetry as a courtier in London. He attracted criticism, not only from Sidney, for his experiments with what Sidney called 'an old rustic language'.[3] In 1580 he published Books I to III of *The Faerie Queene*. Books IV to VI followed in 1595, with a second edition of I to III: the printer was Richard Field, a Stratford man known to Shakespeare.

On Spenser's death in January 1599, the Earl of Essex paid for his funeral in Westminster Abbey, where he was buried near Chaucer: the poets of the age threw elegies into his grave. Queen Elizabeth herself ordered a monument to him, which never materialised. The Countess of Dorset provided one for the Abbey in 1620: though this mistook the dates of birth and death, it did name him 'The Prince of Poets in his Time'. This monument was restored in marble in 1778, with the dates corrected. It may be seen today in Poets' Corner.

In the last decades of Elizabeth's reign, the great men that Spenser knew shared a sense of high enterprise, of discovery of the world and adventure in it. Spenser had that spirit, making high claims for the function of English poetry. He wrote at a time of daunting religious problems, and he can be seen to be occupied not only with the complexities of the formal Elizabethan Settlement, but also with the difficulties produced by dissent from both sides, Protestant and Catholic. Protestants criticised the Church of England, but more, found the Church of Rome to be deviant and heretical. That national Catholic problem, moreover, involved national security. Formidable Jesuit missionaries, trained to persist till death, began to arrive from Douai in the late 1570s, dedicated to undermining the recently excommunicated queen. Any Protestant writer of the time felt free to attack what was understood as a Catholic threat.

Critics of *The Shepherd's Calendar* have been squeamish in understanding that Spenser was a fully Protestant writer. Three of the twelve eclogues, 'May', 'July' and 'September', deal with religious matters. Spenser's speakers are subtle, and the movement within each poem, and within the whole volume, is complex, but even so the parallel between Spenser's position and that of most Protestant writers of the time is powerful'.[4] Commentators have laboured to show a non-existent religious 'balance' in *The Calendar*, and even to 'rescue' Spenser from the Calvinism of the time.[5] This is to assume, from a distorted later perspective, that Calvinism in Elizabeth's court was some sort of reprehensible aberration, and not a norm. Modern historical studies have focused on the conflicts about theories of church government, and certainly from 1570 those issues were both strong and public. More out of sight, however, have been the more central Protestant concerns for an educated, preaching ministry; for further reformation of the Church of England in the light of the Scriptures; and a hatred of episcopal pomp and wealth, with particularly fervent opposition to Roman Catholicism. Spenser can be shown to share the militant Protestantism of the highborn circle in which he moved, particularly of the Earl of Leicester, Lord Grey de Wilton and Sir Philip Sidney. It is hard to read the parable of the Wolf in the 'May' eclogue without seeing that the victim, the young kid, is, as the gloss by Spenser's Cambridge friend 'E. K.' explains 'The simple sort of the faithful and true Christians', deceived by the popish fox.[6] In all three ecclesiastical eclogues, the speakers on both sides are given engaging characteristics. As the dialogues unfold, the flaws in one speaker's argument are steadily exposed. Because Spenser has used the genre of pastoral dialogue, it does not follow that the final effect has to be of ambivalence. 'May', 'July' and 'September' are Protestant in their impetus. They are part of an effect made by the whole of the *Calendar*, relating the work of the poet to that of the pastor. As Spenser concludes the *Calendar*, his purpose has been 'To teach the ruder shepherd how to feed his sheep / And from the falsers fraud his folded flock to keep.'[7]

Spenser's deepest concerns can be seen at their best in 'the great slow swing' of his mind in *The Faerie Queene*.[8] Richly feeding into his poetry more than two thousand years of literature and thought, he was also consciously trying to make a new poetry for England, looking back to the greatness of Chaucer two hundred years before. He wanted poetry to be wholly accessible to the 'vulgar': he did not write in Latin (at all—in this, among the major poets, he was joined only by Shakespeare). He studied how French poetry resolved one Renaissance problem in making national languages capable of carrying the highest subjects. In this respect, of course, he was working parallel to the recent translators of classical authors, and especially the Bible, from the original languages into the vernaculars.

Spenser and Protestant Understanding of the Bible

Though commentators have been unable to avoid Christian significances in *The Faerie Queene*, these have often been seen in terms of recent religious history and doctrine rather than an understanding of particularly Protestant doctrines from the Bible. An example is the passage in Book I Canto II in which the Redcross Knight fights his climactic battle against the dragon, receiving strength from the Well of Life and the Tree of Life (specifically, I. xi. 30) to kill that Devil. These have been taken as standing for the two sacraments of the Church of England, baptism and the eucharist.[9] In Spenser's 'continued allegory and dark conceit,' as he expressed his purpose in his prefatory letter to Sir Walter Raleigh, these are present here, but that identification is too schematic. Both the Well and the Tree stand also for the power of Christ in his Person, best interpreted by Revelation 22:1-2, where the 'river of water of life' is not only the sacrament of baptism but the doctrine of Christ:

> For unto life the dead it could restore,
>   And guilt of sinful crimes clean wash away,
>   Those that with sickness were infected sore,
>   It could recure, and aged long decay
>   Renew, as one were borne that very day. (ix.30)

The Book of Revelation was known to all Bible-reading Protestant Christians, with commentaries and annotations. (These, especially those in the Geneva Bibles available to Spenser, lacked the later seedy assumptions of secular as well as religious cosmic significance adduced from that book which have made modern minds avoid it—as examples, it is said that announced there, in code, are the date and time of the last great victory [at 'Armageddon'] for Christian capitalism, or the date and time of the Second Coming of Jesus Christ.) For Spenser, the Well has healing properties far beyond the once-for-all washing of baptism (and in any case we must assume that the Redcross Knight was baptised long before). It has also been said that the Redcross Knight, rising early on the third day to slay the dragon, becomes Christ himself:[10] when seen in the light of the New Testament, this does not make sense. Spenser's point is that the true Christian life is lived in imitation of Christ, not identification with him. The Redcross Knight, for Spenser's epic to work, has to remain human.

A second Protestant characteristic is that his writing, however rich in significance, is never esoteric. The power of Spenser's poems to explicate themselves is striking. His 'continued allegory' should be taken only to the extent that Scripture-readers understood allegory.

The Bible contains allegories, of a self-explanatory sort—that is how the early churches could accommodate the Song of Songs. Paul himself in Galatians 4:21-6 commends an Old Testament story as to be taken allegorically. But to write anything which baffles the common reader without access to explanations in the rarefied heights of unusual learning is foreign to Protestant writers. One glory of *The Faerie Queene* is that it is understandable. Allegory, there, is not hiding truths. Spenser wrote at a time when this question was current: Sir John Harrington, for example, pressed an esoteric poetic theory; Sidney the reverse. That *The Faerie Queene* was not read esoterically is shown by a little book by Sir Kenelm Digby, published in 1643 and entitled *Observations on the 22nd Stanza in the 9th Canto of the 2nd Book of Spenser's Faerie Queene*. Digby tackles that one stanza simply because it alone does not fit with Spenser's normal method in this enormous allegory, where he (Digby) notes that Spenser 'doth himself declare his own conceptions in such sort as they are obvious to any ordinary capacity'.[11] Similarly the very frequently used images from the Book of Revelation, not only in Book I, are clear in their sense to any reader familiar with that book and its elucidation in the margins of Geneva Bibles. Spenser's remarkable learning draws on a range of literature, history, philosophy, mythography and iconography, as well as biblical commentaries and religious books. Yet all this becomes transmuted into the narratives of recognisable human beings in romance—all the senses in that highly charged genre become imaginatively available.

To approach a third Protestant characteristic one may take as examples the enemies of the Redcross Knight in the first half of Book I. There is no mystery. Two are papists and two are adherents of Mahomet: though they differ, their nature is clear. The followers of Mahomet (Sansfoy and Sansjoy) attack the Redcross Knight physically. They are familiar figures from medieval romance and Italian romantic epic (Sir Beves killed fifty on a single day[12]). The two papists, Archimago and Duessa, however, work differently, by means of fraudulent 'Shewes'. Here is the alarm felt by Protestants about the seductiveness of Catholic casuistry. In these 'shewes' are created or promoted ambiguous spectacles with which the inexperienced knight has to contend: a 'lowly Hermitage' (i.34) and a 'goodly Lady' (ii.13), 'two goodly trees' (ii.28), a 'goodly building, bravely garnished' (iv.2). 'Goodly', of course, is equivocal for Spenser: the Redcross Knight is to blame not for being deceived, but for his persistence in error after 'warning signals have clearly indicated that the phenomenon on hand ought to be rejected . . . after each adventure his mind is more clouded and his heart more tainted by the nature of the experience he has passed through'.[13] So Archimago's hermitage at first seems to offer a true pastoral simplicity of life, and neither Una nor the Redcross Knight can discern its true meaning. There is, however, no difficulty for the reader, as Spenser guides the response.

One of the characteristics of the Spenserian stanza, with its interlocking rhyme scheme and final longer line, is to allow, often within a single stanza, a characteristic movement from something necessarily complex, physical, moral or psychological to final words which make explicit a meaning which the reader has been discovering. In Book I Canto I stanza 35, Una and the Redcross Knight, in some distress, have (to the reader's pleasure) arrived at a welcoming house dedicated to humble contentment. The first words of the stanza are 'arrived there,' which is gratifying: by the ninth line the reader is alarmed.

> Arrived there, the little house they fill,
>   Ne look for entertainment, where none was:
>   Rest is their feast, and all things at their will;
>   The noblest mind the best contentment has.
>   With fair discourse the evening so they passed:
>   For that old man of pleasing words had store,
>   And well could file his tongue as smooth as glass;
>   He told of Saints and Popes, and evermore
> He strowed an *Ave-Mary* after and before.

This stanza prepares for the discovery that the hypocritical hermit is a sorcerer who deals in 'mighty charms, to trouble sleepy minds' (I.i.36)— a sorcery which Protestant writers claimed belonged to papist clergy.[14]

That Spenser was writing at a time of cultural difficulties is clear. In a way that extended Sidney, he was trying to reconcile the richnesses of pagan and medieval culture, with which literature in English was so newly blessed in the new outpouring of printed material, with the special divine insights of Christianity, and especially Protestant Christianity. Spenser is said to have experienced disillusion with Protestant values, a movement which can be detected, it is claimed, in the addition of the two hymns, of heavenly and celestial beauty, to the previously written two of earthly or natural love and beauty, which are entirely Petrarchan and Neoplatonic. In the dedication of these *Foure Hymnes* (1596), to the Puritan Countesses of Cumberland and Warwick, Spenser suggests that the first two were too pagan, even 'poison,' in their 'strong passion.' He begins the second pair of poems by repudiating those earlier follies. According to Fulke Greville, Sidney wanted to destroy *Arcadia* for the same reason.[15] The striking parallel is with Milton who, in *Paradise Regained*, added a fourth temptation to the New Testament's three, in which Christ was tempted to study pagan wisdom. The two, however, divine and pagan, do not have to be absolutes, and there is a large difference of scale between Spenser's youthful ecstasies and the authority of Christ in the wilderness. The criterion, for Protestant writers, is first and always the Bible, which accommodates to religious purposes a good deal of secular writing (the Song of Songs and Esther to look no further). Spenser the epic poet explores large areas of moral, emotional and social experience. The whole of *The Faerie Queene*, as it remains, is built 'in a way which allows neither the protagonist nor the readers to forget the continuing reality of the spiritual realm which is the source and the destiny of moral virtue'.[16]

Sixteenth-Century Liberation

To Protestants, language itself was liberated, the Word of God being always creatively active. A good deal of the explosion of magnificent poetry in the time of Spenser and Shakespeare can be put down not so much to the latest Italian fashions, as Sidney commended in his seminal *Apology for Poetry* in the 1580s, but the firm understanding that, in spite of Plato, poetry was on God's side after all, because God himself wrote poetry, as the Bible had newly shown. Freshly inventing thoughts, forms, styles and even words, was part of a poet being, as Sidney pointed out, a 'maker'[17] and, as the Bible also showed, could be both unfettered and endless. Hamlet, his mind racing with suggestion, is not threatened with a charge of heresy.

A strong feature of the later sixteenth century was the first arrival in English of the great classical texts. One of the half-dozen most significant of these, Ovid's *Metamorphoses*, arrived first complete in English in 1563–7, translated into jogging verse by Arthur Golding. A long introductory Book by Golding himself sets out to show how biblical Ovid is. Golding was more famous at the time as the translator of a dozen major works by Calvin, including volumes of sermons. Ovid's epic arrives in English as a Calvinist work. Golding's Ovid certainly influenced Shakespeare all his life (though he read the original, of course): a long passage, VII.263–89, makes most of Prospero's speech at *The Tempest* 5.I.33–57.

Shakespeare

It is vital to allow Shakespeare a mind that is open.[18] The seventeenth and eighteenth centuries denied him any learning at all: he was a sport, a child of nature rather than of art. Some sort of Divine Being opened a flap in his head and poured it all in: Shakespeare, they passionately maintained, did not read books. Observers in the nineteenth century found he knew the Bible, and then wrote pious books about Shakespeare's biblical knowledge. At the start of the twenty-first century he is allowed to be both learned and thoughtful. His sources are indeed manifold: classical writers, especially Ovid and Plutarch, frequently in the original (including better Greek, as well as Latin, than Ben Jonson could bring himself to allow), and English versions. He used modern French and Italian works, not always translated. He read books on law, medicine, folklore, alchemy, astrology, natural history and much, much else. The English *Chronicles* of Hall and Holinshed gave him plots. Previous and contemporary English writers, especially Chaucer, Marlowe and Lodge influenced him greatly.

We cannot go to the other extreme and make him a universal genius. There were areas he did not address. He was not interested in the contemporary London scene of sexual transaction and its literature, as Jonson and Middleton were: nor in dramatising Old Testament stories, as quite a number of his contemporaries did; nor did he join the majority of his fellow sonneteers in Englishing some of the Psalms. Nevertheless, multiplicity, of sources, interests—and of levels of reading—should be recognised. Shakespeare knew the Bible with an understanding that is in most ways strange to us. It can be seen most obviously in his many quotations, often from places that are unfamiliar.[19] In *The Merchant of Venice*, 1.3, he makes Shylock, in his first scene, recount a strange incident in the story of Laban from Genesis 30. To tell a story from the Hebrew Scriptures is a natural thing for a Jew to do. Shakespeare expects his audience not only to know it, but to ask themselves why Shylock is telling it there. Shakespeare uses Bible references movingly, as Richard II refers to Judas's greeting to Christ (*Richard II*, 4.1.169–71): comically, as Benedick says he would not marry Beatrice though she were endowed with all that Adam had left to him before he transgressed (*Much Ado About Nothing* 2.1.235–6); and indirectly, as Bottom, waking from his dream in *A Midsummer Night's Dream* 4.1.209–12, misquotes St Paul to describe it—'The eye of man hath not heard . . .'. More interestingly, Shakespeare makes assumptions about the biblical understanding of his ordinary hearers and readers that allow him to follow New Testament thought into one of its sixteenth-century developments, the encapsulation of New Testament theology, particularly that of Paul, which became known as Calvinism. Both *Julius Caesar* and *Hamlet*, written close together in 1599 and 1600, are in part Calvinist plays.[20] English translations of Calvin's works were almost beyond comparison the most frequent in Europe. William Perkins's Calvinist sermons in Cambridge between 1592 and 1602 were immensely popular: his Calvinist *Golden Chain* was reprinted twelve times between 1591 and 1600. (Work remains to be done on the causes of national ignorance of Calvin in the past three or four hundred years, and the effects of that on the understanding of English and early American literature.[21])

In the second scene of the second Act of *Measure for Measure*, Isabella retorts to the Deputy's Draconian 'Your brother is forfeit of the law,' with:

> Alas! Alas!
> Why, all the souls that were were forfeit once:
> And He that might the vantage best have took
> Found out the remedy. (72–5)

Her evocation of the biblical account of the blameless life of Christ, and his work of the redemption of the world in his death, as Christians believe, is at that moment in the play subtly resonant. Isabella takes her theology further:

> How would you be
> If He, which is the top of judgement, should
> But judge you as you are? O, think on that;
> And mercy then will breathe within your lips
> Like man new made. (75–9)

Her main nouns and verbs are biblical, especially 'souls', 'judge', 'judgement' and 'mercy'. The whole play, however, hangs on more than a pointed biblical reference. In its working-out of the themes not only of justice and mercy, but also of law and love, of grace, remedy and redemption, it is very close to—indeed, only intelligible in the light of—Paul in the Epistles to the Romans and to the Galatians. Shakespeare was not writing theology: he was a poet and maker of dramas. But he seemed to expect his audience to understand the larger world he is in, and that setting his play in contemporary Vienna allows him to make characters who can reflect the human and divine responsibilities that Paul thrusts at us, and make such characters change and grow.

There are many aspects of Shakespeare's poems and plays which can be seen to reflect not simply a Bible knowledge shared with his audience, but the way in which unique elements in, especially, the New Testament, affect his dramatic writing. His uniquely New Testament understanding of the true union in marriage needs exploration. The biblical nature of his historical patterning, with its political implications, goes beyond, to share strategies of many of the poets of the time to preserve, politically as well as religiously, a degree of independence.[22] This is vital. Shakespeare does his unique things for his own poetic and dramatic reasons. Yet in choosing to write, and to rewrite, English history, he cannot help being in a Protestant stream of providential national historiography. Hall, Grafton, Holinshed and Foxe, to name but four, Protestant rewriters all, were doing that, and they were only the higher end of the culture. In the second half of the century, a strong tradition of anonymous chronicle writing, often in doggerel, used the voice of the people to give historical examples, much as Tyndale does at a more dignified level in *The Practice of Prelates*: most of it is apocalyptic in direction, following John Bale.[23]

There is space here to mention only one further matter. In her book, *Shakespeare's Theory of Drama* (1996), Pauline Kiernan discovers a sort of Shakespearean Defence of Drama by finding that Shakespeare rejected the mimetic aesthetic of Sidney and his late Renaissance humanist peers.[24] Shakespeare, she finds, did something quite different, valuing instead something she notes as 'presence,' the living human body on stage, with its necessarily intensely subjective set of responses. Also in 1996, Debora Shuger, remarking how Shakespeare's religion has been wrongly seen as defending a conservative social order, noted that in fact he gives dramatic life to 'poor and common speech,' the self, as she puts it, as suffering subject: 'Lear's pedigree does not fundamentally alter the fact that he is a powerless and hurt old man tormented by rage, guilt and thankless children . . . the displacing of social discourses of suffering and poverty on to psychological representations' is a legacy peculiarly of Protestant subjectivity.[25]

William Tyndale is relevant here. Always subjective in his responses to the work of the Gospel, in all his writing that is not biblical translation (particularly his *Wicked Mammon* and his *Obedience of a Christian Man*) he allows nothing to stand between the suffering soul and God—and that suffering is often metaphorised by him as either deep poverty or great illness, from both of which the gospel releases the ordinary man or woman or child, he insists, with glorious new and energetic liberty. Secondly, Tyndale translated the Bible for the ploughboy, as he famously remarked, that poor, underprivileged, physically suffering creature. One cannot argue that Shakespeare had read Tyndale's books: but, thirdly, he *had* read Tyndale's translation of the four

Gospels. Naseeb Shaheen has shown that they are easily Shakespeare's most-referred-to biblical books, and whether he read Geneva Bibles (the evidence points that way) or the Bishops' Bible, he was still largely reading Tyndale.

One core of the Gospels is the removal of the religious rituals of exclusion: Jesus shocked the righteous by sitting down for meals with moral outcasts. His bodily presence, as a Messiah, someone with the greatest spiritual power who heals and teaches now, and not in some future, was with fishermen and prostitutes and publicans. As Jesus says so often, the Kingdom of God is now. Any over-ritualised religion since the dawn of time can make its priests say that yes, we know, it's rotten, and hard luck, but just do as we say, keep at the ritual, stick it out, give us your money and you'll end up with the angels in heaven for evermore. The Gospels do not say this. There is a future; but the world of the Kingdom of God, as in so many of the parables, is now, even more than then. The finding of the lost sheep is now. The Prodigal Son returns now. The four Gospels are full of hard sayings, and the modern scholarly teasing-out of the relation between them as texts has been described as one of the most difficult subjects in the humanities.[26] Yet at the same time they are blazingly simple, being full of people, usually poor and suffering people, in the presence of an extraordinary teacher and healer. In the healing is the sudden dramatic conflict between humanity wrong (diseased, ill, deformed) and humanity right. Here is Pauline Kiernan's 'presence'; what, as Debora Shuger pointed out, William Perkins called 'a person of mine own self, under Christ.'[27] Tyndale brought to English readers the strength of the inward, spiritual regiment, presence localised not only in the temporal and secular (that idea originates in Luther) but in the spiritual and subjective, psychologically represented, taken into a body on the stage. The *mimesis* of the later humanists, Sidney and the rest pointed to some ethical value of art. Shakespeare, by contrast, is full of people, quite newly. This came to him from fifty years of increasing subjectivity, through a Protestant fact, everyone knowing the Bible in English, especially the Gospels.

Recent commentators express surprise about how new this was. Harold Bloom, in his introduction to his *Shakespeare: The Invention of the Human*, writes, 'In Shakespeare, characters develop rather than unfold, and they develop because they re-conceive themselves... [as in] no other writer'.[28] Shakespeare's theory of drama is of bodily presence, as Pauline Kiernan shows. That body is in interior, human, conflict. Of Edgar's bedlam beggar and Lear's nakedness in the storm Debora Shuger writes:

> Such characters acquire their psychological depth by assimilating the ancient Christian discourses of social injustice to the structures of the psyche ... within the tragic protagonist, enabling a fundamentally new presentation of the self.... Before Lear, kings did not hallucinate or run around half-naked with flowers in their hair, weeping over their unkind children.[29]

The phrase 'ancient Christian discourses of social injustice' could be focused on four narratives fully available to all English people, the Gospels.

It has for a long time been noticed that Hamlet's language borrows heavily from popular speech, his images being 'drawn from the most common aspects of everyday life ... which ally him to the lower-class figures of the Moralities.'[30] Shakespeare had no need to walk to Coventry to see the mystery plays in order to meet ordinary people ('lower-class figures' in that unfortunate phrase) in dramatic conflict. He could find those everyday images, heavily pregnant with apparently infinite meaning, at home, in the Gospels. Riches of material from the ancient world, the European Renaissance and recent history were borne to Shakespeare on a great tidal wave. But the great shifting of tectonic plates in Europe which produced the Protestant *tsunami* (far greater than a 'tidal wave') that flooded Europe to such depth gave him, through the Bible in English, a Kingdom of Heaven which is immediate; bodily presence on stage. Here is a parable:

> What woman having ten groats, if she lose one, doth not light a candle, and sweep the house, and seek diligently, till she find it? And when she hath found it she calleth her lovers and her neighbours saying: Rejoice with me, for I have found the groat which I had lost.[31]

What could be simpler? Words have changed: 'groats' has gone, and 'lovers' has become entirely sexual: yet Jesus' story is not only clear; it also goes far beyond rational analysis. Luke tells it in the context of the Pharisees murmuring because Jesus is with 'sinners,' and eats with them. The story is not, or not only, about moral outcasts. It is more fully about losing and finding again, an experience that can make one weep, like finding oneself unexpectedly at home again. Jesus uses it to parallel 'joy in the presence of the angels of God', and what *that* means cannot surely be put into rational words at all.

In Hamlet's last desperate seconds, he is fighting for time to tell vital things to the obtuse—and thus suddenly betraying—Horatio:

> Had I but time—as this fell sergeant Death
> Is strict in his arrest—O, I could tell you—
> But let it be. (5.2.328–30)

Shakespeare expresses what might be said given less than a minute to live (unlike Ben Jonson, who expresses what Ben Jonson might say). In that simple language, Hamlet's range of emotion and thought, and the sense of a vast revelation of what it would—will—be like to die, are beyond anything expected. The extraordinary image of the fell sergeant strictly arresting suggests guilt, and martyrdom, and horror, and inevitability, and an arresting being who is both outside and inside the dying body, all in the end of someone's life on earth. Shakespeare is close to Tyndale in that sense of simple words bringing in a new kingdom of possibilities—'This thy brother was dead, and is alive again; was lost, and is found': or 'Now abideth faith, hope and love, even these three: but the chief of these is love.'

Harold Bloom gets this wrong. He rightly says that only the Bible matches Shakespeare, but he finds that 'what the Bible and Shakespeare have in common is rather less than most people suppose . . . only a certain universalism.'[32] Not so. What Shakespeare and the Bible have in common is that language, at the highest moments, of elemental simplicity, from the Gospels. It is suffering and poverty that are interiorised by Shakespeare. In the Gospels it is 'one sick of the palsy' (whose friends, so dense is the crowd, break open the roof of the house and let him down) to whom Jesus says, 'son, thy sins are forgiven thee.' Shakespeare met suffering people, registered in the ordinary language of the people, in the texts of the Gospels in English, ultimately Tyndale's English. He interiorised their suffering, and put them on the stage.

CHAPTER 3

The Problem of Self-Love in Shakespeare's Tragedies and in Renaissance and Reformation Theology

Robert Lanier Reid

Studies of the discourse of desire in Shakespeare's plays and sonnets have, since the 1970s, focused on two main bonds: the romance of sexual opposites and its complement, the companionate bond of sexual equals. Shakespeare's fascination with both, and with the tension between them, persists from *Two Gentlemen of Verona* to *Two Noble Kinsmen*. These bonds may form an envious rivalry or be mutually supportive; and Shakespeare's deepening use of cross-dressed disguise opens a transference and interchange between the two. In evaluating this diverse engagement of Self with Others, scholars have not fully explored how the interplay of courtship and friendship offers each character a means of self-fulfillment. Our fascination with the complexities of gender-based relationships has caused neglect of a third mode of desire which is far more central to Shakespeare's plays, namely, self-love.[1] How did Shakespeare conceive of self-love, and in what forms does it appear in his poems and plays? What were the predominant ideas about self-love among Renaissance and Reformation thinkers, whether of Catholic or Protestant sympathy, and toward which pole did Shakespeare lean in portraying the varied forms of self-love?

We must begin by observing the centrality of self-love in human life and in Shakespeare's works. As Oscar Wilde observed, "Self-love is the beginning of a life-long romance," and Shakespeare's depictions of human nature fully exploit this maxim. We must also grapple with the strangely problematic and frustrating nature of self-love, for this compelling love affair implies a division in the self. In *Oneself as Another* Paul Ricoeur observes how one's own body and mind are perceived as a mysterious "other," awakening a desire to possess and magnify this otherness which is so near and dear (1–26, 113–68).[2] This infatuation, however, gives way to a fearful wound on realizing the body-based self's imperfections, its degrading subjection to ugliness, weakness, mutability, mortality. As a result, one defensively seeks power, bonding, and possessions to palliate the wound of unfulfilled self-love and resultant self-estrangement. Managing this proliferation of defensive, recuperative strategies is central to the quest for self-fulfillment and identity. Thus, while romantic love fades in Shakespeare's histories and grows problematic in the tragedies, self-love persists as a *cause célèbre* in every play and poem.

In Sonnet 62 Shakespeare's main concern is not the adoration of a handsome youth, nor frustration with a dark lady, but an unfulfilled self-adulation:

> Sin of self-love possesseth all mine eye
> And all my soul and all my every part;
> And for this sin there is no remedy,
> It is so grounded inward in my heart. (1–4)[3]

In the first line "eye" puns on the "I" which is the essential self and the "eye" which sees the self reflected in worldly mirrors. Self-love thus knits the outer and inner worlds.

The second quatrain shifts to the self's aggressive fantasy of greatness as a trope of superiority:

> Methinks no face so gracious is as mine,
> No shape so true, no truth of such account,
> And for myself mine own worth do define,
> As I all others in all worths surmount. (5–8)

This assertion of absolute supremacy problematizes the poet's identity, implying an insecure envy which seeks to "surmount" (indeed negate) the significance of "all others." This denial that anyone can mirror him adequately, that he must be *sui generis*, a godlike self-definer, anticipates the contemptuous exclusivity of Macbeth and Coriolanus.

The sestet brings the usual reality check, when a mirror shows the poet wrinkled with age. This humbling discovery completely inverts the experience of Narcissus, yet in privileging material appearances (ensouled body rather than idealized soul), Shakespeare remains true to his customary worldview:

> But when my glass shows me myself indeed,
> Beated and chopped with tanned antiquity,
> Mine own self-love quite contrary I read;
> Self so self-loving were iniquity. (9–12)

Here is perhaps the key to what Keats called the "negative capability" of Shakespeare. Acknowledging his failure to look like Narcissus and, moreover, to realize grandiose eternal selfhood, the playwright will resort to endless imagining of high-born and low-born characters as defensive displacements. Thus in the closing couplet Shakespeare defers to the handsome boy, lauding him as a valid basis for his own self-love since he identifies so completely with the boy's youthful outward beauty:

> 'Tis thee, myself, that for myself I praise,
> Painting my age with beauty of thy days. (13–14)

This conclusive flattery of the beloved, a common pattern in the sonnets, here is used to reformulate the problem of self-love. Instead of deflecting our awareness of the "sin of self-love," the deferential couplet actually enhances the poet's admission of utmost egoism. As Anne Ferry notes in *The Inward Language*, Shakespeare, unlike Sidney, fully acknowledges and explores the implications of his own self-love.[4]

In *The Heresy of Self-Love* (1968), which argues the importance of self-love in Western culture, Paul Zweig considers this motive central to all Shakespeare's sonnets, especially Sonnet 126, apparently addressed to a young man. In the adored youth, Zweig says, the poet seeks to immortalize an idealized image of himself as a defense against time's, and life's, ravages.[5] By repeatedly asserting the power of his art to confer immortality, the poet flatters himself more than the youth. Moreover, the sonnets praise the young man's outward beauty far more than his moral character, which increasingly appears as fickle and self-indulgent.

Thus the critique of self-love in Sonnet 62 seems intended partly as a lesson for the beautiful youth: the opening line thus indicates the poet's fascination with the youth's, as well as the poet's, "sin of self-love." The young man's consummate attractiveness ("beauty of thy days," suggests the allure of both youth and privilege) mirrors the poet's self-love in identifying with him: "'Tis thee, myself, that for myself I praise."

Philosophical fictions which portray the myth as love's origin and the achieving of identity through relationship often begin with an episode of self-mirroring—an event confirming the troubling division in the self. In *Phaedrus* 255D Plato emphasizes self-fulfillment by means of reflections in the beloved;[6] in *The Romance of the Rose* Amant sees his reflection in Narcissus's fountain before engaging with the rose-maiden;[7] in Chaucer's "Squire's Tale" the mirror of Canacee enables her to discern false love in others (132–45, 225–35, 347–75, 499–620);[8] in *The Faerie Queene* Britomart first envisions her beloved in Merlin's mirror (3.2.22–44);[9] and in *Paradise Lost* Eve transposes the glorifying of her own image to admiring Adam's spiritual beauty (4.449–91).[10] All these episodes imply that love grows from an idealized self-image, though each version, especially Milton's, also implies a potential for treacherous self-betrayal in the delightful mirroring and idealizing of oneself. In these mythic fables, as in Shakespeare's Sonnet 62, self-adulation anxiously merges with self-abnegation, a paradox reflected in Narcissus's cry: *inopem me copia fecit* ("my plenty makes me poor").[11] In his study of Shakespeare's sonnets, C. L. Barber praises the "selfless love" of these "wonderfully generous poems" and the "negative capability" which can "create a world resonant with the friend's beauty"; but there is notable contradiction in Barber's praising the poet for "realiz[ing] others with a selflessness" that can be "poignant ... desperate ... ugly ... sublime."[12] Outward or bodily based beauty arouses a hunger that neither the eyes nor any contact with the shadowy world of senses can satisfy. Plato, Plotinus and Ficino saw Narcissus "as a symbol of the human soul searching for its own beauty—a reflection of divine beauty—but unwittingly seduced by the reflection of that beauty in the physical body."[13] Zweig concludes his study by suggesting that Shakespeare resolved his own problem of self-love by turning from the beautiful youth of the sonnets to the multiple personae of drama.[14] I believe, though, that self-love is the central motive, not only of all his sonnets but of every character in his plays.

CONTRARY VIEWS OF SELF-LOVE FROM ANTIQUITY TO THE REFORMATION

Self-love's centrality becomes fully apparent when we consider those leading poets, philosophers, and theologians who focus not only on its perverse corruptions but also on its essentially positive form. Augustine, who returns to self-love endlessly, explores both of its extremes. In *The City of God* and *De genesi ad litteram* he admits self-love's fallen debasement; but in *De doctrina Christiana* and *De Trinitate* he emphasizes the essential goodness of creation and of the human soul, evident in its trinitarian powers.[15] Shakespeare's mature protagonists, in struggling with increasingly complex forms of self-love, reflect the influence of diverse intellectual traditions. On one side, Plotinus, Augustine, and many medieval and Reformation thinkers urge caution for Narcissus's sad fable, lamenting the youth's preoccupation with his fleshly body and urging that love focus on the rational and virtuous self. On the other side, Aristotle, Aquinas and La Primaudaye stress that self-love—including love for one's body—is natural and vital to ethical well-being. Plato, however, in the *Laws* says, "Every man is naturally his own friend,"[16] and Aristotle makes this proverbial dictum the cornerstone doctrine in the *Nicomachean Ethics*. For him all virtues, notably magnanimity, derive from self-interest, and the crowning virtue of friendship is grounded in sensible self-love: "in loving a friend, men love what is good for themselves" (8.5.1157b);[17] "he is related to his friend as to himself (for his friend is another self)"; "the extreme of friendship is likened to one's love for oneself" (9.4.1166a–b). In sum, "the good man should be a lover of self." (9.8.1169a). Aquinas provides a still wider theoretical basis for approving of this good form of self-love. In *Summa Theologiae* he notes "the first movement of every [person's] appetite is towards its own good" (1.2.25.2),[18] and he stresses that, in "loving one's neighbor as oneself, ... the model exceeds the copy"; "the self ... is closer to itself than to another, and therefore constitutes a prior object of love" (2.2.26.4). He adds, "Despite the . . . self-transcending effect of love, the agent 'does not will the good of his friend *more than* his own good . . . and does not [love] another more than himself'" (1.2.28.3 ad 3).

In the Renaissance this positive view of self-love is recited in Shakespeare's favorite encyclopedic source of ideas on human nature. In part 2 of *The French Academie* Pierre de la Primaudaye begins his nineteen-chapter analysis of human passions with a lengthy discourse on "selfe-love," which he treats as the "wel-spring" of all passions and all virtues. Like Aristotle and Aquinas, he insists that "[w]e love ourselves naturally"; "For it is an affection which is as it were a beame of the love that God beareth towards all his creatures, and which he causeth to shine in them, so that it is not possible, that they which are capable of any affection of love, should not love their owne bloud and their like. . . . Wherefore if this love and this affection were well ruled and ordered, it is so farre from being vicious, that contrariwise the spirit of God condemneth as monsters those . . . that want it. And therefore God . . . appointeth it to be the rule of our love towards our neighbour"[19] La Primaudaye acknowledges the dark underside, the potential "unrulinesse" of self-love: "When this love and affection is disordered in us, it is not only vicious, but also as it were the original and fountaine of all other vices and sins, whereas if it were wel-ordered & ruled according to the will and law of God, it would be . . . the originall and wel-spring of all virtues" (459–60).

Augustine too considered good self-love as central to human nature, its norm, yet he emphasizes that original sin has distorted this primal impulse into an ambitious lust to build worldly cities of destruction. Nevertheless, Augustine maintains a belief in the possibility of true self-love, which can draw men to the City of God—if only it allies with communal well-being and if only one prays for divine grace to restore the sense of oneself as *imago dei*. In *On the Trinity* Augustine describes self-love as the memory of the Holy Spirit implanted in the soul at creation, a memory mediated by Christ.[20] Likewise for Aquinas, "proper self-love consists in love for the self 'in God'" (1.6.1 ad 2), as well as reciprocal "bond[s] of affection" and "mutual indwelling" with other souls (1.2.28.1–2).

Many Protestant Reformation theologians, however, deny the possibility of good self-love without intervening grace, and Martin Luther carries this skepticism to an extreme. In *Lectures on Romans* he urges that we replace self-love with self-hate, and cultivate self-sacrifice: "true love for yourself is hatred for yourself. . . . Therefore he who hates himself and loves his neighbor, this person truly loves himself. For he loves himself outside of himself, thus he loves himself purely as long as he loves himself in his neighbor."[21] Only grace, Luther says, can bring true self-love when it "delivers" the self from being "completely curved in" on itself.[22] Luther is referring to the second key scriptural text regarding self-love: not only must we follow the great summary command to love both self and neighbor as a reflection of loving God entirely, but we must live with Jesus' harder command: "If any man wil come after me, let him denye him self, and take up his crosse daily, and followe me. For whosoeuer wil saue his life wil lose it: and whosoeuer wil lose his life for my sake, the same shal saue it" (Luke 9:23-24; *The Geneva Bible*[23]). Luther follows the harsher phrasing of John 12:25: "He that loueth his life, shal lose it, & he that hateth his life in this world, shal kepe it vnto life eternal." Aquinas does not emphasize this passage; he mentions "self-hate" only as "the effective result of false self-love" that undermines the self's true good; he never prescribes self-hate, even rhetorically.[24]

Does Shakespeare in portraying the motives and consequences of self-love draw from Augustine's vision of the dark side of human nature, stressed by Luther and Calvin and broadcast widely by Reformation divines, or does he favor the eudaemonist (happiness-based) tradition of Aristotle and Aquinas, as well as Augustine's brighter vision of humankind in *On the Trinity*, a view which recurs in La Primaudaye, Montaigne, Hooker, and Donne?[25] The latter group envisions good self-love as a normative quest for perfection, a self-esteem which reflects that of God, who (according to the Westminster, Lutheran, Calvin and Heidelberg catechisms), created all things "for his own glory."[26] This mystery of divine self-love is consummately envisioned by the pilgrim Dante at the very end of his quest:

> O eternal light, existing in yourself alone,
> Alone knowing yourself; and who, known to yourself
> And knowing, love and smile upon yourself![27]

Despite Reformation insistence on original sin, Shakespeare could find theological support for a proper, thoughtful glorying in the goodness of oneself and one's offspring, thus appreciating creation and imitating the Creator.

Though Sonnet 62 labels self-love as "sin," Shakespeare's concept of self-love, both in this sonnet and throughout his plays, is as ambivalent as that of philosophers and theologians since antiquity. Helen Vendler in *The Art of Shakespeare's Sonnets* reads Sonnet 62 as severe self-criticism,[28] but Shakespeare's attitude seems more playfully indulgent and flexible, an inner drama in process. Punning on "iniquity" as "inequity," he accepts this "sin" as the ground of his being ("grounded inward in my heart"), and he justifies self-love by his frank homage to the self-loving youth. Note the marvelous complexity of tone—and of personal identity—in the sonnet's penultimate line, "'Tis thee, myself, that for myself I praise": is this a mood of humble self-abasement, proud self-approval, or a disarmingly ironic blend of both?

Three Levels of Self-Love in Shakespeare's Characters

Self-love is universal in Shakespeare's characters but assumes quite distinct forms. The antics of the immature, thoughtless narcissists are comical and poignant, for they remain naively unaware in their self-dotage, even when they are publicly exposed. More fearful is the second group, the cunning, villainous egoists, whose self-aggrandizement and cruelty are intensely rational and intentional, especially in villain-protagonists like Richard III and Macbeth. It is the third group, the generous-spirited and wittily ironic protagonists (not unlike the poet's own voice in Sonnet 62), who are capable of expressing self-love in an attractive manner, refined by the sufferings and joys they share with friends and lovers. As Aquinas says, they establish reciprocal "bonds of affection" and "mutual indwelling" with other souls. In some cases these self-lovers even acknowledge support from divine providence, as in the concluding episodes of *Hamlet* (5.2.10, 157–61), *King Lear* (5.3.16–17, 160–61) and *The Tempest* (5.1.189, 201–13; Epilogue 16–18) in Bevington's fourth edition of Shakespeare.

Shakespeare's immature, delusional egoists, marked by grandiose fantasies and cowardly defenses, are mostly young male aristocrats, but the group includes older men and a few women as well. All resemble one of two Ovidian figures: either the passive Narcissus who drowns in self-contemplation and reduces an admiring maiden to an Echo, or the aggressive Phaethon, whose aspiration consumes him in fire. Self-exhibition so blinds these characters to their own flaws and to the value of others, so deprives them of empathy, humor and wisdom, that their foibles are apparent even to friends, family and servants. Striking examples are Proteus and Valentine in *Two Gentlemen of Verona*, Demetrius and Chiron in *Titus Andronicus*, Tybalt in *Romeo and Juliet*, Hotspur in *1 Henry IV*, Malvolio in *Twelfth Night*, Laertes in *Hamlet*, Achilles and Ajax in *Troilus and Cressida*, Bertram and Parolles in *All's Well* and Cloten in *Cymbeline*.

In *Two Gentlemen of Verona* Valentine's youthful egoism is initially laughable, as when Sylvia urges him to address his artful love letters to himself, a task he greatly enjoys. But in his boast of possessing a mistress of unmatchable worth, he evokes a darker self-love in Proteus, who deserts Julia and slanders Valentine to steal Sylvia's affection. Proteus makes this remark about his bosom-friends, "If I keep them, I needs must lose myself. . . . I to myself am dearer than a friend, For love is still [i.e., always] most precious in itself" (2.6.21, 23–24). Though Aquinas affirms the superiority of self-love over friendship, Proteus does not really love, nor know, himself: his insecure self-promotion, like that of Bertram and Cloten, begins in parental dotage, is stunned by envy, and proceeds in cruel treachery; it is the callous narcissism of a privileged adolescent. A still deadlier self-obsession is that of bullying braggarts like Demetrius and Chiron, Tybalt, Hotspur, Laertes, Ajax, Achilles; and in comic vein, Parolles, Malvolio and Cloten. Their fantasies of self-importance invite others to belittle them in asides and, for the latter three, to shame them with hilarious ruses.

A second type of self-lover, the opportunistic Machiavellian villain, consciously and intentionally exploits and destroys others in order to attain a sole and sterile supremacy. In these figures Shakespeare exploits what Hegel called the "portentous power of the negative."[29] Instead of the rash petulance of the immature egoists, the villains pursue their ends with sharp and malevolent craft. Aaron and Tamora, Richard III, Shylock, Don John, Iago, Goneril-Regan-Cornwall-Oswald-Edmund and Antiochus combine intellectual cunning with contempt for spiritual being, lust for material goods, and reduction of human nature to bestial drives. To aggrandize themselves they slander and destroy others, even spouses and intimate friends; thus their family relationships are incestuous, tyrannical and short-lived, a mere forum for demonstrating their cruel prowess. Centrally motivating these figures is a proud self-love that would displace God and all authority, joined with an envious exclusiveness that destroys all rivals, corrupts all innocence and finally negates its own being. Richard III opens his play with narcissistic fury at his body's deformity: "I that am rudely stamped, and want love's majesty" (1.1.16); and at the end he resists shame for his crimes in a monologue replete with self-love. Facing the angry ghosts of his victims, Richard wonders if he should fear himself: "No," he replies, "Richard loves Richard; that is, I am I" (5.3.183). By affirming the naturalness of his self-love, Richard likens himself to God, the ultimate "I am"; yet Richard's self-assertion is strictly limited: not the universal, open-ended "I AM" that participates in all being, but a rigidly self-enclosed solipsism: "I am [only] I."

Similar but even more satanic is the self-love of Iago, who seems driven less by ambition than by nihilistic contempt, especially for those of magnanimous nature. In the opening he stresses his self-interest and mere pretense of service:

> In following him, I follow but myself—
> Heaven is my judge, not I for love and duty,
> But seeming so for my particular end. (1.1.57–62)

His sneering conclusion, "I am not what I am" (67), is a reveling in duplicity, but it also epitomizes the nihilism of his mode of self-love.

His sinister phrasing negates the confident "I am I" of Richard III, and thus further darkens the parody of divinity. God, the "I am," promotes Being, creating others with similar freedom and power. In contrast, Iago's hate annihilates all others—rivals and superiors, friends and charitable souls, and finally his own heart and voice. His final comment—"From this time forth I never will speak word" (5.2.312)—thus fulfills his initial claim, "I am not what I am" (1.1.67). Is all self-love so limiting as this, so bent on finding power in negation? Our third and most prominent group of Shakespearean characters refutes this derogatory conception of self-love.

Shakespeare's most admired characters show self-love's most complex and engaging face. Audiences delight in the self-glorying pride that animates the combative courtships of Petruchio and Katharina, Titania and Oberon, Beatrice and Benedick, Antony and Cleopatra, and the comic vaunts of Juliet's nurse, Dogberry, Mistress Quickly, and especially Falstaff and Bottom, whose limitless self-love insinuates them into every part, delightfully mimicking and mangling "all humors." The charismatic protagonists in plays of 1596–1599 even begin to struggle with moral correctness. While the spectacular self-vaunters of the first history tetralogy—Suffolk, Margaret, Eleanor, York, Warwick, Joan La Pucelle, the Talbots, Jack Cade, Richard—displayed a shallow, brutal, unaware self-love, in the second tetralogy the quest for personal glory deepens into wonderfully ambivalent self-awareness. Hal predicts his success in messianic terms, "Redeeming time when men think least I will" (*1 Henry IV* 1.2.211); to his father he centrally affirms his confidence (3.2.129–59); and he finally taunts Hotspur, "all the budding honors on thy crest / I'll crop to make a garland for my head" (5.4.72–73). But the self-promotion of this "mirror of all Christian kings" (*Henry V* 2.Pro.6) is shadowed by the less restrained, hence more destructive ambitions of Falstaff, Hotspur, and King Henry. The critics' perplexity over whether Henry V enacts perfect kingship alerts us to the subtleties of self-love, which so easily deludes and enslaves the uncautious soul. During these years Shakespeare's portrayal of self-love also becomes more captivating through cross-dressing that brings bigendered awareness and deeper moral commitment. In the great comedies and tragedies from 1597 onward, women such as Portia, Beatrice, Rosalind, Viola, Helena and Cleopatra share in self-admiring wit and prowess, even as willful women such as Goneril, Regan and Lady Macbeth share in the ruthless appropriation of power through trickery and violence.

SELF-LOVE IN THE MATURE TRAGEDIES

Shakespeare's portrayal of self-love's full complexity, including its essentially positive nature, becomes apparent in the series of great tragedies beginning with *Julius Caesar*. In *Shakespearean Tragedy: Its Art and Christian Premises* Roy Battenhouse provides a severe Protestant perspective when he observes the prominence of self-love in these tragedies, not as a God-implanted motivational core, but as the deadliest of burdens, a Christianized expansion, via original sin, of *hamartia* or the tragic flaw.[30] This dark and self-isolating mode of self-love culminates in the Macbeths and in Coriolanus and Volumnia, who contemptuously assert superiority over others. Friends and foes agree that Coriolanus is "O'ercome with pride, ambitious, past all thinking / Self-loving" (4.6.30–33). With his extreme bent for violence and absolutist vaunts, Coriolanus surpasses the earlier portraits of vain warriors (Tybalt, Hotspur, Ajax, Achilles), providing the fullest study of antagonistic self-aggrandizement, a self-constrictive elitism that leads (as in *Julius Caesar*) to his ritual slaughter by those reduced to envy. *Macbeth* shows the ultimate toll on the psyche of this estranging, murderous mode of self-love: the play evokes the primitive mindset in which "one is either predator or prey, . . . master or slave."[31] Macbeth's effort to erase all dependencies is of course self-defeating, for in assaulting all human bonds (fatherly king, best friend, mother and child) and in attempting to void conscience, the bond with God, he loses his essential being.

Other tragic protagonists, however, show that self-love need not exclude neighbor-love. The struggling egos of Brutus, Hamlet, Othello, King Lear, Antony, Cleopatra and their devoted entourages, though conflicted and often misguided, are repeatedly affirmed in a network of supportive relationships. These plays increasingly exemplify the paradox noted by Aristotle, Augustine and Aquinas *that self-love is fulfilled in loving others*, especially when the conscience of those loved reflects the will of God. Whereas Shakespeare's early plays persistently assign privilege and dominance to self-approving males (Petruchio, Oberon, Henry V), in *Julius Caesar* the self-love of male authority-figures is, for the first time, complexly questioned and explored. Shakespeare displays its many errant forms as well as the attractiveness of its potential goodness, especially in the evolving persona of Brutus.

All characters in *Julius Caesar* show the clamor of self-love, but only Brutus struggles to affirm its positive dimension. Caesar's grandiose self-image, as he maneuvers toward absolute rule, is continually manifested in quotable maxims: "Cowards die many times before their deaths; / The valiant never taste of death but once" (2.2.32–33). He goes to the capitol believing the Senate will "give this day a crown to mighty Caesar" (2.2.93–94), and he confirms his fate by boasting godlike immutability against their pleas for mercy: "I am constant as the northern star, / Of whose true-fixed and resting quality / There is no fellow in the firmament" (3.1.60–62). Against such pride Cassius's narcissistic wound seeks murderous relief as he chafes at Caesar's celebrity: "Why, man, he doth bestride the narrow world / Like a colossus, and we petty men / Walk under his huge legs and peer about / To find ourselves dishonourable graves" (134–37). Caesar self-approvingly notes Cassius's envy: "Such men as he be never at heart's ease / Whiles they behold a greater than themselves" (207–8).

A third self-lover, Antony, attaches himself to Caesar's rising star and skillfully plays out his own ambitions in the aftermath. His funeral oration, one of Shakespeare's finest theatrical coups, enforces the play's central peripety by collectively exploiting the common people's self-love (that is, tempting them with the will) just as Caesar had done; and Antony's adeptness in rousing the crowd (a charismatic eloquence which becomes less manipulative, more spontaneous and likable in *Antony and Cleopatra*) derives from his own sophisticated enjoyment of self-love. Though Antony's closing eulogy for Brutus (like Octavius's concluding praise for Antony and Cleopatra) is self-serving, his consummate encomium for this "noblest Roman of them all" aptly confirms Brutus's superior resolution of the problem of self-love.

Brutus by his name, nature, and family heritage approximates Aristotle's magnanimous man, whose virtues *merit* self-approval; yet he resists Cassius's flattery partly through his proudly confident nobility and partly through a contrary impulse toward modest restraint and self-abnegation. This inner tension, unshared by the other main characters, is what makes Brutus so attractive to Shakespeare, who uses Brutus's inner development to define the play's structure. In acts 1–2 high-minded Brutus is seduced into leading the assassination; in act 3 Brutus's bland public justification shows his naive trust that all others, including Antony and the common people, must share his virtue; in acts 4–5 Brutus's misjudgments in war underscore his moral idealism, and his deepening friendship with Cassius forms the basis for high-minded suicide. Brutus's moral growth is the play's touchstone as he undergoes a full cycle of fall and recovery in dealing with his own self-love. At the beginning of the play he answers Cassius's charge of lessened friendship by pleading self-preoccupation: "If I have veiled my look, / I turn the trouble of my countenance / Merely upon myself" (1.2.37–39). In this celebrated temptation-scene Cassius cleverly builds on that habit of self-withdrawal by flattering Brutus, urging him to see his own virtue:

> it is very much lamented, Brutus,
> That you have no such mirrors as will turn
> Your hidden worthiness into your eye
> That you might see your shadow. (55–58)

In this reference to "mirrors" and "shadow" Cassius evokes the Narcissus story, mimicking the unhealthy dotage in *Venus and Adonis*, where we are told that Narcissus "died to kiss his shadow in the brook" (161), and it recalls the more complex mirror-scene in *Richard II*, where the protagonist, like Narcissus, becomes so aware of his ruinous self-dotage that self-pity intensifies the debilitation: "The shadow of your sorrow hath destroy'd / The shadow of your face" (*Richard II* 4.1.293–94).

Moved by Cassius's flattery of his nobility, family name, and public acclaim, Brutus nevertheless resists vainglory, showing his difference from the other conspirators, the starkest contrast being with Caska, whose babbling contempt for the "rabblement," the "tag-rag people," "the common herd" with their "chopped hands," "sweaty nightcaps," and "stinking breath" ironically displays Caska's vulgarity as he tries to recruit Brutus to the cause. The pretentious elitism of both Caska and Cassius sharply contrasts with Brutus's genuinely noble sensitivity in the next scene, where his inner struggle mingles with courtesy to his servant Lucius. Confident of his own worth, Brutus fears that Caesar's self-love is becoming uncontrollable; yet he generously admits Caesar's customary rational self-control:

> I know no personal cause to spurn at him
> But for the general. He would be crown'd:
> How that might change his nature, there's the question.
> ...
> Th' abuse of greatness is when it disjoins
> Remorse from power; and to speak truth of Caesar
> I have not known when his affections swayed
> More than his reason. But 'tis a common proof
> That lowliness is young ambition's ladder. (2.1.10–12; 18–22)

That Brutus himself resists the baser forms of self-love—Cassius's avaricious materialism, Caesar's overreaching ambition, Antony's glib manipulations—is indicated not only by the universal admiration for Brutus (from conspirators, from his wife and servants, from military colleagues and opponents), but also by the respect he shows to others of every social class, notably in the tender regard for his servant Lucius and for the soldier who assists Brutus in his suicide.

Brutus's moral struggle shows the difficulty of realizing a good self-love. In the temptation-scene of act 1 (1.2.28–322), which serves as the focal point in the first two-act cycle, Cassius lures Brutus into self-adulation as a basis for resenting Caesar. Closely parallel, but with reverse outcome, is their quarrel-scene (4.3.1–123), which serves as the focal point of the final two-act cycle. The quarrel-scene inverts the facile narcissism of the temptation-scene, as Brutus criticizes Cassius's unprincipled avarice and urges him to reclaim a virtuous basis for self-love:

> What, shall one of us,
> That struck the foremost man of this world,
>   ... now
> Contaminate our fingers with base bribes,
> And sell the mighty space of our large honours
> For so much trash as may be grasped thus? (4.3.18–26)

He sternly dismisses Cassius—"Away, slight man!" (37)—for his "proud heart," his greedy, waspish temper, and his vaunting, urging him to associate with "slaves" and "bondmen" rather than with "noble men" (42–54). Brutus lightly echoes Caesar's self-righteousness when he proclaims himself "so armed in honesty" that Cassius's threats "pass by me as the idle wind, / Which I respect not" (67–69); but Brutus's frank and open criticism differs sharply from Caesar's far-off critique of the "lean and hungry" Cassius. Following this stark exposure, Cassius pitifully holds that a friend should overlook such faults, but when Brutus refuses to "flatter," Cassius histrionically admits his faults and offers his proud heart for Brutus to sacrifice along with Caesar's. Brutus again undercuts this pretentious show, and in so doing lays a basis for genuine friendship in the final episodes. In this challenging scene neither Cassius nor Brutus renounces self-love, but they amend it to meet Brutus's high standards: Cassius's inclination to avarice, vaunting and self-deception is subordinated to Brutus's stoic self-restraint, his valorous honesty and, when exposure is complete, his forgiveness of his friend.

In *Julius Caesar* self-love is not discredited and discarded but rather is gradually refined, culminating in a loving gesture which is both self-abnegation and self-fulfilment; hence the overdetermined meaning of the two friends' suicides. As in the love-deaths of Romeo and Juliet, Othello and Desdemona, Antony and Cleopatra, and even the despairful self-immolations of Ophelia and Lady Macbeth, suicide underscores both the power of self-love and the power of relationship. Brutus's suicide partly shows pride in rationally determining his own fate, resisting the parade of conquest:

> Think not, thou noble Roman,
> That ever Brutus will go bound to Rome.
> He bears too great a mind (5.1.110–12).

Yet, along with Cassius, his motivation also builds on their newly deepened friendship in the face of death's mystery:

> Whether we shall meet again, I know not:
> Therefore our everlasting farewell take:
> For ever and for ever farewell, Cassius.
> If we do meet again, why, we shall smile;
> If not, why then this parting was well made. (5.1.115–19)

Brutus's suicide does not emphasize proudly isolated self-governance but rather a consummate valuation of friendship: he asks each military colleague to assist him and receives aid only from Strato as the others plead their love for him. As Brutus works toward a basically positive self-love that culminates in love-death, Portia's death by eating hot coals is a jarringly negative contrast. Her violent self-immolation symbolically emphasizes her remarkable rational prowess, self-possession, and greatness of soul, setting for Brutus and Cassius a severe standard of noble dying. But the fire in her throat also suggests her failure to communicate with Brutus. The contrast of this lonely, brutal suicide with the tender mutuality achieved by Brutus and Cassius suggests Shakespeare's distancing of the female bond in this play, as in *Hamlet*.

In the great tragedies beginning with *Julius Caesar*, Shakespeare thus alters the psychic scenario in which self-love seeks an idealized mirroring other. In the sonnets the aging poet mirrored himself in a handsome youth whose wayward self-indulgence, especially toward the dark lady, is increasingly evident. In *The Merchant of Venice* and *Twelfth Night* the beloved young man (Bassanio, Sebastian) is more morally sensitive than the youth of the sonnets, especially after splitting into bisexual twins; yet this near-androgyny still does not provide an effective mirroring love-object. Neither Bassanio nor Sebastian is fully accessible to sad Antonio; nor is either youth tested and transformed by suffering. That transformation, the fullest refinement of self-love, occurs in the mature tragedies, beginning with *Julius Caesar*, then more radically in *Hamlet*, which is Shakespeare's most mysterious and problematic meditation on this central human struggle.

For Roy Battenhouse, Hamlet fails to achieve maturity because of his "intense subjectivism, self-dramatization, flight from reality, and specious argument," "egoism and self-pity," "homicidal or suicidal mania" (226), above all, "inordinate love of glory for the self": "self-centeredness is the unwitting quality of Hamlet's idealism," as expressed in his idolizing Ophelia (231) and his father (232), and especially his apostrophes to man as "the paragon of animals" (233). But to Ophelia Hamlet admits his errancies:

> I am very
> proud, revengeful, ambitious, with more offenses at
> my beck than I have thoughts to put them in,
> imagination to give them shape, or time to act them
> in. What should such fellows as I do crawling
> between earth and heaven? We are arrant knaves,
> all; believe none of us (3.1.123–28).

In Hamlet's skeptical assault on human nature, and most pointedly women, Shakespeare begins a series of tragedies and bitter comedies that move us far from Brutus's confidence in his nobility.

As Battenhouse maintains, Hamlet's bent for extravagant idealization (in courting Ophelia, mourning his father, praising Horatio)—and equally for extravagant condemnation (of Claudius and Gertrude, Ophelia and her father, Rosencrantz and Guildenstern)—is to some extent a defensive and immature version of self-love, a narcissistic wound. His harkening to a vengeful ghost and his verbal and physical cruelty to others, especially Ophelia, do not betoken a "sweet prince."[32] Nevertheless, we sense many countervailing reasons for finding Hamlet admirable: his delay in revenging and his questioning of the ghost's moral authority; his valid distaste for his mother's hasty remarriage, for former friends and courtiers becoming spies, and for Ophelia's acquiescence in serving as bait; and more positively, his mother's persistent dotage, Ophelia's lavish praise, and Horatio's faithful friendship and exalted elegy. Hamlet's moral excellence is indicated not only by these aristocratic testimonials but also by numerous commoners who find him approachable, likable and respectful of themselves: guards, players, pirates and especially Yorick, whose earthy humor, love of life and love of Hamlet is resurrected in the personality of the gravedigger. These vulgar men lack the courtly pretense and jockeying for power that we sense in Claudius, Polonius, Laertes, Rosencrantz and Guildenstern, and Osric. Hamlet's effort to be reconciled to Laertes and his voicing of providential workings suggest a softening of his earlier disgust for life; and Hamlet's final desire for Horatio to live and to tell his story seems a significant movement toward recovering genuine self-love. *Julius Caesar* and *Hamlet* thus provide an extensive anatomy of self-love, and in the latter play its diverse extremes vie within the complex psyche of a single figure, a "sweet prince" with "bad dreams."

Subsequent tragedies show deepening perspectives on self-love. The problems of corrupt and exclusive self-love are definitively revealed in *Othello*, where most characters, especially males, struggle with wounded narcissism. We noted that Iago insists on serving only his own interests, and he likewise depicts Othello as "loving his own pride and purposes" (1.1.13). Othello's first entrance seems to confirm that view as he refuses to hide from suspicions and eagerly seeks to display himself to the world: "My parts, my title, and my perfect soul / Shall manifest me rightly" (1.2.31–32). Self-love is enmeshed in his rhetorical eloquence, the "Othello music" of self-centered storytelling which makes him so attractive. Desdemona's identification with his venturous spirit, wishing "That heaven had made her such a man" (1.3.165), underscores the naturalness of his ambition and pride, properly glorying in his courageous, responsible identity. This noble self-esteem finds a foil in the shallower self-preening of Cassio. His abuse of Bianca and drunken loss of office help us to appreciate Othello's idealizing of Desdemona and despair at no longer serving her rare virtue (3.3.361, 4.2.59–62). Othello's ardent self-love is thus not mere hubris, not simply a "fatal flaw" for Iago to exploit. Rather, in his initial tender exchanges with Desdemona, Othello shows the magnanimous blossoming of his "great . . . heart" (5.2.361), a self-esteem so maturely managed that it draws Desdemona's devotion: "My heart's subdued / Even to the very quality of my lord" (1.3.251–52). Certainly Othello's self-regard offers a fertile seedbed for Iago's slanderous insinuations, yet, no less than Brutus and Hamlet, Othello struggles to sustain a positive mode of self-love. To perceive his self-love only in a negative sense is to eviscerate the heart of this great tragedy.

The most profound study of self-love occurs in *King Lear*, beginning with the aged sovereign's mythic ritual of self-exaltation: "Which of you shall we say doth love us most?" (1.1.51) (Similarly Cleopatra asks Antony at the outset, "If it be love indeed, tell me how much." [1.1.14]) Like Brutus, Hamlet, and Othello, Lear is centrally motivated by a self-love which deeply evolves in the course of the play, especially since Lear's struggle with self-affirmation is complicated by the burdensome mantle of kingship and by the anxieties of old age and mortality. In his ardent defenses against such temptations and adversaries, Lear finds the most challenging self-mirroring of all in his sexual and moral opposite, Cordelia. This complex handling of self-love in a privileged male carries us far beyond the paralyzing pool of Narcissus—into a distraught, fragmented self which in old age seeks the mirror not of a winsome lad but of a virtuous daughter, an "other" whom he has tried to absorb into himself, yet who shows that she is strong enough to resist the old man's vanity yet devoted enough to sacrifice herself for him. Similarly, in each of the final romances an aging, male authority-figure is mirrored and chastened by a maiden (Marina, Imogen, Perdita, Miranda) who, despite her youth, shows high moral judgment.

Resolving Self-Love: Shakespeare's Magus

As Zweig notes in *The Heresy of Self-Love*, ancient folklore offers a paradigm of self-love in the ambitious heretical magus, Dr. Faustus.[33] It is intriguing that Shakespeare's swansong, *The Tempest*, features Prospero as a reformed Faustus. On behalf of his daughter Miranda, who mirrors the best part of himself, Prospero uses his artful power to reshape human nature and history: a tempest, disappearing banquet, and punitive speech to expose his enemies' sins; transformative songs, an epiphanic meeting, arduous chores, and a sublime wedding masque to guide the young lovers through courtship; and a final reunion of the disparate members of the ship of state. Prospero's final boast suggests the playwright's glory in having staged humankind's wishful fantasies of controlling both the natural world and the destiny of the human soul:

> Ye elves . . . by whose aid . . . I have bedimm'd
> The noontide sun, called forth the mutinous winds,
> And 'twixt the green sea and the azured vault
> Set roaring war; . . . graves at my command
> Have waked their sleepers, oped, and let 'em forth
> By my so potent art. (5.1.33–50)

In surrendering this power, Prospero seeks to control his self-love; and he concludes the play by stressing his reliance on the love of others, his audiences, and on divine grace and forbearance:

> Now my charms are all o'erthrown,
> And what strength I have 's mine own,
> Which is most faint. . . .
> [So] release me from my bands
> With the help of your good hands.
> . . . Now I want
> Spirits to enforce, art to enchant,
> And my ending is despair,
> Unless I be reliev'd by prayer. (Epilogue 1–3, 9–10, 13–16)

The energy of this epilogue—and of *The Tempest* as a whole—is restrained and disarming, for it seeks to displace and contain the wilder energy that so charmed us in earlier plays.

What, then, attracts us so deeply to a self-indulgent clown like Bottom or an insatiable rogue like Falstaff, to sparring lovers like Katharina and Petruchio, Oberon and Titania, Beatrice and Benedick, or to regal minds like Hal, Rosalind, Hamlet, Lear, Cleopatra and Prospero? What else but an extraordinary impulse of self-love, often resorting to self-exhibition (plays within the play) in order to counteract the cruelty of envious rivals and in order to be loved supremely by all. In such characters, self-love achieves maturity or "ripeness" in at least three ways. First, these gregarious, imaginative characters (like the actor-playwright) tend to engage with audiences of all social types, abilities and moral natures, thus providing a mutual mirroring that resembles what Aquinas calls a reciprocal "bond of affection" and "mutual indwelling" with other souls. Second, some of these characters are able to perform or impersonate diverse social types within a masterfully regal identity which is, paradoxically, a self-abnegated identity, thus enacting multiple personalities in a single self: their identification with otherness demonstrates remarkable *powers of self-change*—either through sovereign empathy, through disguise and impersonation, or through chaotic gushings of madness which disclose the vast resources of psyche. Third, occasionally a sublimer form of self-love comes from witnessing the disintegration of life's theatrical stagings and especially from losing an other who mirrors the best part of oneself—hence an epiphany mediated by human faces. Watching these diverse ripenings in such consummate players as Falstaff, Rosalind, Hamlet, Lear, Cleopatra and Prospero evokes our own urge for completeness through active identification, for in their eloquent self-glorying, which so intensifies the being of others, we witness Shakespeare's most suggestive mirroring of God: an unlimited creative and loving power that springs from self-love.

CHAPTER 4

"I Could Not Say 'Amen'": Prayer and Providence in *Macbeth*

Robert S. Miola

Though ancient playwrights believed in different deities and ethical systems, they too depicted human beings struggling with the gods, with fate and free will, crime and punishment, guilt and suffering. Sophocles (5th c. BC) portrays Oedipus, solver of the Sphinx's riddle and King of Thebes, who discovers that all along he has been fulfilling, not fleeing, the curse of Apollo and its dread predictions: "Lead me away, O friends, the utterly lost (*ton meg' olethrion*), most accursed (*ton kataratotaton*), and the one among mortals most hated (*exthrotaton*) by the gods!" (1341–43). In several plays that provided models for *Macbeth*, Seneca (d. 65 AD) presents men and women saying the unsayable, doing the unthinkable and suffering the unimaginable. The witch Medea slays her own children in a horrifying act of revenge. In contrast to Euripides *Medea*, which ends in a choral affirmation of Zeus's justice and order, Seneca's play concludes with Medea's transformation into something inhuman: she leaves the scene of desolation in a chariot drawn by dragons, bearing witness, wherever she goes, that there are gods, *testare nullos esse, qua veheris, deos* (1027). Driven mad by the goddess Juno, Seneca's Hercules in *Hercules Furens* kills his children, then awakens to full recognition of his deed in suicidal grief and remorse. These tragic heroes struggle against the gods and themselves.

Such classical archetypes inform tragedy in the West, with Seneca especially shaping Elizabethan tragedy. *Medea* and *Hercules Furens* partly account for the child-killing so prominent in *Macbeth*. Of course,

Seneca here joins with native traditions of medieval drama, represented powerfully by Herod's massacre of holy innocents. Child-killing, as many have noted, appears both in the stage action of Shakespeare's play—the murder of Macduff's children, the bloody-child apparition—and in its language, Lady Macbeth's terrible hyperbole:

> I have given suck, and know
> How tender 'tis to love the babe that milks me;
> I would, while it was smiling in my face,
> Have plucked my nipple from his boneless gums
> And dashed the brains out, had I so sworn as you
> Have done to this. (1.7.54–59)[1]

Seneca may directly inspire Lady Macbeth herself.[2] Medea invokes the gods, asking them to "drive away feminine fears" (*pelle femineos metus*, 42) from her mind; alone, she rouses herself to a terrible deed of self-creation. In her famous soliloquy, Lady Macbeth asks the spirits (demons? the witches?) to "unsex" her, to "stop up th'access and passage to remorse," to take her "milk for gall" (1.5.36ff.). Of course, the differences between the two women loom large and important. Medea achieves a unique place in *scelus* ("crime"); altering the universe by transgressing the bounds of the natural, she becomes a supernatural creation who flies away like a god. Instead of such apotheosis, however, Lady Macbeth comes crashing down. Tormented by guilt and sleeplessness, she last appears in the sleepwalking scene (5.1), a ghost of her former self, haunted, frightened, broken. Perhaps the most celebrated actress in this role, Sarah Siddons (1755–1831) portrayed Lady Macbeth washing her hands vehemently; she imagined her character, "with wan and haggard countenance, her starry eyes glazed with the ever-burning fever of remorse, and on their lids the shadows of death."[3] Medea transforms herself; Lady Macbeth dies offstage.

Macbeth also experiences a breathtaking rise and crashing fall. He appears first as a classical warrior hero, "valor's minion," the bridegroom of Bellona, Roman goddess of war (1.2.19, 55). At a crucial point in the action he justifies the decision to kill Banquo in Senecan fashion: "Things bad begun make strong themselves by ill" (3.2.57) echoes

Seneca's proverbial saying, *per scelera semper sceleribus tutum est iter* (*Agamemnon*, 115), "the safe way for crime is through more crimes." But there is no safe way for crimes in Macbeth's world; not even Bellona's bridegroom can carve out his passage with brandished steel and bloody execution. Dagger in bloodstained hand, Macbeth suffers like no classical hero at the very moment of his triumphant murder; he hears the sleeping guards awake:

> *Macbeth*:   One cried "God bless us!" and "Amen!" the other,
> As they had seen me with these hangman's hands.
> List'ning their fear, I could not say "Amen"
>
> When they did say "God bless us!"
>
> *Lady Macbeth*: Consider it not so deeply.
>
> *Macbeth*:   But wherefore could not I pronounce "Amen"?
> I had most need of blessing, and "Amen"
>
> Stuck in my throat (2.2.29–36)

In David Garrick's celebrated eighteenth-century performance of this scene the self-reproach ("these hangman's hands") widened into a "wonderful expression of heartfelt horror."[4] Here that self-reproach accompanies an urgent need for God's blessing and the solace of prayer. Unable to say "Amen," Macbeth expresses a childlike incomprehension and astonishment at what he has done and become.

This extraordinary moment marks the differences between Macbeth and his classical predecessors, and from the cruel, remorseless tyrant Shakespeare found in Holinshed's *Chronicles* (1587), the main source of the play. And this moment takes us into the heart of Macbeth's tragedy: he has most need of God's blessing and cannot say "Amen." Confessing his need for God's blessing, of course, Macbeth declares himself an imperfect man in a fallen world. As John Smith put it in a book published about the time of the play, *A Pattern of True Prayer* (1605), everyone needs to obtain "saving blessings" from God through prayer because only those blessing can remove the "secret poison" in the heart caused by original sin:

> Hence it cometh that seeing wicked men do not and cannot pray therefore, though they have many blessings in show, yet in truth they are not so but rather curses, even the very poison and bane of their souls, means to hasten their damnation, and to drench the deeper in the pit of hell another day; whereas contrariwise, the godly asking blessings of god, He in mercy removeth this curse from the righteous man's goods, and makes his blessings saving blessings unto him. (sig. B2)[5]

This context makes precisely legible Macbeth's urgent need for blessing and his incapacity for prayer. Regarding this latter point, both Catholics and Protestants agree on the essential necessity of prayer and its nature. Urging the faithful to pray always, St. John Fisher defines prayer as a turning of the mind and heart toward God, with or without words, that results in the fervor of charity, sweetness of communion, and salvation. Protestant Thomas Becon agrees: prayer is a "lifting up of a pure mind to God, wherein we ask somewhat of him"; citing church fathers—Cyprian, Ambrose, Augustine, Jerome and Gregory—Becon continues: "prayer is not the work of the mouth but of the heart, not of the voice but of the thought, not of the lips but of the mind."[6] Everyone condemned empty prayer, vain babble or mere "lip-labor" (sig. C4) in John Smith's phrase. (Though both sadly accused the other side of lip-labor, with Protestants pointing to the rosary, Office of the Blessed Virgin and Latin Mass; and Catholics to the state-mandated *Book of Common Prayer*, each successive edition prefaced by parliamentary decree.) Claudius in *Hamlet* would prove himself a perfectly unobjectionable theologian to both confessions: "My words fly up, my thoughts remain below. / Words without thoughts never to heaven go" (3.3.97–99). Macbeth cannot say "Amen," anyone could have told him, because he prays with his lips only and not with his heart.

Furthermore, the word "Amen" has a special valence in its cultural moment, having assumed a pivotal position in theological disputes of Reformation. The saying of "Amen" became a crucial point of controversy in the Harding-Jewel debates on the vernacular. Construing Paul (1 Cor 14), John Jewel argued that saying "Amen" only to things understood could constitute a prayer. Saying "Amen" to the eucharistic prayer for Harding signified assent to the doctrine of transubstantiation; for Jewel no such thing, but "a thanksgiving unto God for our delivery by the death of Christ."[7] A number of writers wrote on the significance of "Amen" at the end of the Lord's Prayer. In *The Pathway to Prayer and Piety* (1609), Robert Hill explained that the word "Amen" ("so be it") put a "seal" on a prayer; it is a Hebraism that through long use in Greek, Latin and English provides an appropriate conclusion, if used with earnest desire and full consent, "not in hypocrisy to God." Hill advises readers "not to use this word 'Amen' so unadvisedly as we do now, but to know what it is to which we say 'Amen,' lest by ignorance we seal a curse to ourselves and others."[8] Macbeth's inability to say "Amen" testifies to his hypocrisy and sinfulness; but, more important, his desire to say "Amen" testifies to his goodness, to his deep and deeply denied need for grace and blessings.

Macbeth's abortive prayer thus illustrates the moral world of the play, the ethical universe in which he must live and die. And we must surely share, at first, in his momentary astonishment: why, after all, cannot the man who has just butchered his guest, kinsman, and king manage to mouth an "Amen," even if insincere? What stops him, what sticks the word in his throat—the involuntary reflex of a defeated conscience or some divine refusal to tolerate yet another transgression? The play affords no window through which to look this deeply into Macbeth's soul, but one thing is clear: Macbeth's inability to say "Amen" signals the futility of his crime. Human action and the will to power may prevail in Medea's world but not here, where nature itself gives witness to the immutable order of moral law. Macbeth fears that "the very stones" will prate of his whereabouts (2.1.58). The night of the King's murder is "unruly": chimneys fall, laments and strange screams of death fill the air, the owl clamors, the earth shakes (2.3.48–55). Afterward, an unnatural darkness strangles the sun, a mousing owl kills a falcon, and Duncan's horses eat each other. In the Globe performance of 1611, Simon Forman reports, the blood on Macbeth's hands "could not be washed off by any means, nor from his wife's hands."[9] After Banquo's ghost rises, Macbeth says that stones move, trees speak and birds ("maggot-pies and choughs and rooks") reveal "the secret'st man of blood" (3.4.125–28).

The mix of legend, superstition, and mirabilia here points to divine order; herein the play echoes the popular providentialism Tessa Watt and Alexandra Walsham have well explored, the inscrutable theater of God's judgments made entirely, if fitfully, scrutable in the popular press.[10] Cheap print frequently featured such cosmic disruptions as visible sermons, as signs of God's presence and disapproval. In many pamphlets and broadsides, as in the world of this play, the capricious pagan gods Apollo, Juno and Zeus, do not rule, but the just Judeo-Christian God, the God who will return at the last judgment, the day of the great doom, when the dead rise from their graves and walk like sprites (2.3.74–76).

This God, creator of nature and moral order, figures centrally in Holinshed's *Chronicles*: "almighty God showed himself thereby to be offended most highly for that wicked murder of King Duff, and, surely, unless the offenders were tried forth and punished for that deed, the realm should feel the just indignation of the divine judgment for omitting such punishment as was due for so grievous an offense."[11] And this God makes a surprising number of appearances (fifteen total) in the language of Shakespeare's dark, bloody play, rife with scenes of evil supernaturalism and murderous ambition.

Coleridge noted long ago that the witches "strike the keynote" of the play, but there is an insistent, if quieter, divine counterpoint.[12] Orson Welles heard and amplified this music in his 1948 film version, often employing the symbol of the cross amidst the gnarled trees and stones of his primitive Scotland, adding a Holy Father to conduct a service against Satan and oppose the rising evil. In Shakespeare's text Ross greets Duncan with unintentional irony, "God save the King!" (1.2.48). Immediately after the murder Banquo declares himself to stand "in the great hand of God" (2.3.129) against treasonous malice. Malcolm asks "God above" (4.3.121) to regulate the alliance with Macduff, echoing the lord who hoped that "Him above" (3.6.32) would ratify the rebellion against Macbeth. Witnessing Lady Macbeth sleepwalking, the Doctor does what Macbeth could not: he says a spontaneous prayer: "God, God, forgive us all" (5.1.66). In the opening scene the Captain compares the battle to Golgotha (1.2.40), place of the crucifixion; Malcolm later praises Siward as the best soldier in "Christendom" (4.3.193). Commissioning the murderers, Macbeth pointedly asks, "Are you so gospeled to pray for this good man and for his issue, whose heavy hand hath bowed you to the grave and beggared yours for ever?" (3.1.89–91). Whether or not he alludes specifically to Matthew 5:44 ("Love your enemies and pray for those who persecute you"), Macbeth here invokes the God whom he has disobeyed and the moral order he has violated. And once again, he adverts to prayer, this time thinking it the cowardly alternative to the manly action of murder.

King Macbeth's newfound contempt for the gospel and prayer marks his moral deterioration. "Had I but died an hour before this chance, / I had lived a blessèd time" (2.3.88–89), he himself said earlier. But such blessing as he required and yearned for now lies out of reach and out of mind. Lennox, ironically, hopes that a "swift blessing" (3.6.48) in the form of divine aid and the English army will come to remove / The means that makes us strangers" (4.3.164). In purposeful contrast to King Macbeth, Edward the Confessor is a religious curer who gives "holy prayers" and the "healing benediction" to the afflicted, who has "a heavenly gift of prophecy" (4.3.155–58). "Sundry blessings hang about his throne" (4.3.159), while Macbeth becomes a "hand accursed" (3.6.50), receiving not love and honor but "curses, not loud but deep" (5.3.27).

In the Shakespeare play that most embodies the "principle of contrast" and moves "upon the verge of an abyss," to borrow Hazlitt's fine phrasing, there is a pointed antithesis between blessing and cursing.[13] Cursed by his people, King Macbeth invokes the Prince of Darkness to curse his hapless servant: "The devil damn thee black, thou creamfaced loon!" (5.3.11). He that had once most need of blessing now turns the other way for curses. Here Macbeth echoes his previous imprecation, hurled, illogically perhaps but effectively, at the Weird sisters: "Deny me this [the truth about Banquo's issue], / And an eternal curse fall upon you!" (4.1.104–5). They immediately obey and summon the apparitions. But what supernatural suasion, what purchase of divine or demonic wrath, can this sinning mortal possibly claim? In Welcome Msomi's brilliant retelling *uMabatha*, which transposes the play to Zulu Africa, the threat seems much more appropriate: "If you disobey

/ My warriors will tear out your hearts / And leave your flesh for jackal meat."[14] In Shakespeare's play Macbeth deploys metaphysical rather than physical threat, his choice once again turning prayer into sinful self-assertion and malediction. Macbeth's last words constitute his final curse; instead of repenting, he takes it upon himself to redefine the very terms of salvation and damnation: "Before my body / I throw my warlike shield. Lay on, Macduff, / And damned be him that first cries, 'Hold, enough!'" (5.8.32–34). Identifying "he" as God by pointing toward the heavens, Derek Jacobi's Macbeth pointed the blasphemy by turning the curse against the deity.

Given the company he keeps, we should not be surprised, perhaps, that Macbeth's enemy, Hecate, leader of the witches, delivers the most telling commentary on his spiritual state:

> He shall spurn fate, scorn death, and bear
> His hopes 'bove wisdom, grace, and fear.
> And you all know, security
> Is mortals' chiefest enemy. (3.5.30–33)

Hecate here plays orthodox preacher, echoing numerous homilies and popular theology pamphlets ("you all know") on the dangers of "security," i.e. spiritual overconfidence and complacency, repose in the pleasures of this world. In 1584 John Stockwood published *A Very Fruitful and Necessary Sermon* "to the wakening and stirring up of all such as be lulled asleep in the cradle of security or carelessness."[15] The title page of Johann Habermann's *The Enemy of Security*,[16] exhorts the reader to watch and "pray continually." About the time of Macbeth, William Est preached in *The Scourge of Security* (1609)[17] that neglect of prayer led to the return of the unclean spirit. About the same time Thomas Draxe explained that the substance of security is contained in the words "I sleep" (B1v) and the antidote in the phrase "I sleep but mine heart waketh."[18] This homiletic fervor motivated John Downame's *A Treatise of Security* (1622), written "to rouse up" sinners "out of this sleep or rather lethargy of carnal security" (epistle dedicatory).[19]

Hecate's precise spiritual diagnosis, then, evokes a discrete, clearly outlined, and abundantly available complex of image and exhortation.

Shakespeare fully engages this familiar complex but reverses its basic logic: the sleepless Macbeth ever waketh in his cradle of security, not lulled, but racked "in the affliction of these terrible dreams / That shake us nightly" (3.2.20–21). The pervasive images of sleeplessness in the play have been well remarked, of course—the bewitched insomniac sailor who dwindles, peaks, and pines, to the mysterious cry, "Macbeth hath murdered sleep"; Macbeth's yearnings for "sleep that knits up the raveled sleave of care, / The death of each day's life" (2.2.38–39), the sleepwalking Lady Macbeth. But to contemporary audiences they must have derived their force from Shakespeare's daring inversion of conventional rhetoric and moral formula. His Macbeth is agonizingly and unremittingly awake, stung by the agenbyte of inwit, in full tormenting consciousness of his sin.

As this insomnia indicates, Macbeth's gains are negligible and indistinct, his losses large and clearly articulated: "honor, love, obedience, troops of friends, / I must not look to have" (5.3.25–26). And, correspondingly, the earthly highlights of Scotland are never so precisely mapped as the spiritual landscapes Macbeth traverses. Some of the Scottish references, Saint Colme's Inch (or Inchcolm isle) and Colmekill, even point to the other world, where the real drama transpires: both localities pay nominal tribute to St. Columba (521–97), the abstemious missionary to northern Scotland who preached, worked miracles, and converted the pagan Picts and Druids to Christianity. Appropriately, Duncan's body is carried to the "sacred storehouse of his predecessors" (2.4.35) at Colmekill, the monastic "cell of Columba" in Iona, off the west of Scotland. The forces of Christianity thus align themselves in death as in life against the pagan barbarism of Scotland. Macbeth moves between these two opposed realms, as between blessings and curses, angels and devils, and, like one of Hamlet's crawling fellows, heaven and hell. Lady Macbeth wants the "dunnest smoke of hell" to beshroud the world so that heaven cannot "peep through the blanket of the dark / To cry 'Hold, hold'" (1.5.53–54). "The heavens, as troubled with man's act" (i.e. the murder), threaten "his bloody stage" (2.4.5–6) with natural disruptions and cosmic events. Macduff says that "new sorrows / Strike heaven on the face" (4.3.5–6). Heaven often appears as a metonym for divine providence. Lennox hopes, if it "please heaven" (3.6.19), that Macbeth will not get his hands on Duncan's heirs. The messenger says to the doomed Lady Macduff, "heaven preserve you" (4.2.68); Macduff wonders that heaven looked on at the slaughter of his wife and children (4.3.223–24). Heaven grants the gifts of healing and prophecy to King Edward (4.3.150ff.). Most significantly, heaven appears in contrast to hell as the afterlife abode of the blessed and just, the place of peace and happiness. Again, Macbeth himself points out the moral before the murders of Duncan and Banquo: the ringing bell summons the king "to heaven or to hell" (2.1.64); and Banquo's soul "If it find heaven, must find it out tonight" (3.1.143). On the opposing side, the Porter imagines himself keeping the gate in hell and comments on the condemned residents. Though reviled by Elizabeth Montagu ("entirely absurd"), Samuel Taylor Coleridge ("disgusting") and others, this great serio-comic scene (2.3) appropriately gives the other place a local habitation and a name.[20]

The Macbeths walk the broad and royal road to hell—in fact, they sometimes seem already to live there. Reliving her crimes over and over again, Lady Macbeth, one of the living dead, murmurs "Hell is murky" (5.1.31). Judi Dench turned this line into a discovery, "Hell *is* murky," before letting out a bloodcurdling scream as the abyss opens for her. Macduff calls Macbeth a "hell-kite" and a "hellhound" (4.3.220; 5.8.3), thus echoing his pronouncement, "Not in the legions / Of horrid hell can come a devil more damned / In his evils to top Macbeth" (4.3.56–58).

Damned in evils—*Macbeth* take us on a journey into the heart and soul of the damned. Enacting the morality-play sequence of temptation, sin and death, Shakespeare degrades repentance in this Everyman to a melancholy remorse, leaving both Macbeths to the consequences of their actions, to the "deep damnation of his [Duncan's] taking-off" (1.7.20). The resulting portraits of sin, punishment and damnation stand worthily next to those of Dante's *Inferno*: to Ezzelino the tyrant in Phlegethon, the boiling river of blood (canto 12); to Vanni Fucci, defiant and making an obscene gesture to God (canto 25); to Ugolino, who eats the bodies of his dead children (canto 33); to Fra Alberigo and Branca Doria, whose souls are already in hell though their bodies live on earth (canto 33); to the traitors Judas, Brutus and Cassius, writhing from the mouths of Satan in the ice of Judeccza (canto 34). Such compelling, full-bodied figures all contrast with the sterilized wraiths of the native *de casibus* tradition, tediously moralizing their histories, reciting their faults, and preaching repentance. Dante and Shakespeare portray the sinners themselves, living human beings, groaning, sweating, suffering, cursing, excusing, regretting, all their faults and imperfections on their heads, their sins in full and flagrant blossom. And, like Macbeth, the damned souls throughout the nine circles of Dante's *Inferno* are capable of every kind of speech-noise, eloquence and remorse, save one: they cannot pray.

The play's focus on damnation inspired Derek Jacobi to summarize his conception of the lead role thus: "I tried to plot his journey from the golden boy of the opening to the burnt-out loser accepting his own damnation of the conclusion."[21] This journey, we should remember, Shakespeare consciously constructs from numerous possibilities in Holinshed's account. In his notes for plays and poems, John Milton apparently envisioned a different kind of *Macbeth*; starting with the conference of Malcolm and Macduff (4.3) and including the ghost of Duncan, he imagined perhaps a political play in the form of a classical revenge tragedy. Shakespeare, by contrast, writes a drama of damnation that purposefully evokes and engages contemporary theology, particularly the disputes about divine foreknowledge, human responsibility, the nature of grace, and the freedom of the human will. These disputes occupied preachers in the pulpit as well as the best theological minds of the early modern period. The classic Catholic position, based on Aquinas, appears succinctly in Dante's *Purgatorio* (16): Marco Lombardo there argues that people tend "to assign / to heaven every cause, as if it were / the necessary source of every motion" (*ogne cagion recate / pur suso al cielo, pur come se tutto / movesse seco di necessitate*, 67–69); but if this were so, free will would be destroyed (*fora distrutto / libero arbitrio*) and there would be no justice (*non fora giustizia*, 70–71) in rewarding the good and punishing the wicked.[22] Calvin dissented, of course, in well-known chapters of the *Institutes*, arguing that "it be wrought by the will of god that salvation is freely offered to some and that other some be debarred from coming to it."²³ Asserting the total efficacy of God's foreknowledge and divine grace in his *Thirty-Sixth Article*, Martin Luther emphatically denied the existence of free will:

> I misspoke when I said that free will came before grace in name only; rather I should have simply said "free will is a fiction among real things, a name with no reality" ... All things occur by absolute necessity.²⁴

Erasmus responded to Luther in *De libero arbitrio*, at one point in the voice of a reader of Scripture, speaking to God:

> Why complain of my behavior, when all my actions, good or bad, are performed by you in me regardless of my will? Why reproach me, when I have no power to preserve the good you have given me, or keep out the evil you put into me? Why entreat me, when everything depends on you, and happens as it pleases you? Why bless me, as though I had done my duty, when whatever happens is your work? Why curse me, when I sinned through necessity? What is the purpose of such a vast number of commandments if not a single person has it all in his power to do what is commanded?²⁵

Contending that the doctrine of predestination invalidates God's commandments and renders absurd the concept of divine justice, Erasmus argues that free will elects not to cooperate with divine grace. The controversy provides an illuminating context for the depiction of witches, sin and punishment in Macbeth. First, it summarily disposes of the notion that the Weird sisters can, in any sense, possess or control Macbeth. Those early Protestants and Catholics who believe in such creatures never grant to them such power. The debate on free will centers not on witches or demons but on the nature of God's foreknowledge and providence. To many the play has seemed to reflect Protestant convictions about such matters, specifically portraying reprobation. In her classic essay "Milton's Satan and the Theme of Damnation in Elizabethan Tragedy" (1948), Helen Gardner argues that Macbeth is incapable of repentance or change. Later John Stachniewski provides Protestant chapter and verse in "Calvinist Psychology in Macbeth." Arthur Kinney perceives the doctrine of Calvinist "predestination" throughout the action of the play. Peter Lake argues that Macbeth presents the "interiority of reprobation" and contrasts clearly with his alter-ego Banquo, one of the "elect."[26]

Such astute critics certainly respond to the power of play and to the driving propulsion of the evil there represented. But Macbeth cannot be smoothly co-opted into Protestant predestination schematics. Whatever his personal convictions, Shakespeare here adopts a Catholic view of the action and theology of free will by emphasizing the initial inevitability of the crime, the sheer gratuitousness (as Augustine put it) of the evil freely chosen. He suppresses Holinshed's notice of Duncan's weakness and inefficiency and all notice of the conspiracy to kill the king, endowed instead with an aura of sanctity. Macbeth repeatedly adverts to the terror implicit in free will, in the awesome power to choose good or evil: "I dare do all that may become a man / Who dares do more is none" (1.7.46–47). He never contemplates the predispositions of fate or of the deity but thinks instead on the consequences of his choices and actions, consequences he would desperately evade and deny. Recalling the prophecy about Banquo, he emphasizes his own responsibility and autonomous agency:

> If't be so,
> For Banquo's issue have I filed my mind,
> For them the gracious Duncan have I murdered,
> Put rancors in the vessel of my peace
> Only for them, and mine eternal jewel
> Given to the common enemy of man
> To make them kings, the seeds of Banquo kings! (3.1.66–72)

Macbeth has chosen evil, in his words, "given" his soul to the devil. To emphasize the point, Shakespeare again departs from Holinshed in his depiction of Banquo, who encourages him in jest to "purchase" the crown, and who knows in advance of the assassination.[27] But Shakespeare's Banquo freely and steadfastly resists temptation: Before going to sleep he, unlike Macbeth, prays, "Merciful powers, / Restrain in me the cursèd thoughts that nature / Gives way to in repose" (2.1.7–9). Invoking the powers (the order of angels specifically charged with resisting demons),

Banquo here resists temptations, "cursèd thoughts"; after prayer, he confronts Macbeth directly, asserting that he must lose no honor, must keep his "bosom franchised and allegiance clear" (2.1.26–28).

Shakespeare deploys the Catholic view of free will perhaps from theological conviction, but more certainly from theatrical necessity. For the doctrine of predestination renders human action essentially undramatic: when the end is known, preordained, and absolutely just, there can be no real choice, suspense, conflict or resolution. This conception of human action and divine providence renders pity an impertinence, terror a transgression and tragedy an impossibility. Consider the death of the reprobate, as described by the popular Calvinist William Perkins in *A Golden Chain, a Description of Theology containing the Order of the Causes of Salvation and Damnation* (1591):

> The reprobates when they die become without sense and astonied like unto a stone; or else they are overwhelmed with a terrible horror of conscience, and despairing of their salvation, as it were, with the gulf of the sea overturning them.[28]

Perkins illustrates the first option with the story of Nabal, who hears of God's judgment against him: "his heart died within him; he became like a stone. About ten days later the Lord struck Nabal, and he died" (1 Sam 25:37-38). He illustrates the second with the story of Judas, who hanged himself in despair (Matt 27:5). However these ends may bear comparison with the death of Lady Macbeth offstage, they contrast jarringly with Macbeth's final moments—the somber reflections ("Tomorrow, and tomorrow, and tomorrow," 5.5.19ff.) and the moment of clear moral vision and remorse in the final meeting with Macduff:

> Of all men else I have avoided thee.
> But get thee back. My soul is too much charged
> With blood of thine already! (5.8.4–6)

There is also the defiant resurgence of military valor:

> Though Birnham Wood be come to Dunsinane,
> And thou opposed, being of no woman born,

> Yet I will try the last. Before my body,
> I throw my warlike shield. Lay on, Macduff.... (5.8.30–34)

The vitality and eloquence of Macbeth, here as throughout the play, distinguish him from the reprobate of the popular imagination, the heart-dead stone, Nabal, or the despairing, suicidal Judas. In need of salvation, Macbeth freely chooses "the sweet fruition of an earthly crown," and the spectacle of his sinning and suffering makes up the tragedy of the play.

Defined by unarticulated prayer and providential decree, the potent theology of this spectacle rarely survives translation or adaptation. In his popular seventeenth-century version, Davenant gave the dying Macbeth not a defiant snarl but a belated confession of folly, "Farewell vain world, and what's most vain in it, ambition."[29] That sort of pious bleating constitutes one sort of evasion; another can be witnessed in the final grunting and bellowing of Washizu in Kurosawa's brilliant 1957 film, *Throne of Blood, or The Castle of the Spider's Web*. Volleys of hissing arrows strike and stick in the Japanese Macbeth, staggering desperately on the wall of his castle. A final arrow pierces him in the throat (graphic testimony to what he did not and cannot say?). Despite Davenant's and Kurosawa's considerable achievements, neither represents the vitality and eloquence of Macbeth's final moments or the full terror of eternal damnation. Writing a travesty of Macbeth in the nineteenth century, Francis Talfourd shrewdly seized upon this latter point to turn the play topsy-turvy. In his version Duncan returns from the dead, as do Banquo and Lady Macbeth (with a parasol), arm-in-arm. The slain Macbeth rises from the ground and addresses the king:

> I tender, sir, of course, my resignation,
> Since all's in train for me to leave my station.
> So at your feet I lay my regal diadem
> Without regret, nor wish again that I had 'em.[30]

There is no turning back for Shakespeare's Macbeth, of course, whose inability to say "Amen" stirred his audience's darkest desires and fears.

Chapter 5

Hamlet and Protestant Aural Theater

Grace Tiffany

Over the past half-century, many Shakespeareans have argued either that Protestantism or Catholicism informs the general Christian ethos of *Hamlet*. Dover Wilson, Raymond Waddington and Roland Mushat Frye are among the many who find in King Claudius a Lutheran who, though longing to repent of his fratricide, harbors a trapped, "limed soul" (3.3.68),[1] whose inability to pray, to use Luther's words, "clearly manifest[s] that the endeavor and effect of free will are simply nothing."[2] Peter Milward finds "something Lutheran in [Hamlet's] brooding emphasis on the corruption of human nature,"[3] and Charles Cannon stresses the play's Calvinism, saying that the "the problems of the theater dealt with" in *Hamlet* "lead Shakespeare . . . toward the possibility of predestination."[4] Anthony Low has more recently argued that the play stages the Protestant dismissal of the Catholic doctrine of Purgatory, and in *Hamlet in Purgatory* Stephen Greenblatt echoes Low's claim. Still, in a 2001 *Commonweal* review of Greenblatt's influential book, Edward Oakes approvingly quotes a Jesuit friend's comment on *Hamlet*: "What a *Catholic* play that was!"[5]

My purpose here is not to argue that *Hamlet* is a Catholic or a Protestant play. With David Daniell in "Shakespeare and the Protestant Mind," I agree that Shakespeare's plays declare their author's allegiance to neither faith to the exclusion of the other.[6] Thus I will not assert that Hamlet's oblique instruction to Guildenstern, "Hide fox, and all after" (4.2.30–31), is a cryptic reference to Foxe's *Book of Martyrs*,[7] or that

Horatio's description of "post-haste and romage in the land" (1.1.107) signals Denmark's energetic papalism. I will, however, argue the influence of what Daniell calls Shakespeare's "Protestant inheritance" on *Hamlet*. Both the play and its eponymous hero seem specifically constructed to record and display views on theater's potential for good or for evil, ideas expressed in much English Protestant discourse near the time of the play's creation. Elsewhere I have argued that Shakespeare's exploration of those ideas at the brink of the seventeenth century inspired him to construct his greatest tragedy as a strange "anti-play."[8] Here I will demonstrate that *Hamlet*'s paradoxical anti-theatrical theater may also be described as "aural theater."

I

As Daniell has cogently argued, Shakespeare's Protestant inheritance can logically be inferred from the fact that "[i]n his fifty-two years, Shakespeare lived in a nation that was officially, aggressively, and massively Protestant."[9] Quoting Peter Lake, Daniell writes that, though some late sixteenth-century Catholics "met in barns and private households, the godly inherited the public space of the parish church," in which the "altar was now a communion table" and "the rood loft with its doom images" and "images of saints had been removed. The liturgy was in English, not Latin; the mass had been replaced with a communion service. No trace of the cult of the saints or the notion of Purgatory . . . was left in either the service book or the outward ceremonial face of the Church."[10] Many of the views expressed by the most popular pastors of the age—among them Thomas Playfere; Stephen Egerton; John Field; and Lancelot Andrewes, whose London parish contained "the Fortune and Red Bull theatres," and whose services were "eagerly attended" by some players[11]—showed the influence of John Calvin's theology. In Shakespeare's lifetime, moreover, 142 editions of the Geneva Bible were printed; this, Daniell notes, "ha[d] to do with demand."[12] Whatever Shakespeare's personal beliefs or private instruction may have been, it is inarguable that his environment recurrently exposed him to Protestant strains of thought, and it thus is not surprising that echoes of Protestant moral views are found in his greatest tragedy.

The particular aspect of Protestant thought which I want to trace in *Hamlet* is one Jonas Barish has famously called the "anti-theatrical prejudice." *Hamlet* criticizes morally corrupt types of drama that appeal to the eye and delude their watchers. Of course, the play's enduring paradox is that it is itself composed not only of words but of a series of exciting spectacles, including a ghost's several appearances, a reenacted poisoning, and a fast-paced contest with rapiers. Throughout the play, however, Shakespeare calls witnesses' attention to the false impressions these staged sights create without verbal explanation of their meanings. The silent Ghost might be a malevolent spirit, until his eloquent explanation of his presence to Hamlet convinces the prince "[i]t is an honest ghost" (1.5.138). When Hamlet begins to doubt the Ghost's honesty again, a staged entertainment in which—as I will show—the verbal, explanatory component overshadows the visual restores his faith. And the wild, violent spectacle of the play's last scene will leave crucial facts "unknown," Hamlet tells us, until Horatio "tell[s Hamlet's] story" (5.2.348–49). Words in *Hamlet* are sometimes deceitful—Claudius calls Hamlet his "son," a misnomer which Hamlet quickly corrects, saying "A little more than kin, but less than kind" (1.2.63–65)—but the preponderance of *Hamlet*'s references to deception target suspicious ocular "proofs." To improve spectacular visual shows that by themselves may dangerously mislead us, *Hamlet* offers a morally purgative and strongly emphasized *aural* dimension.

The play's emphasis on the moral superiority of words to images derives from a tradition as old as Plato, but most present to Shakespeare in one strain of the discourse of late sixteenth- and early seventeenth-century radical Protestants. This strain was the anti-theatricalism found in the rhetoric of puritanical Protestant Reformers. Though "anti-theatricalism" has become the catch-phrase for such Renaissance moralists' condemnation of public entertainments, including not only plays but bear-baitings, cockfights, bonfires, dances, puppet-shows and even "fantastic costly apparel,"[13] I wish to argue that these Reformers' criticisms were chiefly directed against the visual aspects of theatrical performances, and that many Reformers implicitly or explicitly championed an alternative, virtue-inspiring aural theater. In England,

Reformers' alternative stress on heard performance resulted in what Bryan Crockett has called the "cult of the ear."[14]

Late sixteenth- and early seventeenth-century English moralists founded their distrust of spectacle not only on the Bible's condemnation of graven images, but on the strain of Neoplatonic thought articulated by Church Fathers who held images and display to be low mimetic forms, attractive to the baser appetites and distracting from virtuous activity. The most influential of the Church Fathers, Augustine, was as important to Catholics as to Protestants, but the portions of his writings which attacked plays were of particular interest to the more radical Reformers. Thus many English anti-theatrical writers, like William Prynne in his preface to *Histrio-Mastix* ("The Player Whipped"), quoted an early passage in Augustine's *Confessions* where Augustine laments that, in his prodigal youth, "[stage]-plays . . . carried me away, full of images of my miseries." Augustine laments that at such entertainments "man . . . desires as a spectator to feel sorrow," "a miserable madness." For "when he compassionates others, then it is mercy. But what sort of compassion is this for feigned and scenical passions?" "[W]hat more miserable than a miserable being . . . weeping the death of Dido for love to Aeneas?"[15] Like Prynne, who scorned such "scenical passions" as "lascivious pictures" (preface), the late sixteenth-century moralist Anthony Munday wrote against the "filthiness of playes and spectacles," which

> [. . .] maketh both the actors and beholders guilty alike. For while [watchers] say nought, but gladly look on, they all by sight and assent be actors, that truly may be applied unto them that saying of the apostle, *How not that only they which commit such things are worthy death, but also which favor them that do them* (Romans 1:31). So that in that representation of whoredom, all the people in mind play the whores. (3)[16]

Munday also warned readers against viewing the gaudy playhouse spectacles, describing the eyes as "two open windows" by which "death breaketh into the soul." Not only the Puritan tract-writers but some Protestant poets wrote in the late sixteenth century against the incitements to carnality arising from deceptive images. In Spenser's *Faerie*

Queene, The Redcrosse Knight is distracted from his virtuous path by the appearance of the lewd Fidessa, "A goodly Lady clad in scarlot red, / Purfled with gold and pearle of rich assay" (book 1, canto 2, *ll*. 110–11), (to the Reforming mind, she is a clear embodiment of the Catholic Church). When Fidessa recounts her dubious story, Redcrosse "in great passion . . . [does] dwell, / More busying his quicke eyes, her face to view, / Then his dull eares, to heare what she did tell" (canto 2, *ll*. 230–32). Redcrosse's moral correction occurs later, in the House of Holiness, when Fidelia, or Faith, instructs him by means of the "sacred Booke" (canto 10, *v*. 19, *l*. 1), not pleasing show.

Clearly, the English Reformers' condemnation of wanton spectacle did not lead them to reject all human attempts at representation. Spenser's criticism of Fidessa is couched in his own allegorical "booke," one as invested in holy scripture as it is in classical mythology and courtly romance tradition; this book's "end . . . is to fashion a gentleman or noble person in vertuous and gentle discipline."[17] Elsewhere I have shown that even the most rabid Renaissance anti-theatricalists structured their condemnatory books and tracts as verbal theater, translating to written form the conventions of the stages they attacked.[18] William Prynne's excoriation of theaters is subtitled *The Actor's Tragedy*, and its primary title, *Histrio-Mastix*, is borrowed from a then thirty-year-old play by John Marston. An anti-theatrical treatise by Stephen Gosson is divided into five parts, as plays were, and titled *Plays Confuted in Five Actions*, or five acts. In such writings, theater's dangerous spectacle is erased, and its rhetorical power employed for pure verbal "theater." Crucial to the legitimacy of this theater is its authors' commitment to and dependence on moral teaching, and chiefly on biblical precepts, as when Munday cites Romans, or Gosson paraphrases Ephesians 4:24: "For God hath made us to his owne likenesse, which likenesse consisteth not in lineaments and proportion of the body"—such as are seen on garish display in the playhouse—"but in . . . [unseen] holiness."[19]

A precedent for the Reformers' embrace of holy verbal theater lay in the writings of Calvin. In his *Commentaries on Exodus*, Calvin wrote, "[T]here is much . . . force in the language when [Moses] introduces the Egyptians as speakers. . . . for thus does the marvellous catastrophe more strikingly affect our minds, when the Egyptians, brought, as it were, on the stage, not only trumpet forth their victory, but insolently give vent to their arrogance and cruelty" (15.9).[20] For Shakespeare, however, the theatrical use of scripture lay closer at hand than Calvin's *Institutes*. It could be found not only in the anti-theatricalists' paradoxically theatrical sermons and pamphlets of the 1580s and 1590s, but in the London churches of those decades, where Protestant pastors performed "verbal pyrotechnics," presenting their audiences with "dizzying [biblical] paradoxes," dramatically expressed.[21] These preachers' sermons brought to life the action Spenser describes in *The Faerie Queene*, when Fidelia revives Redcrosse by reading aloud from scripture: "wonder was to heare her goodly speach: / For she was able, with her words to kill, / And raise againe to life" (canto 10, *ll*. 169–71).

Bryan Crockett has written of the popularity of the gifted late sixteenth- and early seventeenth-century Puritan pastors whose "goodly speach" was, like Fidelia's, a "wonder." Crockett lays particular stress on the aural dimension of these men's homilies, describing how sermons delivered in the 1590s by pastors such as Thomas Playfere were known to bring audiences to tears through their artful use of the spoken word. "Popery is a religion for the eye; ours for the ear," claimed one such pastor, Ralph Brownrig.[22] Objecting to scholarship that "focuses almost exclusively on the Protestants' reliance on the *written* word," Crockett argues that "[t]he usual [Renaissance] Protestant claim is that biblical ideas are imparted not primarily by reading but by the spoken word" of the inspired preacher.[23] In Galatians 3:2, Paul exhorts Christians to believe truth that is "heard." Honoring Paul's emphasis, John Donne preached, "The organ that God hath given the natural man is the eye. . . . The organ that God hath given the Christian is the ear."[24]

II

The ear brings us to *Hamlet*. Shakespeare's play contains more than a score of direct references to the ear. Many of those present this organ as a dangerous channel for corruption, a description of hearing that will seem, at first glance, opposed to the Protestant emphasis on the ear as the avenue to grace. In *Hamlet* ears are the fragile body's portals—old Hamlet describes his own death, born of the "leprous distillment" his brother poured into "the porches of [his] ears" (1.5.64, 63). They are also gateways to the mind, which stand as open to verbal attack as the sleeping king's ears proved to the access of literal poison. Descriptions of speaking as assault underscore the danger of listening. In the play's first scene Barnardo bids Horatio to let him and his fellow watchman Marcellus "assail [Horatio's] ears, / That are so fortified against [the] story" of the Ghost's appearance (1.1.31–32). Later Hamlet asks Horatio not to "do [Hamlet's] ear violence" by speaking ill of himself (1.2.171). Ophelia's honor will be jeopardized if she listens with "too credent ear" to Hamlet's "songs" (1.3.30). The Ghost's full tale of his purgatorial prison house, entering Hamlet's "ears of flesh," would "freeze [Hamlet's] blood" (1.5.22, 16) much as Claudius's poison "curd'led" the Ghost's own (1.5.34). The cock's crow, falling on the Ghost's ear, is a "fearful summons" that makes him "[start]" (1.1.150, 149). "The whole ear of Denmark . . . is abused" by the "forged process of [old Hamlet's] death" (1.5.36), and the fall of Ilium "takes prisoner Pyrrhus' ear," in the words of the traveling player (2.2.477). Hamlet complains that this same overwrought player, given the right cause, would "cleave the general ear with horrid speech" (2.2.563). Another bad actor, according to Hamlet, might "split the ears of the groundlings" (3.2.10). Hamlet himself would "speak daggers" to his mother (3.2.396), and does; his words "like daggers enter [in] her ears" when he "wag[s] his tongue" at her "in noise rude" (3.4.95, 39–40). Hamlet's verbal assault on Gertrude includes a pun on the word "ear": he calls his father a once "wholesome" ear of grain, "blasted" by the "mildewed ear" that is Claudius (3.4.65, 64). Laertes "wants not buzzers to infect his ear / With pestilent speeches of his father's death" (4.5.90–91); his howled grief makes the stars "stand / Like wonder-wounded hearers" in the graveyard scene (5.1.256–57). Hamlet has "words to speak in [Horatio's] ear will make [him] dumb," though those words are "much too light for the bore of the matter" (4.6.24–26): heavier word-guns are wanted. As Thomas Pendleton, James Siemon and Kenneth Gross have each noted, ears in *Hamlet* are vulnerable to attack.[25]

Yet close examination of *Hamlet*'s dialogue and plot shows that the painful assaults suffered by hearers in *Hamlet* are as often purgative as damaging. In *Shakespeare's Noise*, Gross demonstrates that the destructive language that threatens both the "whole ear of Denmark" and the private ears of individual Danes is lies—the sort of poison that Iago will "pour . . . into [Othello's] ear" (*Othello* 2.3.356)—and other critics have noticed this as well.[26] Yet though ears in *Hamlet* are open to abuse through lies, those ears are also the gateways for slander's corrective. In fact, the woeful hearing to which Hamlet's listeners submit most often exposes them, not to slander, but to a violent but necessary truth. Barnardo's and Francisco's revelations about the Ghost "assail" Horatio's ears, but their story must be told in order for the men to find the source of Denmark's corruption. Hearing is painful but morally crucial in *Hamlet*. Hence the numerous exhortations delivered by Horatio, by Hamlet, and by the Ghost to listen, to attend, to hear the truth. Horatio bids Hamlet to "listen with an attent[ive] ear" to his description of the Ghost, and Hamlet responds, "For God's love, let me hear!" (1.2.193, 195). In act 1 the Ghost asks for Hamlet's "serious hearing," and repeats "hear," "hear," "List, list, o, list!" "Now, Hamlet, hear!" (1.5.5, 7, 8, 22, 34). "At each ear a hearer," Hamlet instructs Rosencrantz and Guildenstern (2.2.382), before he relays the paradoxical fact that old Polonius is a big baby. "Do you hear?" Hamlet then urges Polonius, instructing him to treat the players well (2.2.523), and "Dost thou hear?" he later asks Horatio, as he requires his friend to submit to honest, though embarrassing, praise (3.2.62). Later, Laertes will complain that his father's "means of death and obscure funeral . . . Cry to be heard" (4.5.214–17), as does the story of Hamlet's own father's murder.

The evident painfulness of ears' encounters with such truths may obscure the curative value of the truths that are told. Yet it should not. Even the crowing cock, whose "fearful summons" troubles the ear of the wandering Ghost, works to the good. The cock is the "bird of dawning," associated with the anniversary of Christ's birth, a "hallowed" and "gracious" time (1.1.160, 164). His voice jars, but is "wholesome"; when he sings, "no planets strike, / . . . nor witch hath power to charm" (1.1.162–63). Like the cock's crow, the ear-assaulting truths told by the Ghost, by Hamlet, and finally by Horatio offer medicinal wounds. *Othello*'s Brabantio will deny that the "bruis'd heart" may be "pierced," or lanced, "through the ear" (1.3.218–19), but *Hamlet* insists on that curative process. In *Hamlet* the wounded ear is the path to a soul's—or a country's—redemption from rottenness. Oedipus, exposing himself to a painful tale of murder and incest, finds himself on the "brink" of "dreadful hearing," but asserts, "still I must hear."[27] He, like Hamlet, is committed to purgation. Like Oedipus, Hamlet bids the Ghost tell his horrid story, saying, "Speak, I am bound to hear" (1.5.6). Later, Hamlet will "speak daggers" to his mother in an attempt to redeem her "fighting soul" (3.4.113). To apply the words of Martin Luther, Hamlet must "so inflict the [aural] wound" as "to both mitigate and heal it"; he must "be so severe as not to forget to be kind."[28] In Hamlet's own words, he must "be cruel . . . to be kind" (3.4.178).

III

The purgative assault of dreadful revelations about fratricide and incest is some distance from the dazzling descriptions of Christ's resurrection preached by Calvinist pastors, and the pained aural witness of Hamlet, Gertrude and Horatio little resembles the ecstatic listening lent by Thomas Playfere's congregation in the 1590s. Yet Hamlet does indeed demonstrate the cultural influence of the Reformed pastors' stress on the ear as the pathway to salvation, and of the general Protestant distrust of deceptive spectacle. Further, like the anti-theatrical writers, and the pastors whose aurally theatrical churches rivaled the playhouses, or "chappel[s] of Satan," to quote Anthony Munday,[29] Hamlet proposes a morally superior, spoken performativity to displace outrageous spectacle. Authentic performance in Hamlet is puritanically directed at exposing vice and encouraging virtue, and it aims at the ear.

Hamlet's early claim that he has "that within that passes show" (1.2.85) is often presumed to invoke a radical distrust of all theater's capacity to represent inner states of mind. I would suggest, however, that Hamlet's words, taken in their entirety, suggest not that his inner state cannot be represented, but that it cannot be represented visually. He condemns the shows of mourning—the "inky cloak," the "customary suits of solemn black," the "fruitful river of the eye," the "dejected havior of the visage," the "trappings and the suits of woe"—as mere "shapes of grief," inauthentic "actions that a man might play" (1.2.77–84). His description of a grief that "passes show" suggests a Protestant distrust of theater's power to present truth to the eye. Yet Hamlet nowhere suggests that truth might not be *articulated*, when freedom is given to speak. His heart breaks because he "must hold [his] tongue" (1.2.159).

Thus throughout the play we hear Hamlet searching for a verbal register to convey his moral truth. We may better understand his mysterious "antic disposition" (1.5.72) when we observe that feigned madness grants him the liberty to speak in moral paradoxes, some of which echo the Bible-based preaching of English Protestant pastors like Thomas Playfere and Lancelot Andrewes. Hamlet's morbid reminder to Claudius that "[a] man may fish with the worm that hath eat of a king" (4.2.27–28) is like Playfere's riddling observation that Christ "was not counted so good as a live worm, but was buried in the earth a dead lion to be meat for the worms."[30] Further, much of Hamlet's speech, be it riddling or straightforward, exposes the dishonest *visual* theatrical displays of Gertrude, Ophelia and Claudius. His sour description of his mother, "like Niobe, all tears" at his father's funeral (1.2.149); his bitter complaint to Ophelia that God has given painted women "one face" and they "make [themselves] another" (3.1.143–44); and his outraged observation that Claudius might "smile, and smile, and be a villain" (1.5.108) express a Protestant recoil from deceptive spectacle. Hamlet's contempt for the traveling player's performance of Aeneas's tale to Dido is similarly aimed at the Player's unwarranted visual display of emotion. Hamlet finds it "monstrous" that "this player here" could "force his soul so to his own conceit / That from her working all the visage wann'd, / Tears in his eyes, distraction in his aspect" (2.2.551, 553–55). During the staging of *The Mousetrap*, Hamlet urges the actor playing Lucianus to "leave [his] damnable faces and begin": that is, to cease mugging and begin speaking.

Hamlet would "replace bad acting with good acting," as Crockett writes.[31] In the words of Huston Diehl, in "prais[ing] audiences who distance themselves from spectacle and focus on the meaning of the play," Hamlet "articulates the qualities of an ideal *Protestant* theater."[32] Such a theater displaces ocular display with the performance of reasoned speech. Thus the play with which Hamlet determines to scourge Claudius will rely chiefly on rhetoric and only secondarily on spectacle. "[W]e'll hear a play tomorrow," Hamlet says (2.2.535–36). References to "hearing" rather than, as we would say, "seeing" a play are found elsewhere in Shakespeare.[33] Shakespeare's mixed descriptions of drama's aural and visual effects record the difficulty Elizabethan playwrights had in describing how their plays were to be received,[34] and also support Andrew Gurr's claim that the playwrights generally "valued poetry much more than the 'shows' of the common stage."[35] But Hamlet's directions for *The Mousetrap* are notable for their unusual emphasis on that short play's spoken dimension. Hamlet's particular addition to the play will be a "speech of some dozen . . . or sixteen lines" which will become the drama's centerpiece (2.2.541–42). The hearing of this speech, Hamlet hopes, will prompt Claudius's repentance, since "murther, though it have no tongue, will speak / With most miraculous organ" (2.2.593–94). "Speak the speech . . . as I pronounc'd it to you, trippingly on the tongue," he warns the player the next day (3.2.1–2). Play to the audience's ears, and thus "[R]eform" playing altogether, he pleads (*l.* 38).

Huston Diehl has discussed the likeness between Hamlet's and Philip Sidney's arguments for a reasonable theater that avoids excessive theatrical display,[36] and indeed *The Mousetrap* scene, wherein "The Murther of Gonzago" is staged, may owe something to the 1588 *Defence of Poesy*'s specific description of "the abominable tyrant Alexander Pheraeus . . . who without all pity had murdered infinite numbers," but "from whose eyes a tragedy, well made and represented, drew abundance of tears." Sidney, citing Plutarch, recounts that this man "withdrew himself" from "hearkening" to the painful stage-representation of violent actions like his own.[37] (Interestingly, Plutarch, though not Sidney, records that this same tyrant "wept at the sufferings of Hecuba" in Euripides's play.[38] If Shakespeare did consider Sidney's passage, he took note of Sidney's use of the word "hearkening" to describe the attention the tyrant bestowed on tragic performances. It is primarily

Claudius's ear that Hamlet designs his play to affect. "Will the king hear this piece of work?" he asks Polonius (3.2.46–47). Yet "The Murther of Gonzago," which stages the "aural rape" of old Hamlet (to quote Kenneth Gross[39]), is not the "cursed hebona" that Claudius poured into his brother's ear (1.5.62), but a bitter medicine that Hamlet calls "wormwood" (3.2.181), a plant "good for worms in a man's ear," according to a popular sixteenth-century manual authored by the herbalist Richard Banckes.[40] During the Renaissance the word was often used to describe biting satire. In 1616 Ben Jonson writes that his moral epigrams may be thought "Wormwood."[41] A decade after *Hamlet*, Shakespeare would synesthetically employ the metaphor of the harsh herb to suggest curative speech. In *The Winter's Tale* Paulina rebukes Leontes for his past cruelty to Hermione; Leontes replies that her just censure is "as bitter on [her] tongue as in my thought" (5.1.18–19) Hamlet's "wormwood" is also a bitter aural chastisement. Hamlet's wormwood is not just the staged reenactment of Claudius's crime but the prince's harsh spoken interpretation of that crime's meaning, and of the meaning of Gertrude's sin as well.

Although scholars have disagreed on which part of "The Murther of Gonzago" is the "speech of some dozen or sixteen lines" written by Hamlet, or even on whether the players manage to reach those lines before Claudius interrupts the play, I propose that the passage which begins with the Player Queen's interruption of the Player King at line 177, includes the Player King's lengthy speech on the difficulty of doing what one purposes, and culminates in the Player Queen's final protestations of eternal fidelity at line 223 is meant to be understood as Hamlet's contribution. Notwithstanding that this passage is not one set speech but a dialogue, and is considerably longer than sixteen lines—unsurprising, from a character as verbose as Hamlet—the passage recapitulates moral themes so central to Hamlet's earlier private conversations and soliloquies that it strongly suggests itself as Hamlet's rhetorical enlargement of the "extant" play (3.2.262). At line 177 the Player Queen cuts short the Player King's prospective blessings on her possible remarriage after his death with a spirited declaration that such remarriage would be "treason" (*l*. 178), and discredits the occasions of second marriage as "base respects of thrift" (*l.* 183). This last line echoes Hamlet's dry comment to Horatio that out of "thrift," the "bak'd-meats" from his father's funeral "Did coldly furnish forth the marriage tables" at Gertrude's and Claudius's wedding (1.2.180–81). The Player King's response to the Player Queen elaborates on the difficulty of bringing virtuous purposes to fruition, in terms which recall Hamlet's great soliloquy of the prior scene. "What to ourselves in passion we propose, / The passion ending doth the purpose lose" (3.2.193–94) is less eloquent than "Thus enterprises of great pitch and moment / With this regard their currents turn awry, / And lose the name of action" (3.1.85–87), but the ideas the two passages frame are nearly identical, though the Player King's words describe not a revenger's ebbing rage but a wife's weak intent to remain virtuous.

Hamlet's high hopes for this dialogue's redemptive effect on Gertrude are expressed in the enthusiastic "If she should break [her vow] now!" and the impatient "Madam, how like you this play?" with which he comments on the drama (3.2.224, 229). A few lines later he explains the play-murder of the Player King even as Claudius watches it: "'A poisons him i' th' garden for his estate" (3.2.261), Hamlet says helpfully. Hamlet mutters "Wormwood!" when the Player Queen protests her deathless love for the Player King, invoking, besides the medicinal meaning I have mentioned above, a passage in Proverbs: "For the lips of a strange woman drop as an honeycomb. . . . But the end of her is bitter as worme wood" (5:3-4). In *The Mousetrap*, the whoredom described in Proverbs becomes the violation of marriage, an institution whose sacredness, always honored by medieval English Catholics, acquired even stronger emphasis in Reformed English culture.[42] The dignity of marriage is invoked elsewhere in *Hamlet* by both Hamlet and his father's Ghost (3.4.55–63, 1.5.47–50). Anthony Munday warned that through watching plays' "representation of [such] whoredom, all the people in mind play the whores," and with "Wormwood!" Hamlet invokes the Bible to break the Player Queen's visual charm: to remind the audience of the proper Christian context by which to judge her infidelity.

Indeed, as I have argued elsewhere, Hamlet himself, "as good as a chorus" (3.2.245), interrupts the play long before Claudius does with these illuminating comments on its moral import.[43] In what way is Hamlet as good as a chorus? In the plays of Aeschylus and Sophocles, the chorus commented on spectacular actions that had been kept from the audience's view. Clytemnestra's infidelity, Agamemnon's and Clytemnestra's murders, and Oedipus's self-blinding are not witnessed but described, and in each case the moral context of the action is verbally clarified by the chorus. Unlike the earliest Greek tragedies, *The Mousetrap* does stage horrid actions, but its Elizabethan chorus, Hamlet, explains these actions so as to control their effects on watchers. Hamlet is eager, in Ophelia's words, to "tell us what this show mean[s]" (3.2.143). Even though he has already expanded *The Mousetrap*'s verbal content, he seems to fear the play's dangerous capacity to decline from didactic exercise to spectacular entertainment.

Hence Hamlet's first interruption comes early, following the unwelcome dumb show that precedes the spoken play. This dumb show, which silently enacts the king's murder before the play proper can contextualize the crime, is "minching mallecho," or mischief, as Hamlet immediately tells Ophelia (3.2.138). As J. Dover Wilson has said, Hamlet is "exceedingly annoyed at the dumbshow," which delays his purpose of "tent[ing]" Claudius's ear with "horrid speech" (2.2.597, 563).[44] In his speech to the players Hamlet has mocked "inexplicable dumb shows" (3.2.12), and this one does prove inexplicable to Claudius, who remains oddly unprovoked by its silent, graphic representation of a murder just like the one he did, complete with *"poison in the sleeper's ears"* (s.d. 3.2.135).[45] After the show's conclusion, Claudius can still ask Hamlet whether Hamlet has "heard the [play's] argument" (3.2.232). His question reminds us that the goal of both Hamlet's soon-to-be-played additions to the work and Hamlet's interruptions of those additions is moral argument, designed to bring Claudius to his knees.

"Argument," of course, meant "plot summary" to the Elizabethans (as when Rosencrantz describes playgoers' pennies as "money bid for argument" [2.2.355]), and Claudius here may merely intend to test Hamlet's knowledge of the story to be enacted. Yet the phrase *"heard the argument"* (my emphasis), and the *debat* form of much of *Gonzago*'s immediately ensuing dialogue, shifts "argument's" meaning here to the province of Renaissance *disputatio*: the posing and answering of difficult moral questions, like "To be or not to be?"[46] In any case, whatever portion of *The Mousetrap*'s argument we are meant to think prompts Claudius to rise, flee the performance, and try to pray, Hamlet's view is that his own spoken glosses have "tent[ed]" his uncle "to the quick" (2.2.597). Claudius started, Hamlet exults to Horatio, "Upon the *talk* of the poisoning" (3.2.289, my emphasis): that is, in response to Hamlet's extra-dramatic comment, "A poisons him in the garden for his estate." Words trump spectacle as the purveyor of painful truth.

This proves so for Gertrude as well, although the carefully scripted speech in *The Mousetrap* fails to move her. As I have noted, Hamlet "speaks daggers" to his mother as he lectures her in her closet, and describes his harsh but salutary jeremiad in the terms he earlier used to describe moral theater. "[T]he purpose of playing," he told the players, is "to hold . . . the mirror up to nature: to show virtue her feature, scorn her own image" (3.2.21–23). Yet the mirror he holds up to Gertrude's soul is a verbal *speculum*. "You go not till I set you up a glass / Where you may see the inmost part of you," he commands (3.4.19–20), and then preaches bluntly against Claudius's villainy and her own shameful behavior. His mirror, or "glass," is this sermon, and Gertrude "see[s]" her sin through hearing it ("O Hamlet, speak no more! / Thou turn'st my eyes into my very soul" [3.4.89–90]).

The fact that Hamlet's lecture to his mother repeats much of the Ghost's own prior description of Claudius's and Gertrude's crimes draws our attention to a last crucial dimension of aural theater in *Hamlet*: the purgative, testimonial telling of a true story. I have touched on some of this. Laertes, for example, claims that Polonius's "means of death" and "obscure funeral / Cry to be heard" (4.5.214–17). The Ghost is driven to beg Hamlet's "serious hearing" of his tale, which recounts Gertrude's decline from him to Claudius and describes a wife who, though "to a radiant angel link'd," would "prey on garbage" (1.5.55, 57). In Gertrude's closet, Hamlet invokes a like comparison between old Hamlet and Claudius, calling his father a man on whom "every god did seem to set his seal," next to whose image his brother seems "a mildewed ear" (3.4.61, 64). Hamlet's moral impulse, then, is to share his father's painful story now that he judges it to be true. In doing so, he finds verbal expression for his own pent outrage. For Hamlet's own hidden story has long since merged with his father's tale.

IV

The charity or redemptiveness of listening to an important true story is everywhere emphasized in *Hamlet*, as it is in the Bible. "Lord ... Let thine ears attend to the voice of my prayers," says the psalmist in the *Geneva* version (Ps 130:2).[47] "List, list, o, list!" says the Ghost (1.5.22), and Horatio bids Hamlet listen "with an attent ear" to his "deliver[y]" of the tale of the Ghost's appearance (1.2.193, 195). "He that hath ears to hear, let him ear," Christ tells the listening crowd (Matt 11:15, *The Geneva Bible*). "[L]et me speak to th'yet unknowing world [of Hamlet's story]," says Horatio, and Fortinbras replies, "Let us haste to hear it" (5.2.279, 386). The ubiquitousness of biblical exhortations to tell and hear truth makes it difficult to establish specific links between scriptural references to hearing and *Hamlet*, and the psalmist's anguished prayer or, at least, the joyful story of Christ's sacrifice is far removed from the "carnal, bloody, and unnatural acts" of which Hamlet's hidden tale is composed. Thus my purpose is and has been only to argue that the Reformed emphasis, first, on what the Bible actually said, and, next, on speaking and hearing rather than on showing and seeing, influenced Shakespeare's presentation of all truth's communication in *Hamlet*. Further, my purpose has been and is to show the theatrical dimension of virtuous telling and listening as Shakespeare presents them. Again to quote Bryan Crockett, although in Elizabethan England "the ear displace[d] the eye as the primary organ of devotion"[48] the late sixteenth and early seventeenth centuries in England were also "the great age of the performance."[49] Thus the moral digesting of painful true stories in *Hamlet* occurs and is to occur not through reading, but through listening to performed speech.

Consequently Hamlet shows initial excitement about the instructive possibilities of Aeneas's tale to Dido as performed by the traveling player. "[A]n excellent play, well digested in the scenes," Hamlet calls the Virgil-based drama from which the tale derives, and he is particularly anxious that the player "speak [him] a speech" from that play which itself enacts the telling of a brutal tale (2.2.439, 434).[50] Yet, as I suggested earlier, afterwards Hamlet thinks the player's performance "monstrous" because any truth the story might convey has been overborne by the visual distractions offered in the player's recitation. The "visage wann'd," the "[t]ears in his eyes," the "distraction in his aspect" (2.2.554–55) display and provoke a "dream of passion" for "nothing": "What's Hecuba to him, or he to [Hecuba] / That he should weep for her? What would he do / Had he the motive and the cue for passion / That I have?" (2.2.559–62). Hamlet's complaint recalls the Augustinian criticism so popular among the Reformers: "Stage-plays ... carried me away, full of *images* of my miseries," Augustine wrote,[51] but "what more miserable being who ... weep[s] the death of Dido for love to Aeneas, but weep[s] not his own death for want of love to Thee, O God."[52] It is after the Player's performance of Aeneas's tale to Dido that Hamlet resolves that told stories must be true stories, and must be conveyed with an emphasis on the auditory rather than on the seductive and misleading ocular dimension. What follows are the revisions to Gonzago's script that I have already discussed.

Hamlet's final displacement of passionate visual portrayal to aural theater is predicted in the play's last scene. He dies unable to recount his own tale, and charges Horatio—whose name suggests his importance as orator[53]—"in this harsh world" to "draw [his] breath in pain / To tell [Hamlet's] story" (5.2.388–89). When Fortinbras appears on stage immediately thereafter, the Norwegian conqueror exhibits a misplaced desire to see the bloody spectacle of the dead Danes ("Where is this sight?" [5.2.362]). He is chastened by Horatio the orator: "What is it you would see?" (5.2.362). The truth is not expressed by the awful sprawled bodies, indeed cannot be apprehended by sight. Instead it inheres in a story that Horatio will tell. "So shall you hear / Of accidental judgments, casual slaughters, / ... all this can I truly deliver" (5.2.380–86). As earlier, when Horatio begged leave to "deliver" a marvelous ghost story to Hamlet, Horatio now presents his voice as midwife at the birth of a painful true tale. Yet, in asserting the greater honesty of the spoken account, Horatio will not relinquish the narrative's theatrical dimension. "[G]ive order that these bodies / High on a stage be placed to the view," he tells Fortinbras, "And let me speak to th' yet unknowing world / How these things came about" (5.2.377–80). Here in the court, Fortinbras says in the play's penultimate line, the dead "[show] much amiss" (5.2.402). But on the scaffold, where men will "speak loudly for [Hamlet]" (5.2.400), the shocking spectacle of the bodies will be tamed, put in its place. The quiet and composed corpses will serve as backdrop to the recounted tale. That tale's speaker will control the stage.

Consider two lines uttered just prior to this moment, when Hamlet speaks his last. Hamlet bequeaths Fortinbras his "dying voice" (5.2.356), and, just before, gasps, "The potent poison quite o'er-crows my spirit" (5.2.352). The phrase "dying voice" points, once more, to the importance of voice and hearing in *Hamlet*. The complaint that poison "o'er-*crows*" Hamlet's ghost presents an echo of the play's first scene, wherein Hamlet's spirit father was summoned by the voice of the dawn bird, the *crowing* cock. Since then Ophelia's mad song has made of the cock a symbol of God ("By Cock, they are to blame" [4.5.61]). Now, in Hamlet's curious dying phrase, the potent poison killing him becomes the cry of that bird of dawning, summoning him with divine power, as it did his father, to an undiscovered country. In Hamlet's line again resounds the Protestant emphasis on the moral authority of true things said and heard. Like the Ghost, Hamlet responds to an aural summons, and bequeaths Horatio and Fortinbras not a misleading show but an honest voice.

CHAPTER 6

Providence in *Julius Caesar*

John W. Mahon

Some years ago, drawn to Hamlet's lines about the "divinity that shapes our ends" (5.2.10)[1] and prompted by my own belief in a divine providence (as well as an invitation to prepare a paper for an Iona conference on *Hamlet*), I wrote "Providential Visitations in *Hamlet*," later published in *Hamlet Studies*.[2] In this article, I suggest that the action of providence in *Hamlet* is primarily visible in the unexpected visitors to the court at Elsinore, where all the action is set. The Ghost, of course, is the most important unexpected visitor, but the players are also unexpected, as is—in act 5—Hamlet himself (he has been sent to England in act 4, to die there), and, to a lesser extent, Fortinbras at the end. These visitors have a real impact on the plot and advance it toward the providential goal of a state ruled by a legitimate monarch. Hamlet's own role as a "visitor" marks his transformation from half-crazed son convinced that he alone can "set it right" (1.5.189) to confident prince, "Hamlet the Dane" (5.1.258), trusting in providence to restore order to Denmark.

Shakespeare's audience, gifted with hindsight and persuaded (whether Protestant or Catholic) that God moves history toward a final goal, the incorporation of all creation into himself, could perhaps see the working of providence in *Julius Caesar*. After all, "the pagan story is told with reference to Elizabethan bibles and Elizabethan religious experience."[3] The action in the play moves Rome closer to the time when it will host the birth of Jesus and support (even, ironically, through its efforts at suppression) the growth of the Jesus movement into the Christian church. David Daniell writes, "Understood biblically, even the geography of the Caesar story [Philippi, site of the decisive battle in Shakespeare's play, was Christianity's first outpost on the European continent, as Paul's letter suggests] points to it being in the Providence of God, preparing for the coming of Christ. Shakespeare's age was not squeamish about seeing the Christian God using 'pagan' events."[4]

Many Elizabethans would argue that the most desirable government was monarchy, a stable and strong central authority that could support and enhance conditions of peace and prosperity. Such conditions were always sought, as much in 1599 as in 44 B.C. From this perspective, Elizabethans would view as a good thing the development of Rome from what William Fulbecke in a 1601 title calls *"the continuall factions, Tumults, and Massacres of the Romans and Italians during the space of one hundred and twentie yeares next before the peaceable Empire of Augustus Caesar."*[5] Fulbecke declares that his history reveals the "mischiefes of discord and civil dissension," brought on by ambition, a "seede" that leads to a "harvest of evils," and remedied "by humble estimation of ourselves, by living well, not by lurking well; by conversing in the light of the common weale with equals, not by complotting in darke conventicles against superiors."[6] This attitude is evident also in a 1578 translation of Appian's *Civil Wars* which includes "an evident demonstration, that peoples rule must give place, and Princes power prevayle." And Richard Reynolds in 1571 published a *Chronicle of all the noble Emperours of the Romaines, from Julius Caesar . . . Setting forth the great power, and divine providence of almighty God, in preserving the godly Princes and common wealthes.*[7] Looking at Shakespeare's Roman plays, Spencer concludes that "[i]n *Julius Caesar,* it seems to me, [Shakespeare] is almost precisely in step with sound Renaissance opinion on the subject."[8]

After thinking on some of the preceding events and statements, I decided to study *Julius Caesar,* looking—as I did earlier with *Hamlet*—for the action of providence in the play. There is no pattern of visitations here, nor do we encounter the dramatic interventions found in *Macbeth*—with its witches, bloody ghost, and miracle-working king—but there is, nevertheless, evidence of the action of providence in the play, in omens, wild weather and extraordinary phenomena, auguries, dreams, and at least one ghostly visitation. For English Christians of every shade of theological opinion, these elements would carry providential significance. Their presence in the play emphasizes the belief—clearly shared by Romans and Englishmen—that there is a reality beyond the one we perceive. In this regard, Elizabethans were much closer to the Romans than to us. Contemporary commentators speak about the challenge of staging *Macbeth*'s witches or *Hamlet*'s ghost (consider the lengths to which Kenneth Branagh goes in his film to make the ghost real) presumably because moderns doubt these phenomena. Shakespeare's audience was prepared to encounter ghosts and witches, meaningful dreams and weather fraught with significance, fairies in the wood and miracles on the battlefield.

In *Julius Caesar*, divine providence advances primarily through the agency of two of the characters. If many agreed that Augustus was God's agent in establishing the best conditions for the birth of God's Son, then God's agents in *Julius Caesar*, the characters who advance God's providential design by making Augustus "sole sir o' th' world,"[9] are, most especially, Cassius and Antony. In successively pivotal and decisive actions, they move the plot toward its conclusion. Both of them act primarily through their influence on others: Cassius through Brutus, Antony through Brutus again and then the Roman mob. The "main action," says Harley Granville-Barker, of the play begins with Cassius's approach to Brutus. Cassius's recruitment of Brutus contributes decisively to the legitimacy and the success of the conspiracy against Caesar. After the assassination, "the mainspring of the renewed action will lie, of course, in the creation of Antony,"[10] whose masterful manipulation of the conspirators, especially of Brutus, and of the mob opens the way for Octavius's successful assumption as Caesar of the mantle of dead Julius. While neither character can be considered the play's protagonist, they both function crucially as enablers. Their significance supports approaches to the play that resist identifying a traditional protagonist. There is no Richard III, Richard II, or Hamlet here, nor is fate the crucial player as in *Romeo and Juliet*.

While many would agree that "it cannot seriously be doubted that Brutus is the focus [of the play],"[11] it is noteworthy that Marvin Spevack avoids the term "hero" for Brutus. A recent thread on SHAKSPER debated the identity of the protagonist in the play, and John Velz, in his posting, noted that several characters could be considered the protagonist, but that the real hero of the Roman plays is Rome itself. "Sharply defined by recognizable localities such as the Capitol, marketplace, and walls, Rome is the central protagonist of the play."[12] Rome as hero, and the realization of its destiny as "universal landlord,"[13] is advanced in this play through the agency of Cassius and Antony. Their actions push Rome toward the ultimate settlement of decades of civil strife with the victory of Octavius as sole ruler in *Antony and Cleopatra*. Dante condemned Brutus and Cassius to the bottom of the *Inferno*, with Judas, because they murdered the man who had brought stability to Rome, but Shakespeare's play shows us a Rome divided about Caesar, willing to accept him as dictator but hesitant to restore the long-before discredited monarchy. It takes Caesar's assassination and the turmoil subsequent to it to turn Rome definitively and without hesitation toward the one-man rule adumbrated in Caesar's triumph and celebrated in many Elizabethan histories.

In an analysis of human behavior that focuses on what he calls mimetic action and the scapegoat mentality in all cultures, René Girard argues that human beings, imitative by nature, too often imitate the wrong behavior, are motivated by envy and emulation, and seek release from competition by isolating one individual as a victim, making that one the scapegoat. He further argues that *Julius Caesar* is a play "about collective violence,"[14] and the focus of this violence is what Girard calls the "founding murder"—a murder that forms the basis for the development of a culture. In Roman terms, Romulus murders Remus and Rome results, the first Brutus expels Tarquin and the republic results, while in Shakespeare's play the conspirators murder Caesar and the empire results. Girard notes that in Livy's history Remus's death is collective: *In turba cecidit* (he fell into the mob), "just like Tarquin, just like Caesar, just like Cinna."[15] Girard assumes that the play refers only to Tarquin and Caesar, perhaps unaware that the feast of the Lupercalia "commemorates the suckling of Romulus and Remus by a she-wolf"; Robert Miola concludes that "in his concern with the Lupercalia, in his desire for progeny (a detail not in Plutarch), Caesar recalls Romulus, who initiated the Lupercalia and started a line of kings."[16]

Naomi Liebler's investigations into the Lupercalia suggest that in Caesar's Rome "traditional observance[s]" of the feast "were vitiated and little respected beyond their empty ceremonial forms." Liebler argues that "without proper observance of the appropriate purgative ritual, some other ceremony, or the semblance of one, appears in its place"—one reason, perhaps, that Caesar tried to reorient the festival by adding himself to the celebration, equating himself with Romulus and thus justifying Cassius's observation that Caesar "[i]s now become a god" (1.2.116). Brutus's effort to ritualize the assassination and Antony's identification of Caesar as a sacrificial victim suggest a search for meaningful ritual. *Caesar*'s audience could have seen what Liebler calls "this Rome-in-transition"[17] and its rituals as ripe for replacement by the Christian message about to be born. The juxtaposition between this troubled period depicted in the play and that of the future *Pax Romana* is suggested in the opening scene of *Hamlet*, when Horatio recalls that

> A little ere the mightiest Julius fell,
> The graves stood tenantless and the sheeted dead
> Did squeak and gibber in the Roman streets. (1.1.114–16)

Moments later, Marcellus reports that "ever 'gainst that season comes / Wherein our Saviour's birth is celebrated," "no spirit dare stir abroad, / The nights are wholesome" (1.1.158–59; 161–62).

For Girard, both Cassius and Antony are characters motivated by envy and emulation, competitiveness and vengefulness. Cassius and Antony, furthermore, are both intimately connected with the "founding murder" of the play. Cassius of course denigrates Caesar and manipulates Brutus into joining a conspiracy against the dictator, while Antony begins the process of divinizing Caesar, so that the hideous knifewounds that Calpurnia foresees in her dream become mouths begging for revenge from the populace. Girard notes that Caesar's report of Calpurnia's dream, and Decius Brutus's flattering interpretation that follows, "seem to contradict each other but in reality they both are true. The first corresponds to what Caesar's murder *is* during the play, a source of extreme disorder, and the second to what the same murder *becomes* in the conclusion, the source of the new imperial order."[18] In a later study, Girard expands on his concept of the "founding murder" in *Julius Caesar* in statements such as the following:

> The successive emperors draw their authority from the sacrificial power that emanates from the deity whose name they bear, the first Caesar, who was assassinated by numerous murderers. So like every sacred monarchy, the [Roman] empire is based upon a collective victim who is divinized. . . .[19]

The dramatist centered his tragedy of Caesar in the murder of the hero and defined quite explicitly the founding, sacrificial virtues of an event that he both connected and opposed to its counterpart in the distant past: the violent expulsion of the last king of Rome.

One of the most revealing passages is the interpretation of the sinister dream Caesar's wife has the night before the assassination. The interpreter clearly announces the founding character, or rather "re-founding" character, of this event:

> It was a vision fair and fortunate:
> Your statue spouting blood in many pipes,
> In which so many smiling Romans bathed,
> Signifies that from you great Rome shall suck
> Reviving blood, and that great men shall press
> For tinctures, stains, relics, and cognizance. (2.2.83–90)

The cult of the emperor explicitly reassumes the primitive scheme of the founding murder.[20]

In other words, Decius Brutus ironically but accurately predicts the impact of Caesar's murder on future events. The characters in the play, as so often, fail to understand the real meaning of events or omens—when Casca worries about the meaning of the wild happenings overnight, Cicero wisely comments that "men may construe things after their fashion, / Clean from the purpose of the things themselves" (1.3.34–35). Moments later, Cassius tells Casca that the strange events are a warning of "some monstrous state" (1.3.71)—a tyranny under Caesar. But when Cassius lies dead on the battlefield of Philippi, Titinius observes, "Alas, thou has misconstrued everything" (5.3.84), a judgment that applies to most of the characters. So in *Hamlet*, the Player King will tell his queen,

> Our wills and fates do so contrary run
> That our devices still are overthrown,
> Our thoughts are ours, their ends none of our own. (3.2.211–13)

Hamlet, deluded by grief and the need to prove himself, thinks that he alone can restore Denmark but, confronted by the power of providence on his sea voyage, he adjusts his perspective. Maynard Mack speaks of the failure of rationalism in *Julius Caesar*, the impact of the soothsayer in whose "soberly reiterated warning" Shakespeare "allows us to catch a hint of something else, something far more primitive and mysterious, from which rationalism in this play keeps vainly trying to cut itself away."[21] The conspirators think that they can control the consequences of their act—Cassius and Brutus both think, to quote Cassius, that "Men at some time are masters of their fates" (1.2.139). In 1.3, Cassius asserts to Casca that, if Caesar is named king, "Cassius from bondage will deliver Cassius"—he cannot realize that he will indeed commit suicide, but in very different circumstances from those he imagines in act 1. Confronted by reality, the most self-assured and rational characters, Caesar and Cassius, both reconsider their cynicism about signs and wonders. The conspirators fail to control the aftermath of their act, at least partly because they do not take feeling, the nonrational side of things, into account. The play argues for "a degree of determinism in history, whether we call it cultural, fatal, or providential, which *helps* to shape our ends, 'Rough-hew them how we will' (*Ham.* 5.2.11)."[22]

Despite its classical setting *Julius Caesar* demonstrates the same conviction about the role of divine providence evident in the English history plays and in such tragedies as *Hamlet* and *Macbeth*. In the structure of the play, Cassius and Antony are crucial agents of the change that serves the providential design working itself out, unknown to these characters. Cassius and Antony are important structural elements in the play (like the unexpected visitors in *Hamlet*). There are of course other such elements. George Walton Williams, for example, offers an especially interesting consideration of structure with an analysis of the role of Pompey in the play, pointing out that Pompey is recalled "at the three most important places in the play, at the structural nodes of the play—the beginning, the middle, and the end."[23] John Velz's "Undular Structure in *Julius Caesar*" demonstrates that "the dynamic of *Julius Caesar* is a sequence of rises to prominence and of declines from it."[24] This sequence marks the path between Pompey, his sons recently defeated and still championed at the start of the action, and Octavius, recently victorious and already at the center of power at the close. Cassius and Antony are primarily responsible for Octavius's success.

Another commentator notes how much of a role envy plays in the action and relates this fact to a central argument in Machiavelli's *Discourses*, where "ingratitude, envy and emulation are the pre-eminent destabilizing political force.... The corrosive effect of envy and emulation are the leitmotif of the *Discourses*, from its preface to its longest section 'On Conspiracies'."[25] For Steve Sohmer, *Julius Caesar* is *Shakespeare's Mystery Play*. He suggests that the calendar is central to the structure because Shakespeare and his contemporaries were, quite literally, trapped in the same Julian calendar that Caesar had introduced in Rome not long before his murder: England refused to adopt the new Gregorian calendar because of its papal inspiration. "Time is the subject of Shakespeare's story in *Julius Caesar*."[26] In 2.1, Brutus is confused about the date because the Julian calendar was new (Julius had added ninety days to the year 46 B.C.. in order to bring the calendar into line with astronomical realities). Similarly, Englishmen were frustrated with a situation which, in 1598, meant that they celebrated Easter almost five weeks later than their fellow Christians elsewhere in western Europe. Sohmer also links various references in *Julius Caesar* to the feasts and seasons of the Christian liturgical year. When they speak of liturgical time Christians are speaking of providential time, time outside of earthly time, time that touches eternity. (Thomas Cranmer's *Book of Common Prayer* had preserved, on a reduced scale, the rhythms of the traditional liturgical year.) A play itself operates in a time outside of time, somewhat like liturgical time. Mark Rose argues that *Julius Caesar*, "like the Mass, . . . centers upon a sacrificial death that initiates a new era in history, the emergence of imperial Rome."[27] Indeed, "an audience may well feel that it is not only witnessing but participating in a kind of ceremony." This "ritual quality," after all, "is directly related to the special historical status of this play's subject: for the Elizabethans as for ourselves, the assassination of Julius Caesar was probably the single most famous event in ancient history." Furthermore, if magic had been banished from the church by the Reformation, "magic reappeared in the ostensibly circumscribed and make-believe world of the theater. If sixteenth-century Englishmen could no longer experience the real physical presence of God on the altar in church, they could still experience the pretended physical manifestation of demons and spirits in the theater."[28] The same audiences would recognize the providential design that helps to structure *Julius Caesar*.

"In those days a decree went out from Caesar Augustus that the whole world should be enrolled." A commentary suggests the importance of these words in Luke's Gospel (2:1):

> According to Greek inscriptions, Augustus was regarded in the Roman Empire as "savior" and "god," and he was credited with establishing a time of peace, the *pax Augusta*, throughout the Roman world during his long reign. It is not by chance that Luke relates the birth of Jesus to the time of Caesar Augustus; the real savior and peace-bearer is the child born in Bethlehem. The great emperor is simply God's agent who provides the occasion for God's purposes to be accomplished.[29]

In *Julius Caesar*, Cassius and Antony bring closer to reality the imperial future of Rome under Octavius.

People in Early Modern England assumed that there is such a thing as God's providence (literally, *pro+videre*, "to see before, foresight"), God's foreknowing, beneficent, and efficient concern, that it determines the ultimate outcome of all human activity, and that we can never gain more than glimpses into its operation from our human vantage point. Recognizing human limitations, John Milton concludes his invocation to *Paradise Lost* by asking the Holy Spirit:

> . . . what in me is dark
> Illumine, what is low raise and support;
> That to the height of this great argument
> I may assert Eternal Providence,
> And justify the ways of God to men. (1.22–26)

When he came to write *Julius Caesar* Shakespeare had just completed his second set of four plays about English history between 1399 and 1485, plays in which the role of providence is often explored. Many people believed that the rewards and punishments experienced by most of society somehow reflected God's will. A crude version of the doctrine of providence commonly held that "God's working day was largely occupied with the distribution of thunderbolts, fire from heaven, earthquakes, and other 'acts of God,'" so that one could "interpret any apparently accidental disaster that befell a sinner as an instance of divine vengeance and, hence, as a demonstration of the truth of divine providence."[30] Such a conception sees providence "as an arbitrary force, indistinguishable (at least to the eye of reason) from Fortune," so that in *2 Henry VI*, "Henry, Gloucester, and Say are all under the illusion that the truth of divine providence means that the innocent never suffer unjustly."[31] Michael Quinn argues that Shakespeare's "own conception of providence, as it emerges from the action of the plays, can best be understood by accepting, as a hypothesis, the scholastic distinction between a general providence and a particular providence. The story of the wars of the Roses, as Shakespeare found it in Hall and Holinshed, was already shaped into a rough demonstration of the truth of a general providence: crime is ultimately punished and time inevitably brings in the triumph of virtue."[32] "But Shakespeare's conception of particular providence in these plays is nothing like so clear-cut and absolute as that of general providence," so that he does show the guilty punished "but, with the notable exception of Richmond, their executioners are themselves equally guilty."[33] Unlike Job's comforters, Shakespeare is unwilling to make simple equivalences between human experiences and God's providential design. Nevertheless, the very nature of drama means that the audience has a sense of the "big picture," the ultimate working out of heaven's design, denied to the characters on stage. The audience is given a God's-eye view of events, and this contrast between what we know and what the characters know only enhances the dramatic irony in the plays.

Another commentator notes that the Christian idea of reward and punishment after death, "when all the inequalities of this life will be adjusted,"[34] assuages the human desire to make connections between divine providence and the experiences of individuals. Henry Ansgar Kelly argues that belief in an afterlife allows for God's justice finally to be "reconciled with the events of everyday reality, and at the same time it remained impossible to state with any certainty the ultimate divine reason for any specific disaster."[35] In *The City of God*, St. Augustine holds that, although God generally reserves his judgment for the afterlife, he does occasionally allow his providence to appear in earthly contexts, since "if no sin received now a plainly divine punishment, it would be concluded that there is no divine providence at all."[36] Most people agreed "that absolutely everything that happened, happened through the causation and concurrence of Providence, and furthermore it was agreed that God's ways were mysterious and unsearchable, in spite of (and because of) the general principle that they were in accord with wisdom and justice and mercy,"[37] since humans have, at best, an imperfect grasp of wisdom, justice and mercy.

In dealing with the "matter of Rome," as much as when dealing with English history, the Elizabethans knew how the story would turn out, and they could appreciate the role of divine providence in the outcome. When he came to write *Julius Caesar*, Shakespeare would have known that the events of 44 B.C. had a profound impact on the world: the assassination of Caesar and its aftermath led not only to the birth of the Roman Empire but to the creation of conditions ideal for Jesus' birth and for the growth of the movement that developed after his death and resurrection. Just as it is no accident that Luke relates Jesus' birth to the reign of Augustus, it is probably no accident that Shakespeare chooses to write about that reign—its beginnings in *Julius Caesar*, its triumph in *Antony and Cleopatra*, and its travails in *Cymbeline*.

Robert Miola has argued for the unity among Shakespeare's Roman works, all six of them (*Titus Andronicus, The Rape of Lucrece, Julius*

Caesar, Coriolanus, Antony and Cleopatra, Cymbeline);[38] and the three that involve Augustus explore the earliest days of empire, of special interest to all Christians as the seedbed of their faith. The empire established under Augustus, a "Prince of Peace," was an epoch providentially arranged to afford a suitable setting for the advent of another "Prince of Peace." What this meant, in the language of the title-page to a 1578 English edition of Appian's *Civil Wars*, was that the "action" represented in *Julius Caesar* and *Antony and Cleopatra* could be discerned in golden hindsight as a "prophane Tragedie, whereof flowed our divine Comoedie." In other words, "a sequence of events that meant one thing to a pre-Christian Roman such as Brutus, Antony or Octavius could have a radically different significance to a later era accustomed to explaining all of human history in light of a divine plan in which even God's enemies were constrained to play a role in fulfilling his designs."[39] In fact, pagans and Christians agreed that human history was a succession of four empires, and for Christians the fourth empire, Rome, was simply a preparation for the fifth, eternal empire to follow the Second Coming of Christ.

This arc of three plays works well geographically as well as chronologically. The first, *Julius Caesar*, is set in Rome and leaves the city only to determine, on a Greek battlefield, who controls Rome. The second, *Antony and Cleopatra*, moves back and forth between Rome and the East, Egypt; while the third, *Cymbeline*, focuses on Britain but also moves back and forth between Rome and the West, Britain. If these three plays are linked, the operation of providence is clear. Whatever the machinations of individuals, providence moves Rome-as-hero toward the strong rule of empire. In this empire, Christianity grows and eventually becomes accepted, indeed becomes the state religion, prepared to fill the vacuum left by the collapse of Roman power in the West even as it remained a central element in the Eastern Roman Empire. At the same time, the continued existence of the Holy Roman Emperor in the West kept alive the notion of empire born under Octavius as Caesar Augustus. Add to all this the enormous influence on Shakespeare and his contemporaries of one writer and one book, Virgil and his *Aeneid* (which survives, possibly, because of Augustus's direct intervention to prevent its destruction after Virgil's untimely death), and the era of Augustus takes on added significance.

In this context, then, Cassius and Antony operate, advancing God's providence in their role as instigators of action. We can certainly see Brutus in a similar role—as John Velz argues, when Brutus refers late in the play to a "tide" in the affairs of men, he has already missed taking his own tide "at the flood."[40] His moment, the crest of his wave, comes with the assassination and the period immediately following, but it flounders against the successful manipulation of Antony. Indeed, Antony is on the scene virtually immediately after the murder of Caesar. So, Brutus moves the action forward, but he does not instigate in quite the same way as Cassius and Antony. (These three characters, interestingly, are the ones who soliloquize.) Brutus has the longest part in the play—5,394 words—while Cassius has the second longest part, with 3,709 words; and Antony is third, with 2,540 words.[41] This perspective on Cassius and Antony also helps to explain what may seem to be the anticlimactic quality of acts 4 and 5—this second part lacks the driving force of the obsessions that motivate both Cassius and Antony. Although both characters remain in the play, their power as agents is circumscribed: for the former by Brutus, for the latter by Octavius. Like everyone else in the play once Octavius appears, both are moved along by a seemingly inevitable process toward Philippi (the end for Cassius) and, for Antony, Actium.

Although Shakespeare shows us that none of these characters really understands where events will lead, we can speak of relative perception. Among the four principals, Brutus is the least perceptive, either about himself or about those around him, and Caesar is little better. Brutus and Caesar have many things in common, including a poor grasp of reality. By comparison, Cassius and Antony understand their surroundings and take control of situations. David Daniell has noted the linguistic uniqueness of each—Cassius uses the most modern vocabulary in the play, words "first recorded in the 1590s or later." Brutus, by contrast, uses more established language. "Cassius' trick of modern speech appears most sharply in his dialogues with Brutus when he is manipulating him."[42] Antony's uniqueness is that "by contrast to everyone else in the play, his language over long periods is apparently driven by feeling for someone else."[43] Again, as Daniell notes, Antony begins his first significant speech in the play, "uniquely for any speaker in the play ... at a loss for words.... Momentarily he thinks, Cassius-like, of himself, 'Either a coward or a flatterer' (3.1.193). Then the following seventeen lines are addressed in love to Caesar and his spirit."[44] Antony's soliloquy, notes Daniell, is Shakespeare's "first soliloquy of grief."[45] Cassius's "newfangledness" in vocabulary and Antony's grief-stricken, other-directed words link them as original, creative speakers.

There is a tension in the play between its classical, restrained, highly rhetorical style and its violent subject, a tension particularly evident in the speeches of Cassius and Antony, who rarely violate decorum even while urging murder and mayhem. Their soliloquies maintain this classical decorum yet also reveal both the manipulative approach they share and their willingness to sacrifice honor (Cassius at 1.2.309) and peace (Antony at 3.1.259ff.) in order to achieve their goals.

Cassius's goal is to eliminate Caesar—he draws Brutus in and then fades, seemingly unable to override the blind Brutus. Antony seeks to avenge Caesar, so he creates the conditions favorable to the rise of a new dictator. In welcoming Octavius, Antony, like Cassius, fades, unable to master his rival. Both men provide an opportunity to another. Cassius recruits Brutus because he thinks Brutus possesses the moral authority to make the conspiracy succeed, and then he defers to Brutus's judgment, even when he knows that Brutus is wrong. By the same token, Antony's welcome to Octavius dooms him because Octavius, not interested in triumvirates or any other form of shared rule, moves in the vacuum left by Brutus's failure and Antony's inability to consolidate his advantage. "Antony's energy, which flared suddenly and brilliantly in the third act, starts to die [in act 4]. In the play's final irony, the Caesarians compete for the privilege of honoring Brutus, with Antony giving the oration and Caesar claiming the body. The echo of [Julius] Caesar's funeral orations, in which Brutus had fine and dignified words but Antony had the body, bodes ill for Antony now. And it is [Octavius] Caesar, not Antony, who takes the practical step of enlisting Brutus's friends in his service. The future belongs to a character we had not even heard of till the play was half over."⁴⁶ Octavius, significantly, has the last words in the play. In Joseph Mankiewicz's 1953 film version, the last two speeches are reversed: Marlon Brando as Antony speaks last, offering his generous epitaph over the fallen Brutus. In a similar directorial amendment, Stuart Burge's 1970 film drops the final speech, so that Charlton Heston as Antony has the last word.

At the beginning of the play, Cassius speaks only one line before he engages Brutus in conversation. When Caesar orders that the soothsayer be set before him, it is Cassius who does Caesar's bidding, "Fellow, come from the throng, look upon Caesar" (1.2.21). Left alone onstage with Brutus, Cassius initiates their conversation. He motivates Brutus, who seems content to remain on the sidelines, into consideration of a course of action. Cassius, like Iago, is a superb manipulator, and Brutus, like Othello, can be manipulated because he is open to suggestion. And yet Cassius is not a villain in the way that Iago is, any more than Antony is a villain. Both men are opportunists, and it is the opportunists who control the first three acts.

Cassius is sincere in his protestations of friendship for Brutus—they are, after all, related, since Cassius is married to Junia, Brutus's sister. Cassius's affection for Brutus seems genuine, especially in the succession of descriptive modifiers he uses in referring to his brother-in-law, first as "good Brutus" (1.2.51), then as "noble Brutus" (1.2.62), "good Brutus" (1.2.66) again, then "gentle Brutus" (1.2.71). He is only partly disingenuous when he declares, "I am glad that my weak words / Have struck but thus much show of fire from Brutus" (1.2.176–77). Yet his motives for seeking Caesar's death are hardly noble. In his eulogy for Brutus, Antony says that the other conspirators "[d]id that they did in envy of great Caesar" (5.5.70), and this is certainly true of Cassius, whose envy is apparent throughout his conversation with Brutus. But Brutus is not really listening to Cassius, working instead on his own problems with Caesar.

This "encounter of Brutus and Cassius [1.2.25–177, concluded at 1.2.295–307] marks the midpoint of the opening action [of the play]. Two pairs of parallel scenes frame the meeting: on the inside are two processional marches; on the outside are two conversations, one between the tribunes and commoners [1.1], and the other [1.2.215–94] among Casca, Brutus, and Cassius."[47] In his "temptation" of Brutus, Cassius develops a biased portrait of Caesar as the *pater patriae*, the Anchises figure who is to be destroyed. We know from Caesar himself in his ample commentaries on his accomplishments, but also from independent observers including Plutarch, that Caesar had earned the eminence that is his at the beginning of the play, as a brave and enterprising general and a clever politician. But Cassius in his envy focuses on the great man's flaws, even going so far as to pervert a famous image in order to prove his point. During their competitive swim across the Tiber, when an exhausted Caesar cries for help, Cassius says that "as Aeneas, our great ancestor, / Did from the flames of Troy upon his shoulder / The old Anchises bear, so from the waves of Tiber / Did I the tired Caesar" (1.2.112–15). The image of Aeneas carrying his father from the burning city encapsulates all that Virgil means by *pietas*, and we know that the picture had a powerful impact on early moderns. Shakespeare himself probably refers to the incident in *As You Like It*, written around this time, when Orlando, in an act of *pietas*, carries Adam on his back into the forest camp of Duke Senior. In *Julius Caesar*, however, as Miola notes, Cassius "replaces the articulated emblem of *pietas*, the image of the son saving the father, with the unarticulated emblem of *impietas*, the image of the son slaying the father."[48] Cassius thus supports the tribunes and Casca in contemning Caesar, but his brutality in recollecting the famous scene from the *Aeneid* is chilling in this context.

Cassius's "program soliloquy" closes out these early scenes. Again he calls Brutus "noble" (1.2.308) and speaks of his "honourable mettle" (1.2.309), implying that he himself is somewhat less than noble. He admits to himself that, were he in Caesar's favor as Brutus is, no malcontent would persuade him to surrender his position, no matter the justification, and he explains his strategy for following up on his efforts to divert Brutus from the honorable course. For all of his self-absorption, Caesar takes the measure of Cassius accurately, and does so in conversation with Antony, who is virtually silent in the play until after the murder of Caesar. On the other hand, by the time Antony faces the triumphant conspirators, "there have already been no less than seven separate references to him, all significant."⁴⁹

Antony speaks only thirty words in scene 2 of act 1, and a mere five words at Caesar's house in scene 2 of act 2. Half of his words in 1.2 are a response to Caesar's observation that Cassius "thinks too much: such men are dangerous" (1.2.195). "Fear him not, Caesar," says Antony; "he's not dangerous. / He is a noble Roman, and well given" (1.2.196–97)— T. S. Dorsch notes that this is Antony's "last error of judgment" in the play.⁵⁰ Antony is far more impressive physically than intellectually or verbally in his first scene in the play. Caesar's response is perceptive, and deliberately juxtaposes Antony to Cassius; Cassius, he says, "reads much, / He is a great observer, and he looks / Quite through the deeds of men. He loves no plays / As thou dost, Antony; he hears no music" (1.2.201–4). Caesar's remark about Cassius as a "great observer" is evident over and over again in the scenes that follow, first in the storm scene (1.3), where Cassius recognizes Casca "by your voice" (1.3.41; "Your ear is good," says Casca), and then Cinna, "I do know him by his gait" (1.3.132); but most notably in the orchard scene, where Cassius suggests that Cicero be brought into the conspiracy (2.1.141–42), then that Antony should "fall together" with Caesar (2.1.161). In expressing fear of Antony, Cassius is far more observant than Antony has been so far. His characterization of Antony as "a shrewd contriver" (2.1.158) fits Antony (and, incidentally, himself) perfectly, especially as we see Antony perform in the days ahead. And Cassius remains observant to the end. He objects to Brutus's folly in allowing Antony to speak at Caesar's funeral, and he—the more seasoned soldier—knows that Brutus is wrong to march on Philippi. It should also be noted that Cassius instigates the conspiracy not only by recruiting Brutus but by recruiting most of the others as well, in each instance demonstrating real skill in manipulating his target. "When Cassius denies that he is 'a common laugher,' 'fawning' on men with the intention of later 'scandalling' them, he is no doubt comparing himself, not altogether unjustly, with such as Antony."⁵¹ Just before the final battle at Philippi, Cassius derides Antony as "a masker and a reveler" and Antony retorts, "Old Cassius still" (5.1.62–63). Ironically, while Cassius and Antony appear to human perception as deadly enemies, *sub specie aeternitatis* they are unwitting allies.

Everything about Antony's performance after the murder bespeaks his abilities as a manipulator. The assassination seems to galvanize him, and to provide him with a clear understanding of Cassius. The two primary agents of the play now understand each other perfectly, because, just like Brutus and Caesar, appearances to the contrary notwithstanding, they are more like each other than either would recognize or admit. Antony cannot fool Cassius, who says just before Antony reappears, "I have a mind / That fears him much, and my misgiving still / Falls shrewdly to the purpose" (3.1.144–46). But he is able completely to hoodwink Brutus, who has earlier dismissed Antony as "but a limb of Caesar" (2.1.165). Antony's servant "comes ahead" of his master, to test the waters, as it were, and, quoting Antony, he describes Brutus as "noble, wise, valiant, and honest"(3.1.126)—Brutus characteristically reflects back on Antony the same qualities, telling the servant that his master is "a wise and valiant Roman" (3.1.137). If Cassius has genuine affection for Brutus, then Antony has genuine love for Julius Caesar, and there is no reason to doubt the sincerity of his sorrow over his mentor's death. But, like Cassius, Antony is an opportunist, and he goes for the main chance. At the decisive moment, the turning-point of the action, as the conspirators look on awestruck at Caesar's bleeding corpse, Antony steps in. Years ago, Kenneth Burke imagined Antony looking back on this moment: "upon me fell the burden of keeping things going," to me was "assigned the definite task of continuing our peripety."[52] Jonathan Goldberg has noted that Antony's first appearance in the play anticipates his later role: as he runs in the race during the Lupercalia in 1.2, "Antony's role is to be the echo of Caesar, the fulfillment of his word, embodied in performance. Antony takes upon himself to extend himself to represent Caesar."[53]

Remarkable about Antony's first significant words in the play is their boldness—joining the "knot" of conspirators around Caesar's bleeding corpse, he ignores the living and addresses himself to his master. He quickly recovers his composure and manages to converse with the killers, but moments later he is again overcome and declares,

> Pardon me, Julius! Here wast thou bayed, brave heart.
> Here didst thou fall. And here thy hunters stand
> Signed in thy spoil and crimsoned in thy lethe. (3.1.204–6)

Rather frank words in such a perilous situation, so much so that Cassius rightly recognizes how dangerous Antony is. But Brutus is blind to the threat. Now that Cassius is so thoroughly negated, Antony comes into the flood tide of his power in the play, as he makes clear in his soliloquy that Caesar's "butchers" will pay for their deed; indeed all of Rome will pay in blood, destruction, the havoc of war. Antony's "aloneness" here "comes as a sudden contrast" to the crowded scenes that precede the soliloquy. "It is a moment of unexpected quiet which indicates that the counteraction is already underway. . . . The conspirators have shed Caesar's 'costly' (precious) blood, which will indeed prove 'costly' (dear, expensive) to them."[54]

It is really a short journey from these sentiments to the masterful manipulation of the Roman mob that so many generations have admired for its skill. No sooner has Antony sent the mob on its way to destroy Cinna the poet in an orgy of murder that imitates the slaughter of Caesar than he confronts a servant who reports that "Octavius is already come to Rome" (3.2.262), even as Brutus and Cassius have fled from the city. Antony does not see Octavius as a threat. He says that Octavius came to Rome "upon a wish. Fortune is merry / And in this mood will give us anything" (3.2.266–67).

Just as Cassius has provided Brutus with a conspiracy ready-made to carry out the assassination of Caesar, so Antony provides Octavius with a city ready for his arrival. By the end of act 3, both men have accomplished their role in the providential plan. In later action, both Cassius and Brutus will be humanized in their quarrel, but Cassius again defers to Brutus's judgment, despite his claims to greater military experience. Similarly, Antony tells Octavius that he has "seen more days" (4.1.18), but when Octavius insists on leading his troops to the right of the battlefield, Antony acquiesces. It is interesting to note that Antony expected Brutus and Cassius to stay away from Philippi and force him and Octavius to pursue them—Antony and Cassius share a certain military prowess. Just before the decisive battle, Cassius and Antony converse for only the second time in the play. Their first conversation came in 3.1, where Cassius recalled Antony from his blunt reverie over Caesar's corpse and pressed him to declare his intentions. Now they trade insults, even as Cassius reminds Brutus that, had things gone Cassius's way, they would not now be faced with Antony.

Cassius and Antony as providential agents in the play trace a similar course, one following upon the other: Cassius is at his best early in the action, skillfully drawing Brutus into the conspiracy, just as Antony is at his best immediately after the assassination, skillfully playing on Brutus to gain the upper hand. Later, both men find themselves overruled by those they have helped, and both die earlier than either Brutus or Octavius. The story of Cassius ends in his suicide at Philippi, where he uses on himself the same dagger that had helped to kill Caesar. Shakespeare leaves Antony's story incomplete, to end after more battles lost. But Octavius's ultimate triumph springs directly from the actions of Cassius and Antony in *Julius Caesar*. Cassius gives Rome the martyred leader whose title *Caesar* takes on meaning after his death, and Antony clears the way for the Caesar who will preside over "the time of universal peace" (*Antony and Cleopatra* 4.6.4), as divine providence works itself out. Both Catholics and Protestants basically agree on the role of providence in *Julius Caesar*. The role is prominent, but evidence of Shakespeare's leaning toward either Protestantism or Catholicism is not apparent; yet the presence of both is undeniable.

CHAPTER 7

Cobbling Souls in Shakespeare's *Julius Caesar*

Maurice Hunt

Opening speeches of Shakespeare's plays sometimes include allusions to certain Christian ideas important for appreciating a characterization of a later motif. In *1 Henry IV*, for example, the titular monarch focuses his guilty desire to redirect the aggression of Englishmen embroiled in the civil war occasioned by his kingship into a crusade to free Jerusalem from pagan rule. Readers—if not auditors—of this speech, in which King Henry IV styles himself a soldier of Christ (1.1.18–20), gather the depth of Henry's desire to atone for sin not only from his mentioning "those blessed feet / Which fourteen hundred years ago were nailed / For our advantage to the bitter cross" (25–27), but also from the fact that his speech numbers thirty-three lines of poetry. "Thirty-three is traditionally the age of Christ at his death," David Daniell notes in the 1998 Arden edition of Shakespeare's *Julius Caesar*.[1] This tradition reflects an emphasis on the Christian symbolism of the number three. Christ's three-year ministry and death after thirty years of life, among other things, stress the Trinitarian mystery of three-in-one and one-in-three. Multiplied together, the two digits of 33 equal 9, the Trinity thrice over. Henry IV expresses his desire to atone for sin in a poetic utterance in which the number of lines equals the number of years Christ is traditionally supposed to have lived—his presence on earth making atonement possible.

Steve Sohmer has argued that an allusion to Christ's supposed age at the time of his crucifixion occurs in *Julius Caesar*, when Octavius reports that Cassius, Brutus, and the other conspirators gave Caesar's body thirty-three mortal wounds (5.1.51–54).[2] Plutarch, in his "Life of Julius Caesar" (as recorded in Shakespeare's dramatic source *Plutarch's Lives of the Noble Grecians and Romans Englished by Sir Thomas North*), claims that Caesar had twenty-three wounds when he was assassinated.[3] Shakespeare, through this change, shows an awareness of the legendary association of Julius Caesar and Jesus Christ.[4] For Shakespeare's predecessors and contemporaries, the fact that both men's names begin with the same initials—"J.C."—supernaturally underscored this association,[5] most memorably drawn in the *Inferno*, where Dante places Cassius and Brutus next to Judas Iscariot in Satan's mouth at the center of hell.[6] That Shakespeare should have his Julius Caesar stabbed to death at the ninth hour (2.4.23), the hour of the crucifixion, is thus not surprising.[7] I want to do more here than simply confirm what many commentators—most notably David Kaula, Marshall Bradley and Steve Sohmer—have previously noted: that Christian values inform Shakespeare's depiction of a famous moment in Rome's history.[8] In what follows, I shall be suggesting that Shakespeare's association of Caesar and Christ is at times a positive rather than a uniformly parodic relationship,[9] and I do so by starting with some unexplored Christian overtones in minor characters' play-opening dialogue, talk partly concerned with "cobbling souls." This phrase becomes important later in the play, when Julius Caesar precipitates soul-cobbling—the fabricating or mending of souls—among Romans touched in some way by his revolutionary presence, both in the flesh and then in the spirit. While this pagan soul-making is imperfect (as the word "cobbling" implies), it acquires Christian resonance when Brutus and Cassius forge a soulful brotherhood in the urgency of having to react to Caesar's mobilizing spirit. Brutus and Cassius's soul-cobbling represents the culmination of a concept introduced lightly by a cobbler in act 1, scene 1.

Two Roman tribunes, Marellus and Flavius, open the play by asking two plebeians to identify themselves through their crafts. After they learn that the first is a carpenter, Marellus asks the second: "what trade are you?"

> *Cobbler*: Truly, sir, in respect of a fine workman, I am but as you would say, a cobbler.
>
> *Marellus*: But what trade art thou? Answer me directly.
>
> *Cobbler*: A trade, sir, that I hope I may use with a safe conscience, which is indeed, sir, a mender of bad soles.
>
> *Flavius*: What trade, thou knave? Thou naughty knave, what trade?
>
> *Cobbler*: Nay I beseech you, sir, be not out with me: yet if you be out, sir, I can mend you.
>
> *Marellus*: What mean'st thou by that? Mend me, thou saucy fellow?
>
> *Cobbler*: Why, sir, cobble you.
>
> *Flavius*: Thou art a cobbler, art thou?
>
> *Cobbler*: Truly, sir, all that I live by, is with the awl: I meddle with no tradesman's matters, nor women's matters; but withal I am indeed, sir, a surgeon to old shoes; when they are in great danger, I recover them. As proper men as ever trod upon neat's leather have gone upon my handiwork. (1.1.9–27)

For Elizabethans, a cobbler mended shoes, often roughly or clumsily (*OED* v1b).[10] But the word more generally could refer to anyone who "put [something] together or joined [parts] roughly or clumsily" (*OED* v2). The humor in the early part of this dialogue depends upon Marellus's understanding of cobbler in this sense, as "botcher." But botcher of what? Thus Marellus asks the commoner again to identify his trade. The subversive, quick-witted Cobbler then makes a familiar Elizabethan pun on "sole" / "soul," claiming to be able to mend not simply the soles of Marellus's shoes but his inner soul as well. But the thick-witted tribune misses this jest, interpreting the plebeian's claim that he can mend him as "patch him up roughly," as though he were a material object in such disrepair that he needs the services of a botcher. While the dense, offended Marellus then drives the joking Cobbler to admit that he repairs shoes, Shakespeare through the citizen's language has introduced into Julius Caesar the notion of the mending or joining together of souls.

Certain details of the opening scene of the play involving the Cobbler, Carpenter, and the Roman tribunes suggest that the Cobbler's reference to the soul in this context amounts to a Christian anachronism on Shakespeare's part. Admittedly, the ancient Greeks as early as Heraclitus had given profundity and immortality to a concept of the human soul (*psyche*), and Cicero among Roman writers had focused in texts such as *De finibus bonorum et malorum* and *De amicitia* on the soul, especially in its dichotomous relationship to the body.[11] Some literate members of the Globe audiences of Shakespeare's play were aware of classical texts that include a mention of the soul and thus most likely gave little or no second thought to the Cobbler's pun. And yet playgoers on a second or third viewing of *Julius Caesar*, and especially readers with the opportunity for leisurely analysis, are inclined to hear the Cobbler's pun as one of the first of many Christian allusions in this Roman tragedy. A sixteenth-century English association of cobbling and the Christian priesthood reinforces this inclination of playgoers and readers. In "A Replycacion" (1525), John Skelton wrote the following verses concerning the preaching of a group of young scholars,

> Ye cobble and ye clout,
> Holy Scripture so about,
> That people are in great dout
> And feare lest they be out
> Of all good Christian order.[12] (1.222–26)

This association may have contributed to the brief opening of a metaphysical dimension in the minds of auditors hearing the Cobbler's jest that "[t]ruly, sir, all that I live by, is with the awl: I meddle with no tradesman's matters, nor women's matters." The Cobbler's pun on "all" / "awl" is both sacred and profane, a Renaissance trope in this sense. A pointed tool for boring holes, the awl was in Elizabethan literature the subject of sexually obscene puns, a symbol of something that meddles with "women's matters."[13] On the profane level, the Cobbler jests that sex preoccupies him: "all that I live by, is with the awl [phallus]." (He immediately disclaims this preoccupation in his remark that he "meddles[s] with no . . . women's matters.") On the sacred level, he says that all he lives by is an all-encompassing principle that infuses his life with meaning. As a devout mender of souls, the Cobbler indeed meddles with no tradesman's matters, but with metaphysical and indeed—in his attempt to mediate Marellus's understanding of "all"—with priestly matters. The Christian overtones resonating from the Cobbler are incidentally reinforced in the scene by his companion's trade. Commenting on the Carpenter's part in the opening dialogue, David Daniell notes that "this first encounter may carry a suggestion that what follows is a dramatic sacrificial story with some association with the Bible passion narratives."[14]

Reading North's translation of *Plutarch's Lives* of Brutus, Caesar, and Mark Antony reveals Shakespeare's originality in making the notion of cobbling souls a dramatic motif in *Julius Caesar*. Focusing upon the anonymous written pleas against tyranny that Brutus discovers addressed to him, Plutarch's Cassius asks Brutus, "Thinkest thou that they be *cobblers*, tapsters, or suche like base *mechanicall* people, that wrtye these billes and scrowles which are found dayly in the Praetor's chaire, and not the noblest men and best citizens that doe it?"[15] The tribune Flavius asks the Carpenter and Cobbler in the opening lines of Shakespeare's *Julius Caesar*, "What, know you not / "Being mechanical [artisans]) you ought not walk / Upon a labouring day . . . ?" (1.1.2–4). The depth of the influence of North's Plutarch on the composition of *Julius Caesar* can be ascertained by the likelihood that the collocation of the words "mechanical" and "cobbler" in Shakespeare's text subliminally derives from the same collocation in North's *Plutarch*. In this respect, the fact that the word "soul" never appears near the collocation in North's text—nor anywhere else in the relevant "Englished" *Lives of Plutarch*—is significant. The metaphoric phenomenon of cobbling souls appears to be wholly Shakespeare's.

What does it mean to possess "soul" in Shakespeare's *Julius Caesar*? What is the relation of "cobbling" to the creation and obsession of "soul" in this play? Caska's report of an offstage scene includes ideas that constitute an answer to these questions. When Caesar, caught up in the excitement surrounding Antony's thrice offering him an emperor's crown, suffers an epileptic seizure, he tells the Roman crowd that "if he has done or said anything amiss, he desired their worships to think it was his infirmity" (1.2.268–70). These words are Caska's, but playgoers understand them to be Caesar's. Thereupon "three or four wenches . . . cried, 'Alas, good soul,' and forgave him with all their hearts" (270–72).

Shakespeare suggests that Antony and Caesar's business of the offered and refused crown resembles a staged play, with the Roman citizens' constituting a gullible audience.[16] Like London commoners moved by actors playing on the thrust stage of Shakespeare's Globe, the Romans, transported by the scenario of the crown, "uttered such a deal of stinking breath because Caesar refused the crown that it almost choked Caesar; for he swooned and fell down at it" (1.2.245–47). "If the tag-rag people did not clap [Caesar] and hiss him according as he pleased and displeased them, as they use to do the players in the theatre, I am no true man" (257–60), Caska reports. Caught up in the spirit of Roman acting, Caesar, "when he perceived the common herd was glad he refused the crown . . . plucked . . . open his doublet and offered them his throat to cut" (263–65). It is at this point that the crowd roars, precipitating Caesar's swoon.[17]

Occasionally, Elizabethans use the word "cobbling" to describe a writer's patching or joining words together. George Puttenham, in the widely read *Arte of English Poesie* (1589), refers to "the Greeks . . . cobling many words together" (quoted in the *OED*), and William Fulke, in his 1575 *Confutation of the Doctrine of Purgatory*, alludes to "the cobbling counterfecter of [certain] epistles" (quoted in the *OED*). Some Elizabethans acquainted with Christopher Marlowe may have associated his artistry with his father's craft of cobbling. And if Shakespeare in London began his professional life as a patcher and mender of other men's plays, more than one of his acquaintances may have thought of him as a cobbler.[18] By their improvisational scripting and acting, Antony and Caesar (and through them Shakespeare) "cobble souls"; that is to say, their cobbled playlet elicits the souls of the wenches, who in turn imagine that Julius Caesar possesses a "good soul."[19] The crass political motives partly informing this manipulative playlet, coupled with the possibility Caesar might not in fact possess soul, seriously qualify the value of this spiritual cobbling.

Nevertheless, this episode establishes what it means to possess soul in ancient Rome. Those who can empathize with the human infirmities of others and forgive them their frailties and generally weep when they hear them ask for forgiveness—those persons possess soul. Shakespeare weaves Christian allusions more densely into the fabric of *Julius Caesar* than he does in any of his other Elizabethan plays and poems with classical settings, and yet, paradoxically, he introduces the word "soul" into the play only seven times. Nevertheless, later usage appears calculated to sustain the sense of soul described at the beginning of this paragraph, a sense that makes the final dramatization of cobbling souls act 4, scene 3 of *Julius Caesar* especially poignant for the Epicurean Cassius and the Stoic Brutus. Shakespeare sharpens the specific sense of soul and the value of cobbling souls in *Julius Caesar* by contrast with frequent voicings on forms of the word "spirit," none of which carries the above-described meanings of "soul." Whereas the eleven articulations of "soul" in *The Comedy of Errors* accompany only two of "spirit," with the figures fifteen versus two for *Titus Andronicus* and sixteen versus four for *The Rape of Lucrece*,[20] twenty-three voicings of forms of the word "spirit" in *Julius Caesar* serve to set off and focus the fewer utterances of "soul."[21]

Shakespeare essentially confirms our initial sense of soul during Antony's celebrated funeral oration, delivered over Caesar's corpse. Antony's oratorical artistry—his brilliant use of rhetorical techniques—represents a more masterful joining together of words, a more memorable cobbling, than his and Caesar's playlet does.[22] Like it, the speech evokes soul, in both orator and auditors. "Poor soul," Second Plebeian says of Antony is an expert dissimulator, and he may have made himself weep in order to further incline Romans against Caesar's assassins. But Antony loved Caesar.[23] In part, Antony weeps because his cobbling—his artistry—is so strong that it has made him genuinely empathize with the pitiful end of Caesar and so evoked soul within him. That it has the same effect on his audience is evident from these later words of Antony's concerning the listening citizens:

> O, now you weep, and I perceive you feel
> The dint of pity: these are gracious drops.
> Kind souls, what weep you when you but behold
> Our Caesar's vesture wounded? Look you here,
> Here is himself, marred as you see with traitors. (3.2.191–95)

This concept of soul qualifies our negative assessment of Caesar's character. It is tempting to stereotype Shakespeare's Julius Caesar as a prototype of pride. Edmund Spenser certainly did so in book 1 of *The Faerie Queen*. Una's dwarf discovers, among other haughty "antique ruins," "High *Caesar*, great *Pompey*, and fierce *Antonius*" imprisoned in Lucifera's House of Pride (1.5.49.9).[24] Consumed by the desire to be emperor, to be a constant godlike man, worshiped in his relics, Shakespeare's Caesar in fact is frail—deaf in one ear, subject to fevers and fits of epilepsy, unable to swim distances. Thus his likening himself to the singular, unmoving northern star by boasting that he is "Unshaken of motion" (3.1.58–70, esp. 70) appears hypocritically vain. "Th'abuse of greatness," Brutus asserts with regard to Caesar, "is when it disjoins / Remorse [compassion] from power" (3.1.18–19). Caesar's turning a deaf ear to Metellus Cimber's plea, just before the assassination, that he show pity to Metellus's brother and repeal his banishment seems designed to be an allusion of remorse from power. But, as Plutarch amply testifies, Caesar from the beginning of his political career had a close bond with the Roman people, whom he initially served as their master of festivities. Thus his leaving in his will seventy-five drachmas to every male citizen and to the citizenry as a whole "all his walks, / His private arbours and new-planted orchards, / On this side Tiber" (3.2.235–40) as a park wherein they might "recreate themselves" (242) signals his enduring affection for the commoners.[25] "When that the poor have cried, Caesar hath wept" (3.2.92), Antony says during his oration. While we never witness this event, we have no reason to believe that it has never happened. When he wept for the tears of the poor, Caesar at that moment could be said to possess a soul.[26]

This possible complication of Caesar's character stresses a disturbing fact about the possession of soul in Shakespeare's *Julius Caesar*. It flares for a moment, conjured by artistic cobbling. Caesar may have wept for the poor, but he generally appears coldhearted or heartless, as Mark Antony does most of the time. Antony may weep over Caesar's pitiful end, but as part of a political bargain he soon condemns his nephew Publius to death (4.1.14–15). Roman citizens, moved by Antony's rhetoric, may weep over Caesar's wounds, but their compassion almost immediately converts to rage and they kill the innocent poet Cinna simply because he bears the name of Cinna the conspirator. One could conclude that the evanescence of the aforementioned expressions of soul in *Julius Caesar* contributes to the tragic effect of the play.

A more enduring, authoritative expression of soul occurs late in act 4 when Cassius and Brutus cobble a soulful brotherhood essentially by themselves, without the special on-stage agency of art. Cassius and Brutus, the leaders of separate armies, pursued by Antony's and Octavius's legions, before the decisive battle of Philippi threaten to turn their swords on one another. Brutus accuses Cassius of greed, in selling offices and excusing bribe-taking, as well as betrayal, in withholding monies from him when he asked for them to pay his soldiers. Brutus attacks Cassius through his physical infirmities, his notorious choleric temperament and his leanness of body (4.3.37). Stung, Cassius exclaims, "A friend should bear his friend's infirmities" (4.3.85).[27] The ability to do so, and to forgive compassionately another for his or her frailties, has been the touchstone for discovering soul in the play. When Cassius pronounces "You love me not," and Brutus coldly replies, "I do not like your faults" (4.3.88), despondent Cassius utters his most emotionally authentic speech in the play:

> Come, Antony, and young Octavius, come,
> Revenge yourselves alone on Cassius,
> For Cassius is a-weary of the world:
> Hated by one he loves, braved by his brother,
> Check'd like a bondman; all his faults observed,
> Set in a notebook, learned and conned by rote
> To cast into my teeth. O I could weep
> My spirit from mine eyes! There is my dagger,
> And here my naked breast; within, a heart

> Dearer than Pluto's mine, richer than gold.
> If that thou be'st a Roman, take it forth.
> I that denied thee gold will give my heart.
> Strike as thou didst at Caesar; for I know when thou didst hate him worst, than lovedst him better
> Than ever thou lovedst Cassius. (4.3.92–106)

In this speech, Cassius reveals signs of a late revolution of character, of a desire for an ideal friendship free of selfish calculation. Playgoers aware of the special value that Epicureans placed on friendship might argue, however, that Cassius's character revolution in this respect never occurs. Just before the Battle of Philippi, Cassius tells Messala,

> You know that I held Epicurus strong
> And his opinion: now I change my mind
> And partly credit things that do presage. (5.1.76–78)

Cassius's late-play remark tells playgoers that a reconsideration of this character's words and deeds in the first four acts of the play would almost certainly illustrate one or more traits of philosophical Epicureanism. In the above-quoted speech, Cassius abandons his Epicurean opinion that the gods, indifferent to human affairs, never speak to mortals through omens. Shakespeare begins characterizing Cassius's philosophical Epicureanism in act 1, when this Roman seemingly offers unqualified friendship to Brutus:

> Brutus, I do observe you now of late.
> I have not from your eyes that gentleness
> And show of love as I was wont to have.
> You bear too stubborn and too strange a hand
> Over your friend, that loves you. (1.2.32–36)

Stephen Buhler has asserted that "[f]ailure to recognize the centrality of friendship in the Epicurean scheme of things has led [more than one commentator on the play] to judge Cassius as psychologically unstable in his devotion to Brutus."[28] According to Buhler, "what replaces the political relationship that exists between and among human beings in the wake of the Epicurean renunciation of the *polis* is exactly friendship."[29] Cassius's friendship with Brutus in the earlier acts of the play violates this ideal to a large extent, however, for Cassius is not above using his friend for revolutionary political purposes. Were Cassius the noble Epicurean friend of Brutus, he would not say in soliloquy,

> Well, Brutus, thou art noble: yet I see
> Thy honourable mettle may be wrought
> From that it is disposed. Therefore it is meet
> That noble minds keep ever with their likes;
> For who so firm that cannot be seduced?
> Caesar doth bear me hard, but he loves Brutus.
> If I were Brutus now, and he were Cassius,
> He should not humor me. (1.2.307–14)

Some commentators on this speech such as John Dove and Peter Gamble believe that Cassius is not referring to himself but to Caesar as the seducer of Brutus's noble mind.[30] Others (the majority), such as Coppélia Kahn, assert that Cassius, privately disclaiming a noble mind, alludes to himself as Brutus's manipulator.[31] But David Daniell, in a note on this passage, argues that, even if an auditor believes that Cassius speaks of Caesar as seducer, "Cassius is [tacitly] admitting that he can himself seduce Brutus to his own destructive hatred of Caesar: the question [posed in 1.2.310–11] suggests that that [thought] is to Cassius a pleasurable challenge."[32] Thus Cassius in either case presents himself as Brutus's cunning inveigler, someone other than a true friend.

The self-sufficient image of himself that Cassius generally projects causes Harley Granville-Barker to believe that Cassius's act 1 scene 2 complaint about unreciprocated friendship is the expression of an egoist, "jealous and thick-skinned."[33] Later, in act 4, the wild, unexpected results of the assassination have shaken Cassius, to the extent that this Roman who boasted of his self-suffiency soon marvels that Brutus can bear the news of Portia's death as well as he does and begins to credit omens of personal doom, contrary to the teaching of his revered Epicurus. Adversity has refined Cassius's notion of friendship and thrust upon him a heartfelt need to practice it genuinely. His late world-weariness reflects a gathering sense of his death's imminence. Shaken from his practice of policy, Cassius reaches out to Brutus in untainted friendship. It now constitutes all that a hunted, lonely man has. His suicidal gesture, indicated in the above-quoted speech, is genuine rather than coldly calculated. After all, what political motive could be strong enough to make him risk his life in a dagger thrust from angry, insulted Brutus?

Significantly, Cassius uses the word "spirit" rather than "soul" in his cry, "O I could weep / My spirit from mine eyes!" In this context, the word "spirit" carries the psychological meaning of "vital spirits."[34] Cassius's statement that he could weep his spirit from his eyes implies that he has the potential to weep but that he does not do so. Nevertheless, those audiences of productions of the play wherein the eyes of the actor playing Cassius are tearful by the end of his speech never contemplate this possibility, so natural his weeping seems. Ironically, Cassius comes close in his above-quoted exclamation to voicing a touchstone for soul in *Julius Caesar*. And yet his tears, if he weeps any, are out of frustration or angry self-pity, rather than compassion for the suffering or frailty of another. Whatever the case with Cassius, Brutus certainly does not weep. For this fact, one could blame his Stoicism. Brutus's stoical repression of tears during his and Messala's reports of his wife Portia's death precludes the display of tears for Cassius's frailties. But Brutus's dry eyes do not mean that Cassius's attempt to cobble together their souls is unsuccessful. Cassius's self-pitying aria, while it does not make Brutus weep, nevertheless moves Brutus to take the blame for their quarrel upon himself, upon his own imputed flashes of wrath (4.3.106–12). Cassius then acknowledges an inherited inclination to choleric behavior as a cause of their rift. Each clasps the other, and, in a gesture resonant with Christian overtones, they eventually drink to brotherly love from a shared bowl of wine. Before he departs, Cassius exclaims, "O my dear brother,"

> This was an ill beginning of the night.
> Never come such division 'tween our souls.
> Let it not, Brutus. (*ll.* 231–33)

Until this episode, Cassius has been the most spiritually skeptical Roman,[35] but here his and Brutus's cobbling together a brotherly bond becomes for him a union of souls rather than spirits or selves. Cassius's and Brutus's manifestation of soul may lack the signature of tears, but it is a reality nevertheless. Perceiving a frailty in themselves, these Romans have forgiven a fault of another who has pained them. Cassius, according to Plutarch, had married Junia, Brutus's sister, and so they were brothers-in-law. But Brutus's affectionate reference to Cassius as his "brother" three times within seventy lines after Cassius's momentous wish, which begins with the address "O, my dear brother" (*l.* 233) invests Brutus's and Cassius's soul-bond with brotherly love.[36] Nothing in the spoken or physical behavior of either Roman during the remainder of the play calls into question the profundity of their cobbling of souls.

Shakespeare stresses the intentionality of this soulful cobbling by lightly suggesting that the contribution of a third party's onstage artistry is unnecessary. The theatricals of Antony and Cleopatra and the creative rhetoric of Antony served as poetic agents for evoking Roman commoners' souls. But in Cassius's and Brutus's case, a poet is unwanted. Immediately after they have forgiven each other's (and their own) infirmities, they laugh off the stage an intrusive poet determined to reconcile them, primarily by means of "jigging" rhymes as "Love and be friends, as two such men should be, / For I have seen more years, I'm sure than ye" (4.3.129–30). This couplet represents Shakespeare's revision of North's translation of Plutarch's transformation of Nestor's attempt to reconcile quarrelling Agamemnon and Achilles in book 1 of Homer's *Iliad*. Whereas Nestor—in Richard Lattimore's translation—advises, "Yet be persuaded. Both of you are younger than I am. / Yes, and in my time I have dealt with better men than / you are" (1.259–61),[37] North's *Plutarch*'s Marcus Phaonius turns Nestor's words into this couplet: "My lords, I pray you harken both to mee, / For I have seene moe yeares than suchye three."[38] Shakespeare's revision of this couplet retains its "jigging"—metrically thumping—quality. As a result, Homer's honey-tongued Nestor devolves to a singsong artist. In adapting this episode from Plutarch, Shakespeare transforms the would-be peacemaker from Marcus Phaonius, a "counterfeate" philosopher into a nameless poet, specifically—I would argue—to highlight the fact that Cassius's and Brutus's cobbling of souls is mutually willed, mutually generated, and thus more abiding because not needing the vehicle of onstage artistry.[39] Of course, there is sensitive poetic artistry in Cassius's and Brutus's mutual cobbling of souls, but it is Shakespeare's, posing as the impassioned talk of two troubled Romans. In this sense, no identifiable on-stage artistic vehicle such as a playlet or formal oration facilitates their soulful cobbling.

While Cassius discovers soul on the eve of his death, Brutus implicitly refines his preexisting notion of the faculty as a result of their poignant reconciliation. Ligarius's calling Brutus before the assassination the "Soul of Rome" (2.1.320) squares with Shakespeare's depiction of Brutus as an ethical, most idealistic Roman. Ligarius asserts that the "Soul of Rome"—Brutus—"like an exorcist has conjured up / My mortified spirit" (2.1.323–24) to the task of assassination. Late in *Julius Caesar*, the phenomenon of cobbling souls represents a positive contrast to an earlier, questionable conjuring of spirits. Brutus's two voicings of the word "souls" significantly occur in juxtaposition with the word "spirits." If ". . . the face of men, / The sufferance of [their] souls, the time's abuse . . . be motives weak" for conspiracy, Brutus tells Cassius, then they should break off their plot. But Brutus straightway says that their motives "bear fire enough / To kindle cowards, and to steel with valour / The melting spirits of women" (2.1.113–15, 119–21). He then argues that the justness of their cause precludes a conspiratorial oath:

> Swear priests and cowards, and men cautelous,
> Old feeble carrions, and such suffering souls
> That welcome wrongs . . .
> . . . But do not stain
> The even virtue of our enterprise,
> Nor th' insuppressive mettle of our spirits,
> To think that or our cause or our performance
> Did need an oath. (2.1.128–35)

Clearly Brutus's concept of soul is of a suffering faculty. Here, however, he mentions "soul" only to play it off against the idea of a manly, brave spirit, which he prefers. For Brutus, "soul" thus amounts to a passive entity that interferes with a Roman's mustering and expression of courageous spirit. When Brutus later hears Cassius's wish that nothing ever again might cause "division 'tween our souls," (4.3.233), he implicitly is offered the opportunity to reflect upon his notion of soul and positively refine it. Shakespeare encourages playgoers to imagine that he does so by having Brutus respond "Let [division] not" to Cassius's wish and by affectionately calling him "good brother" in his following farewell—and then "my brother Cassius" in his following farewell—and then "my brother Cassius" in conversation soon afterwards (4.3.234, 235, 246).

It remains to place Shakespeare's interest in *Julius Caesar* in evoking and developing soul in two larger contexts: one consonant with the play's many Christian allusions and the other consisting of the usage of the word "soul" in the dramatist's classical plays and poems antedating *Julius Caesar*. After the battle of Philippi, North's *Plutarch* provides this commentary: "Howebeit the state of Rome (in my opinion) being now brought to that passé, that it could no more abide to be governed by many Lordes, but required one only absolute Governor: God, to prevent Brutus that it shoulde not come to his government, kept this victorie from his knowledge, though in deede it came a little too late."[40] An Elizabethan, reading the word "God" in this passage, would have instinctively thought of the Judeo-Christian God rather than of Jupiter.[41] Late in the play, Brutus speaks of "arming [himself] with patience / To stay the providence of some higher powers / That govern us below" (5.1.105–7). A Christian tradition reaching back into the Middle Ages construed the defeat of Julius Caesar's assassins and the ascendancy of an absolute ruler, Augustus Caesar, as necessary for the establishment of the so-called *Pax Romana*, the universal peace cited in Isaiah 39:8ff. as requisite for the Messiah's birth.[42] Christian providence entailed the defeat of Cassius and Brutus; otherwise, Roman civil war would prolong or make impossible the creation of this peace. The taper burns dim in the tent of Shakespeare's Brutus as the ghost of Caesar approaches, indicating to playgoers that the walking spirit is a reality and not a hallucination. The Judeo-Christian God sends Caesar's ghost walking to weaken Brutus, to predispose him to defeat. That Shakespeare should show Caesar's assassins attractively cobbling a soul-bond with each other ironically, poignantly, heightens their personal tragedies by revealing a growth of character wasted by their almost immediate deaths. In this respect, Shakespeare does not subversively question the justice of Judeo-Christian providence so much as he remarkably demonstrates how close—and yet how painfully distant—the classical age was in relation to the supreme validator of a brotherhood of souls.

In the plays and poems with sustained, distinctive classical settings that he wrote prior to the composition of *Julius Caesar*, Shakespeare never characterizes soul as the capacity for empathizing with the frailties and sufferings of others—usually tearfully so—and for forgiving them their faults. Even though forms of the word "soul" appear numerous times in *Titus Andronicus* and *The Comedy of Errors* (as was previously mentioned), analysis fails to yield an emphasis in these plays upon soul as a dramatic motif in its own right. In other words, characters in these two classical dramas tend to use the word "soul" casually as a signifier for a precious inner essence that is incorruptible (*Titus* 3.1.9) and beyond which nothing is dearer (*Titus* 3.1.102), that validates oaths (*Titus* 3.1.278), that witches can kill (*Errors* 3.2.37), and so on.[43] With the *Rape of Lucrece*, however, the case is different.

In this popular Elizabethan complaint, Shakespeare dwells upon the effect of Tarquin's rape on his and especially Lucrece's souls, primarily in terms of a repeated soul/body dichotomy. After ravishing Lucrece, guilt-ridden Tarquin imagines hearing his soul say that his passions

> Have battered down her consecrated wall,
> And by their mortal fault brought in subjection
> Her immortality, and made her thrall
> To living death and pain perpetual (*ll.* 723–26)

Later, Lucrece contemplates suicide in terms of its effects upon her body and soul:

> "To kill myself," quoth she, "alack, what were it
> But with my body my poor *soul's* pollution?
> They that lose half with greater patience bear it

> Than they whose whole is swallowed in confusion,
> What mother tries a merciless conclusion
> Who having two sweet babes, when death takes one,
> Will slay the other and be nurse to none.
>
> "My body or my *soul*, which was the dearer,
> When the one pure, the other made divine?
> Whose love of either to myself was nearer,
> When both were kept for heaven and Collatine?
> Ay me! The bark peel'd from the lofty pine,
> His leaves will wither and his sap decay;
> So must my *soul*, her bark being peel'd away.
>
> "Her house is sacked, her quiet interrupted,
> Her mansion battered by the enemy,
> Her sacred temple spotted, spoiled, corrupted,
> Grossly engirt with daring infamy.
> Then let it not be called impiety
> If in this blemished fort I make some hole
> Through which I may convey this *troubled soul*." (*ll.* 1156–76, my italics)

Robert Miola has argued that in *Julius Caesar* Brutus's belief that the conspirators regrettably cannot kill Caesar's supposedly polluted spirit without killing his body (2.1.166–70) is reminiscent of the above-quoted passage wherein Lucrece "bases the decision to commit suicide on the conviction that her chaste soul is tied to her polluted body."[44] "This brief abridgment of my will I make," Lucrece concludes; "My soul and body to the skies and ground" (*ll.* 1198–99). The final stress on soul in *The Rape of Lucrece* falls upon its life freed from Lucrece's dying body:

> Even here she sheathed in her harmless breast
> A harmful knife, that thence her soul unsheathed.
> That blow did bail it from the deep unrest
> Of that polluted prison where it breathed.
> Her contrite sighs unto the clouds bequeathed.
> Her winged sprite, and through her wounds doth fly
> Life's lasting date from cancelled destiny. (*ll.* 1723–29)

Nowhere, then, in this ambitious poem does Shakespeare explicitly associate the possession of soul with the related capacities for tearful empathy for another's suffering, for forgiveness of another's faults, or for forging bonds of brotherly love.

That is not to say that characters in Shakespeare's narrative poem do not weep. Seeing her mistress's sorrowful face but not knowing the cause of its burden, Lucrece's maid weeps:

> But as the earth doth weep, the sun being set,
> Each flower moistened like a melting eye,
> Even so the maid with swelling drops 'gan wet
> Her circled eyne, enforced by sympathy
> Of those fair suns set in her mistress' sky,
> Who in a salt-waved ocean quench their light,
> Which makes the maid weep like the dewy night. (*ll.* 1226–32)

Shakespeare nevertheless mentions soul in connection with the maid's and Lucrece's tears. In fact, he blocks any inclination the reader might have to weep with the maid over Lucrece's tragic sorrow by digressing into an "objective" account of the psychological reasons for women's proneness to tears, chiefly the impressionability of their "waxen" minds, and by vigorously blaming abusive men for "weak-made" women's tears (*ll.* 1237–60). The playwright never emphatically draws the reader into Lucrece's tragedy, so that the reader's soul tearfully responds to her fate.

Shakespeare's composition of *Julius Caesar*, presumably in 1599, included a revision of soul as that concept had appeared in his previous plays and poems with ancient settings. This revision did not result from an evolution of the playwright's metaphysical ideas. Shakespeare—had he wanted to—could have given soul the values it acquires in *Julius Caesar* to manifestations of the faculty in any one of his plays, early or late, pagan or otherwise. That he did so in *Julius Caesar* may have been a consequence of his decision to incorporate a multitude of Christian allusions and subtexts into his tragedy. Disclaiming any cause-and-effect relationship between plays for my subject, or programmatic place for it within Shakespeare's artistry, I conclude by noting nevertheless the illuminating intermediate position of *Julius Caesar* with regard to soul between *The Rape of Lucrece* and *Hamlet*, usually dated around 1600 or 1601.

The importance of the soul's empathetic, tearful function for *Hamlet* can be gathered from comparing the representation of the fall of Troy and of suffering Hecuba in *Hamlet* with its counterpart in *The Rape of Lucrece*. In *Hamlet*, First Player's impassioned word-picture of Hecuba's pathetic, dehumanizing end (2.2.502–18) makes Hamlet turn pale and brings tears to his eyes (519–20). That is a working of his soul we deduce from Hamlet's own description of the abuse of this evocative process. "Is it not monstrous," (551) he soon asks himself, "that this player here,"

> But in a fiction, in a dream of passion,
> Could force his *soul* so to his own conceit
> That from her working [the soul's] all his visage wanned,
> *Tears in his eyes*, distraction in his aspect,
> A broken voice, and his whole function suiting
> With forms to his conceit? (551–57, my italics)

In the great tapestry of the fall of Troy, grieving Lucrece finds objective correlatives for her misery (*Lucrece* 1366–1582) which absorb her attention, and "On this sad shadow Lucrece spends her eyes" (1457). For the sake of wracked Hecuba, Lucrece wishes "with [her] tears [to] quench Troy that burns so long" (1468). Nowhere in his segment of the poem does Shakespeare either assert or imply that Lucrece's weeping over Hecuba's naked frailties either evokes or defines her soul. That connection appears in the intervening tragedy *Julius Caesar*. If we want to understand more fully the spiritual faculty that is wasted by melancholy and lost in Hamlet in his premature death, we might look again at the poignant, admirable evocation of souls in Cassius and Brutus.

Notes

Chapter 1

1 James L. Calderwood, *Shakespearean Metadrama: The Argument of the Play in* Titus Andronicus, Lover's Labor's Lost, Romeo and Juliet, A Midsummer Night's Dream *and* Richard II (Minneapolis: University of Minnesota Press, 1971).

2 "Shakespeare," in Matthew Arnold, *Poems* (London: Brown Green & Longmans, 1853).

3 A recent book that ventures to look beyond the "horizon of Hamlet" is Stephen Greenblatt's *Hamlet in Purgatory* (Princeton: Princeton University Press, 2001).

4 This nonchalance in Shakespeare's choice of titles for his comedies is variously interpreted by G. K. Chesterton and G. B. Shaw in the former's essay "On *A Midsummer Night's Dream,*" in his *The Common Man* (London: Faber & Faber, 1950), 10–21.

5 T. S. Eliot, *Hamlet* (1919), in *Selected Essays*, 2nd ed. (London: Faber, 1934) defines the "objective correlative" as "a set of objects, a situation, a chain of events which shall be the formula of that *particular* emotion" (145).

6 All Shakespearean quotations are from *The Oxford Shakespeare*, edited by W. J. Craig (Oxford: Oxford University Press, 1954).

7 The inglorious end of the Elizabethan age is partly to be explained by the aging queen's refusal to discuss the important question of the succession,

partly by her own decline in health, culminating in her fearful death, as related by one of her ladies in waiting, Lady Southwell. (Agnes Strickland, "Elizabeth, Second Queen Regent of England and Ireland," in *Lives of the Queens of England* [Philadelphia: Lea & Blanchard, 1848], esp. 223.)

8 Introduction to Nicholas Rowe's edition of *Shakespeare* (London: Jacob Jonson, 1709).

9 The word "enterprise" as used by Hamlet in the phrase "[a]nd enterprises of great pitch and moment" (3.1.87), has an almost technical reference to such Catholic plots as those planned against England by the Duke de Guise in France and King Philip II in Spain. As for the subsequent Essex Rebellion and the Gunpowder Plot, it is not often realized that the same Catholic gentlemen, Robert Catesby, Francis Tresham and John Wright, had parts in both. No doubt they were forgiven for their parts in the former on condition that they cooperated with Sir Robert Cecil in the latter.

10 The role of Ben Jonson as government spy is studied at length by B. N. De Luna in his *Jonson's Romish Plot* (Oxford: Clarendon, 1967).

11 The Catholic interpretation of *Hamlet* is well, if briefly, presented by Christopher Devlin in his *Hamlet's Divinity* (Carbondale: Southern Illinois University Press, 1963).

12 I have devoted a monograph to a discussion of the influence of St. Ignatius's *Spiritual Exercises* on the plays of Shakespeare; see *The Plays and the Exercises* (Tokyo: Renaissance Institute, Sophia University, 2002), with a chapter on the "Three Classes of Men."

13 Paradoxically, Hamlet's lack of any real conscience is proven by his two protests in the same scene: the first concerning his sending Rosencrantz and Guildenstern to certain death in England, "They are not near my conscience" (5.2); the second concerning Claudius, "Is't not perfect conscience / To quit him with this arm?" (5.2).

14 For William Allen, in his *Defence of English Catholics* (Rouen: Fr. Parsons' Press, 1584), the great evil in Elizabethan England was that so many Englishmen were forced to speak and act against their real consciences.

15 Cf. my "Homiletic Tradition in *Hamlet*," in *Shakespeare's Other Dimension* (Tokyo: Renaissance Institute, Sophia University, 1987).

16 Peter Milward, *Shakespeare's Religious Background* (Bloomington: Indiana University Press, 1973).

17 The main thesis of Roland Frye in his *Shakespeare and Christian Doctrine* (Princeton: Princeton University Press, 1963) is that even from a Christian point of view, as represented by the eminent Protestant theologians of the age, Luther, Calvin and Hooker, Shakespeare's plays may be regarded as "resolutely secular"—for all their reference to the Bible and Christian tradition. His view is, moreover, supported by the Anglican Helen Gardner, in her T. S. Eliot Memorial Lectures, compiled in *Religion and Literature* (Oxford: Oxford University Press, 1971). I have published a critique of "Shakespeare and Christian Doctrine," in *Shakespeare Studies* 4 (1965–1966), 36–56.

18 "*Doctor Faustus* is a morality play of damnation. Discuss." Such is the challenging statement required for discussion in an examination paper I remember from my days at Oxford.

19 John Vyvyan I regard as unique among Shakespeare critics, though not a professional, in his insistence on interpreting the tragedies in the light of the medieval passion play, as stated in his book *The Shakespearian Ethic* (London: Chatto & Windus, 1959), 149–54.

20 Judas's greeting is given in Matthew 26:49 as "Hail!" but the form "All hail!" is Jesus' greeting to the holy women after his resurrection in Matthew 28:9. It is also the form used by Richard in the deposition scene of *Richard II* 4.1, and derived not so much from the Bible as from the mystery play of the betrayal. It is given as an example of Shakespeare's defective knowledge of the Bible by Richmond Noble, in *Shakespeare's Biblical Knowledge* (London: SPCK, 1935), 103–4.

21 The transition in biblical imagery from Judas to Satan, as implied in the cases of both Macbeth and Iago, is traced in my *Biblical Influences in Shakespeare's Great Tragedies* (Bloomington: Indiana University Press, 1985). As for the Satanic implication in "Stars, hide your fires!" (1.4.50), this comes from the tradition (based on Heb 1:6) that the fall of Lucifer occurred when God required the angels to adore the Son as Messiah (pp. 120–21).

22 G. K. Chesterton, *Chaucer* (London: Faber & Faber, 1932).

23 The influence of the mystery play *The Harrowing of Hell* on the porter scene is ably treated by Soji Iwasaki in his *The Sword and the Word* (Tokyo: Shinszki Shorin, 1973), in a section on "The Descent into Hell," 133–44.

24 For a discussion of the true Jesuit theory of equivocation, as contrasted with the numerous scholarly misconceptions, see my chapter "English Jesuits," in *Shakespeare's Religious Background*, 61–67. Also see P. Caraman, *Henry Garnet, 1555–1606, and the Gunpowder Plot* (London: Longmans, 1964), 247–66. The words of Sir Edward Coke for the prosecution are given in full in *The true and perfect relation of the whole proceeding against the late most barbarous traitors, Garnet a Iesuite and his confederats* (1606) which was a probably source of Macbeth. Cf. Milward, *Shakespeare's Religious Background*, 62.

25 Cf. Francis Edwards, *Guy Fawkes—The Real Story of the Gunpowder Plot?* (London: Rupert Davis, 1969).

26 For Shakespeare's Catholic formation in Stratford, the basic study is still J. H. de Groot's *The Shakespeares and "The Old Faith"* (New York: Books for Libraries Press, 1946).

27 The "Shakeshafte theory" of Shakespeare's years in Lancashire has been vindicated by E. A. J. Honigmann, in his *Shakespeare: The Lost Years* (Manchester: Manchester University Press, 1985).

28 I express my gratitude to my publisher, the Renaissance Institute of Sophia University, for several statements of this paper from my book, *Shakespeare's Meta-drama—Hamlet and Macbeth* (Tokyo: Renaissance Institute, Sophia University, 2003).

Chapter 2

Editor's Note: We are basing these references on the chapter's original setting. We have corrected a few mistakes and have added, on a few occasions, information in brackets that will inform readers of original sources.

1 John Keats, 'Ode to a Nightingale', stanza VII.

2 William Wordsworth, *The Prelude*, Book III (1805), lines 281–4.

3 Sir Philip Sidney, *An Apology for Poetry* (probably early 1580s), ed. Geoffrey Shepherd (1965), 133.

4 See Hume, 1984, *passim*. [Anthea Hume, *Edmund Spenser: Protestant Poet* (Cambridge: Cambridge University Press, 1984)].

5 Rosemond Tuve, quoted in ibid., 4.

6   Quoted in ibid., 25.

7   *Spenser's Minor Poems*, ed. Ernest de Sélincourt (Oxford, 1970), 121, lines 239–40.

8   *Spenser: Selections from the Minor Poems and the Faerie Queene*, chosen and edited by Frank Kermode (Oxford, 1965), 19. This twenty-six-page 'Introduction' is one of the clearest brief accounts of Spenser's mind.

9   Hume, 1984, 105. Spenser quotations are from Spenser's *Faerie Queene*, ed. J. C. Smith, 2 vols (Oxford, 1909).

10 Explicated and challenged by Rosemond Tuve in her *Allegorical Imagery* (Princeton, NJ, 1966), 404.

11 Digby, op. cit., sig. A4. Quoted in Hume, 1984, 183.

12 *The Romance of Sir Beues of Hamtoun* (c. 1300), ed. E. Kölbing, E. E. T. S. Extra Series, xlvi, xlviii, lxv (1885–94), 30. Noted in Hume, 1984, 81 and 190.

13 Hume, 1984, 81.

14 John Bale ?1545 291: quoted in Hume, 1984, 82.

15 See Ronald A. Rebholz, *The Life of Fulke Greville, First Lord Brooke* (Oxford, 1971), 75–77.

16 Hume, 1984, 144.

17 Sidney, 1965, 99.

18 The regular revival of an old fashion for maintaining that Shakespeare was a Catholic is based on no reliable external evidence that will stand up. Shakespeare was baptised, married and buried a Protestant, and he lived and worked in a late-Elizabethan and Jacobean cultural world that was overwhelmingly Protestant. To try to draw any facts about his personal beliefs from his poems and plays is not legitimate.

19 See above, Chapter 22, pp. 374–5 [in David Daniell's *The Bible in English* (New Haven: Yale University Press, 2003] and Naseeb Shaheen (1999) [Naseeb Shaheen, *Biblical References in Shakespeare's Plays* (Newark: University of Delaware Press, 1999)].

20 See *The Arden Shakespeare: Julius Caesar*, ed. David Daniell (1998), 6; and on Hamlet see chapter 17, n. 37 above [in Daniell's *The Bible in English*].

21 *The Cambridge Bibliography of English Literature*, ed. F. W. Bateson in five large volumes (1969). This standard reference work has three entries under 'Calvin'. Even Francesco Guicciardini, obscure for English literature, has more.

22 Norbrook, 1984, 6 [David Norbrook, *Poetry and Politics in the English Renaissance* (London: Routledge, 1984)].

23 See Betteridge, 1996, 10, 51–79 [Thomas Betteridge, *Tudor Histories of the English Reformation 1530–1583* (Aldershot: Ashgate, 1996)].

24 Kiernan, 1996, 58, 61 [Pauline Kiernan, *Shakespeare's Theory of Drama* (Cambridge: Cambridge University Press, 1996)].

25 Shuger, 1996, 55 [Debora Shuger, "Subversive Faiths and Suffering Subjects: Shakespeare and Christianity," in *Religion, Literature and Politics in Post-Reformation England, 1540–1688*, ed. Donna B. Hamilton and Richard Strier (Cambridge: Cambridge University Press, 1996), 46–69].

26 Sanders and Davies, 1989, vii [E. P. Sanders and Margaret Davies, *Studying the Synoptic Gospels* (London: SCM Press, 1989)].

27 Shuger, 1996, 55–7.

28 Bloom, 1999, xvii [Harold Bloom, *Shakespeare: The Invention of the Human* (New York: Riverhead Books, 1998)].

29 Shuger, 1996, 57.

30 Annabel Patterson, quoted in Shuger, 1996, 57.

31 *TNT*, 116 [*Tyndale's New Testament* (New Haven: Yale University Press, 1989)].

32 Bloom, 1999, 3.

Chapter 3

1 A notable exception is W. Thomas MacCary, *Friends and Lovers: The Phenomenology of Desire in Shakespearean Comedy* (New York: Columbia University Press, 1985), who, despite his title, highlights the centrality of

self-love in Shakespeare's comedies, comparing it with the less conflicted narcissism in the comedies of Aristophanes, Plautus and Terence. Valerie Traub, however, in "Desire and the Difference it Makes" (in *The Matter of Difference: Materialist Feminist Criticism of Shakespeare*, ed. Valerie Wayne [Ithaca: Cornell University Press, 1991]) correctly chides MacCary, along with Leonard Tennenhouse and Joel Fineman, for exclusively linking narcissism with homoeroticism, for narcissism is central to all discourses of desire. For other astute studies of the tension between friendship and courtship in Shakespeare's plays, see bibliography: Coppélia Kahn, Arthur Kirsch, Marianne Novy, Peter Erickson, Kay Stockholder, Joseph Porter, Bruce Smith and Maurice Charney.

2   In *Oneself as Another* (trans. Kathleen Blamey [Chicago: University of Chicago Press, 1992]), Ricouer explains the fundamental self-division in personhood (see, e.g., "The Primitive Concept of Person," 35–39); he analyzes self-love's perverse modalities (215–18) and its remediation in friendship and justice (329–41); and he affirms a remark in Bernanos's *Journal d'un curé de compagne*: "It is easier than one thinks to hate oneself. Grace means forgetting oneself. But if all pride were dead in us, the grace of graces would be to love oneself humbly, as one would any of the suffering members of Jesus Christ" (24).

3   All Shakespeare quotations are taken from *The Complete Works of Shakespeare*, ed. David Bevington, 4th ed. (New York: Longman, 1997).

4   Anne Ferry in *The Inward Language: Sonnets of Wyatt, Sidney, Shakespeare, Donne* (Chicago: University of Chicago Press, 1994) notes that Shakespeare's Sonnet 62 echoes Sidney's Sonnet 27:

> Because I oft in dark abstracted guise
> Seem most alone in greatest company
> With dearth of words, or answers quite awry,
> To them that would make speech of speech arise.
> They deem, and of their doom the rumor flies,
> That poison foul of bubbling pride doth lie
> So in my swelling breast that only I
> Fawn on myself, and others do despise:
> Yet pride I think doth not my soul possess,
> Which looks too oft in his unflatt'ring glass:
> But one worse fault, ambition, I confess,

>That makes me oft my best friends overpass,
>Unseen, unheard, while thought to highest place
>Bends all his powers, even unto Stella's grace.

In both sonnets' use the unflattering mirror of self-awareness makes self-love untenable; but Ferry notes that Sidney, unlike Shakespeare, cannot admit his self-love; it is gossipy courtiers who spread rumors of a "poison foul of bubbling pride" that makes the poet fawn on himself and despise others—a charge he denies by blaming his "dark abstracted guise" on love for Stella, his only "ambition" being to gain her favor. [These erring critics also appear in Sonnet 23 ("harder judges judge ambition's rage"); and Sidney repeats his self-defense in Sonnets 61 ("wholly hers, all selfness he forbears") and 90 ("think not that I by verse seek fame, / Who seek, who hope, who love, who live but thee; / Thine eyes my pride, thy lips my history: / If you praise not, all other praise is shame. / Nor so ambitious am I, as to frame / A nest for praise in my young laurel tree").] In short, in his sonnets Sidney never accepts the charge of self-love; nor does he explore its impact on the forming of self and of relationship. Only in the fictive remove of Arcadia does Sidney extensively explore the corruptions of self-love (*philautia*) in courtly lovers and rulers.

5 Paul Zweig, *The Heresy of Self-Love: A Study of Subversive Individualism* (1968; repr. Princeton: Princeton University Press, 1980), 107–8. Besides the astute studies of self-love by Zweig and MacCary, Philip Martin addresses it in *Shakespeare's Sonnets: Self, Love, and Art* (Cambridge: Cambridge University Press, 1972). But he ignores self-love's literary and intellectual history, and he never defines it as a feature of human nature, nor explains its bearing on the three principles of the sonnets, thus leaving it undeveloped.

6 Plato, in *Phaedrus* says, "He loves, but does not know whom or what; he does not understand, he cannot tell what has happened to him" . . . "as in a mirror, in his lover he beholds himself and does not know it," trans. W. C. Helmbold, and W. G. Rabinowitz (New York: Macmillan, 1956), 40.

7 In Guillaume de Lorris's *The Romance of the Rose*, Amant sees in the fountain of his passions two crystal stones (his own eyes, signifying his projective self-awareness) before seeing the rose-maiden: "Two crystal stones within the fountain's depths / Attentively I noted"; "So wonderful / Are they that by their power is all the place . . . / Transfigured . . . / Just as a mirror will reflect each thing that near is placed"; "the mirror Perilous it is, where proud Narcissus saw his face and his grey eyes"; "Whatever

thing appears before one's eyes, / While at these stones he looks, / He straightway love" (trans. Harry W. Robbins [New York: E. P. Dutton, 1962], 29–33).

8   The story of Canacee's mirror, exposing false love in "gentil" courtship, is too indirectly expressed in bad symbolism to cite concisely. See "The Squire's Tale," in *The Works of Geoffrey Chaucer*, ed. F. N. Robinson, 2nd ed. (1933; repr. Boston: Houghton Mifflin, 1957), 154–62.

9   Spenser's account of Merlin's mirror, which shows Britomart her soulmate Artegall, clearly recalls the transfiguring crystal stones of *The Romance of the Rose:* "It vertue had to shew in perfect sight / What ever thing was in the world cantynd, / ... So that it to the looker appertaynd; / ... Like to the world it selfe, and seemd a world of glas" [*The Complete Poetical Works of Spenser*, ed. R. E. Neil Dodge (Boston: Houghton Mifflin, 1908; repr. 1936), 337]. For Britomart's extensive turmoil over this mirror-initiation of her love-quest, including a horrified self-comparison with Narcissus, see *The Fairie Queene*, 3.2.17–3.3.62.

10   In *Paradise Lost* (4.449–91) Milton burdens Eve with the faulty Narcissus-impulse, which must be redirected by an angel: "What there thou seest fair Creature is thyself, / With thee it comes and goes: but follow me, / And I will bring thee where no shadow stays / Thy coming, and thy soft imbraces, hee / Whose image thou art, him thou shalt enjoy / Inseparably thine" (4.467–73, 289). To counteract it, Raphael instructs Adam in a rational, virtuous form of self-love: "weigh with her thyself; / Then value: Oft-times nothing profits more / Than self-esteem, grounded on just and right / Well manag'd" (8.570–73, p. 375–76) in John Milton, *Complete Poems and Major Prose*, ed. Merritt Y. Hughes (New York: Odyssey Press, 1957).

11   In *September* (25–46 and concluding emblem), *Amoretti* 35 and *The Faerie Queene* (1.4.29) Spenser repeats Narcissus's despairing paradoxical cry, *"inopem me copia fecit,"* which Golding renders as "my plentie makes me poore" (*Shakespeare's Ovid: Arthur Golding's Translation of the Metamorphoses*, ed. W. H. D. Rouse (New York: W. W. Norton, 1966), 3.587. Since the fable warns against fruitless self-obsession and physical possessiveness, the same cry is repeated by Avarice (*The Faerie Queene* 1.4.29).

For other literary permutations of Narcissus, see Louise Vinge, *The Narcissus Theme in Western European Literature up to the Early Nineteenth Century*, trans. Robert Dewsnap (Lund, Sweden: University of Lund, 1967); Frederick Goldin, *The Mirror of Narcissus in the Courtly Love Lyric*

(Ithaca: Cornell University Press, 1967); Lynn de Gerenday, "The Problem of Self-Reflective Love in Book III of *The Fairie Queene*," *Literature and Psychology* 26 (1976): 37–48; William Elford Rogers, "Narcissus in *Amoretti* xxxv," *American Notes and Queries* 15 (1976): 18–20; Calvin R. Edwards, "The Narcissus Myth in Spenser's Poetry," *Studies in Philology* 74 (1977): 63–88; and "Narcissus," in *The Spenser Encyclopedia*, ed. A. C. Hamilton et al. (Toronto: University of Toronto Press, 1990) 496–97; Robert Wiltenburg, *Ben Jonson and Self-Love: The Subtlest Maze of All* (Columbia: University of Missouri Press, 1990); Valerie Traub, *Desire and Anxiety: Circulations of Sexuality in Shakespearean Drama* (London: Routledge, 1992); John Guillory, "Milton, Narcissism, Gender: On the Genealogy of Male Self-Esteem," in *Critical Essays on John Milton*, ed. Christopher Kendrick (New York: G. K. Hall, 1995), 194–233.

12 C. L. Barber, "An Essay on Shakespeare's Sonnets," in *Shakespeare's Sonnets*, ed. Harold Bloom (New York: Chelsea House, 1987), 7–9, 21–25.

13 Edwards, "Narcissus," 496.

14 Zweig, 107–8.

15 See, e.g., Augustine, *On Christian Doctrine*, 23–27, in *The Confessions, The City of God, On Christian Doctrine*, trans. Marcus Dods and J. F. Shaw (Chicago: Encyclopedia Britannica, 1952), 630–31. And see Oliver O'Donovan, *The Problem of Self-Love in St. Augustine* (New Haven: Yale University Press, 1980), 1–9, 37–59, 75–111, 137–59.

16 "There is an evil, great above all others, which most men have, implanted in their souls ... saying that every man is by nature a lover of self, and that it is right that he should be such. But the truth is that the cause of all sins in every case lies in the person's excessive love of self.... Wherefore every man must shun excessive self-love, and ever follow after him that is better than himself" (Plato, *Laws*, trans. R. G. Bury [London: Heinemann, 1926], I, 339).

17 *Ethica Nicomachea* in *Introduction to Aristotle*, ed. Richard McKeon (New York: Modern Library, 1947), book 8, ch. 5, 1157b, p. 477.

18 *The Summa Theologia of Saint Thomas Aquinas*, trans. Fathers of the English Dominican Province, rev. by Daniel J. Sullivan (New York: Benziger, 1947), I–II.25.2, pp. 731–32. See Stephen Pope, "Expressive Individualism and True Self-Love: A Thomistic Perspective," *Journal of Religion* 71 (1991), 384–99.

19 Pierre de la Primaudaye, *The Second Part of the French Academie* (London, 1618; orig. Paris, 1586), 458–61.

20 For Augustine's intricate justification of self-love in *On the Trinity*, books 8–14, see O'Donovan, 75–111, 127–36.

21 *Luther's Works*, trans. Walter G. Tillmanns and Jacob A. O. Preus (St. Louis: Concordia, 1972), 512. Subsequent Luther citations are taken from this work.

22 Ibid., 291, 313, 512–13.

23 The quotations of Luke 9:23-24 and John 12:25 are taken from *The Geneva Bible: A Facsimile of the 1560 Edition* (Madison: University of Wisconsin Press, 1969).

24 See *Summa Theologiae* 1–2.29.4: "Whether a man can hate himself"; and see Pope, "Expressive Individualism," 396; and for Augustine's rebuttal of self-hatred, see O'Donovan, 43f., 54f., 88f., 109f.

25 La Primaudaye, *The French Academie, Part 2*, 458–61. Montaigne avoids cares of greatness and glory because "I love myself too well": *The Complete Essays of Montaigne*, trans. Donald Frame (Stanford: Stanford University Press, 1958), 699; and see "Of not communicating one's glory" (187–89) and "Of the disadvantage of greatness" (699–703). Throughout his essays, e.g., "Of vanity" (721–66) and "The Apology of Raymond Sebond" (318–457), he uses pragmatic irony and humor to avert "bad self-love." For Hooker's moderation between proper and improper self-love, see "A Learned Sermon on the Nature of Pride," in Richard Hooker, *Tractates and Sermons*, ed. L. Yeardle and E. Grislis (Cambridge, Mass.: Harvard University Press, 1990), 315–17, 328, 333–34, 652–54. For Donne's playfulness with self-love's ambivalence, see "Self-Love," "The Cross," and "Devotion XVII," in *The Complete Poetry and Selected Prose of John Donne*, ed. Charles M. Coffin (New York: Random House, 1952), 55, 233–35, 440–41; and *The Sermons of John Donne*, eds. George R. Potter and Evelyn M. Simpson, 10 vols. (Berkeley: University of California Press, 1953–1962), 4:319, 330; 5:159–60; 6:209; 7:273; 8:236; 9:373. For Donne's effort to reform self-love through imitating Christ crucified, see Paul W. Harland, " 'A True Substantiation': Donne, Self-Love, and the Passion," in *John Donne's Religious Imagination: Essays in Honor of John T. Shawcross*, ed. Raymond-Jean Frontain and Frances M. Malpezzi (Conway, Ark.: University of Conway Press, 1995), 162–80.

26 The Heidelberg and Westminster catechisms, deeply influenced by *Calvin's Catechism* (1537, 1560), stress that creation, providence, and all God's acts are *for His own glory*: "God has all life, glory, goodness, blessedness in and of himself; and is alone in and unto himself all-sufficient, not standing in need of any creatures which he has made, nor deriving any glory from them, but only manifesting his own glory" (*The Westminster Shorter Catechism* [Phillipsburg, NJ: P & R Publishing, 2003], 2.2; and cf. 1.5, 1.6, 2.1, 3.3, 3.5, 3.7, 4.1, 5.1, 6.1, 16.2). Luther's catechism does not stress God's self-sufficiency and self-glorying but rather his relation to creatures ("He does all this out of pure love and goodness, without our merit, as a benevolent Father"); he emphasizes how humbling it is to acknowledge such extraordinary unearned gifts (Martin Luther, *The Large Catechism* [1530] in *Triglot Concordia: The Symbolical Books of the Evangelical Lutheran Church* [St. Louis: Concordia Publishing House, 1921], 590).

27 *Paradiso* 33.124–26, in Dante Alighieri, *The Divine Comedy*, trans. C. H. Sisson (Oxford: Oxford University Press, 1998).

28 Helen Vendler, *The Art of Shakespeare's Sonnets* (Cambridge: Harvard University Press, 1997), 291–94.

29 "Preface to the Phenomenology of Mind," *Hegel Selections*, ed. J. Loewenberg (New York: Charles Scribner's Sons, 1969), 28–29: "that an accident as such, when cut loose from its containing circumference . . . should get an existence all its own, gain freedom and independence on its own account—this is the portentous power of the negative; it is the energy of thought, of pure ego. Death . . . is the most terrible thing. . . . But the life of the mind is not one that shuns death. . . . It only wins to its truth when it finds itself in utter desolation; . . . mind is this power only by looking the negative in the face and dwelling with it. This dwelling beside it is the magical power that converts the negative into being." In his mature tragedies Shakespeare's "dwelling beside" the negative is unsurpassed.

30 Roy Battenhouse, "Hamartia in Aristotle, Christian Doctrine, and *Hamlet*," in *Shakespearean Tragedy: Its Art and Christian Premises* (Bloomington: Indiana University Press, 1969), 204–66.

31 See Lawrence Josephs, *Character Structure and the Organization of the Self* (New York: Columbia University Press, 1992), ch. 5, "The Archaic Relational Matrix."

32 Battenhouse, 226, 231–33.

Chapter 4

33 Zweig: "The European legend of Faust descends ultimately from this 'arch-heretic' of the first centuries (Simon Magus of Acts 8:5-24). Faust's lust for power represents one of the most constant passions of the European psyche: the longing for a final, all-powerful solitude to which the world itself must submit" (21, and see 3–21).

1 Here and below I quote from my Norton edition, *Macbeth* (New York, 2004); quotations from other works of Shakespeare are cited to *Complete Works*, ed. David Bevington, 5th edn. (New York, 2003). I gratefully acknowledge Norton for permission to reprint parts of my introduction in this essay.

2 See Inga-Stina Ewbank, "The Fiend-like Queen: A Note on *Macbeth* and Seneca's *Medea*," *Shakespeare Survey* 19 (1966), 82–89.

3 Thomas Campbell, *Life of Mrs. Siddons*, 2 vols. (London, 1834), as excerpted in the Norton *Macbeth*, 236.

4 Thomas Davies, *Dramatic Miscellanies*, 3 vols. (London, 1783–1784), as excerpted in the Norton *Macbeth*, 217.

5 John Smith, *A Pattern of True Prayer*, 1605.

6 Thomas Becon, *The Early Works of Thomas Becon*, ed. John Ayre, 3 vols. (Cambridge, The Parker Society 1843–1844) 1:130, 134.

7 John Jewel, *The Works of John Jewel, Bishop of Salisbury*, ed. John Ayre, 4 vols. (Cambridge: Cambridge University Press, 1845–1850), 1:284–86; 2: 699.

8 Robert Hill, *The Pathway to Prayer and Piety*, 6th ed. (London: William Barrett, 1615).

9 Simon Forman, *Booke of Plaies* (MS Ashmole 208), as transcribed in the Norton *Macbeth*, 205.

10 Tessa Watt, *Cheap Print and Popular Piety, 1550–1640* (Cambridge: Cambridge University Press, 1991); Alexandra Walsham, *Providence in Early Modern England* (Oxford: Oxford University Press, 1999).

11 Raphael Holinshed, *The First and Second Volumes of Chronicles* (London, 1587), vol. 2, *The History of Scotland*, as excerpted in the Norton *Macbeth*, 101.

12 *The Literary Remains of Samuel Taylor Coleridge*, ed. Henry Nelson Coleridge, vol. 2 (London, 1836), as excerpted in the Norton *Macbeth*, 101.

13 William Hazlitt, *Characters of Shakespear's Plays* (London, 1817), as excerpted in the Norton *Macbeth*, 225.

14 Welcome Msomi, *uMabatha: An Adaptation of Shakespeare's "Macbeth"* (Praetoria, South Africa: 1996), as excerpted in the Norton *Macbeth*, 197.

15 John Stockwood, *A Very Faithful and Necessary Sermon* (London: Thomas Dawson, 1584), title page.

16 Johann Habermann, *The Enemy of Security*, trans. by Thomas Rogers (London: R. Yaraley & P. Short, 1591), n.p.

17 William Est, *The Scourge of Security* (London: Thomas Creede, 1609).

18 Thomas Draxe, *The Church's Security* (London: George Edd, 1608), sigs. B1v–B2.

19 John Downame, *A Treatise of Security* (London: Felix Kingston & William Stansby, 1622).

20 Elizabeth Montagu, *An Essay on the Writings and Genius of Shakespeare* (London, 1769), and Samuel Taylor Coleridge, n. 10, as excerpted in the Norton *Macbeth*, 215, 218.

21 Derek Jacobi, *Players of Shakespeare 4: Further Essays in Shakespearian Performance by Players with the Royal Shakespeare Company*, ed. Robert Smallwood (Cambridge, Cambridge University Press, 1998), as reprinted in the Norton *Macbeth*, 342.

22 Dante Alighieri, *The Divine Comedy*, trans. Allen Mandelbaum, 3 vols., paper (New York: Bantam, 1982–1986).

23 Jean Calvin, *The Institution of the Christian Religion*, trans. Thomas Norton (London, 1611), 448.

24 Martin Luther, *Assertio omnium articulorum* (1520/1521), as excerpted in the Norton *Macbeth*, 119.

25 Desiderius Erasmus, *De libero arbitrio* (1524), as excerpted in the Norton *Macbeth*, 124.

26 Helen Gardner, "Milton's 'Satan' and the Theme of Damnation in Elizabethan Tragedy," *English Association Essays and Studies* 1 (1948): 46–66; John Stachniewski, "Calvinist Psychology in *Macbeth*," *Shakespeare Studies*, 20 (1988): 169–89; Arthur Kinney, *Lies Like Truth: Shakespeare, Macbeth, and the Cultural Moment* (Detroit: Wayne University Press, 2001): 215–30; Peter Lake with Michael Questier, *The Antichrist's Lewd Hat: Protestants, Papists and Players in Post-Reformation England* (New Haven: Yale University Press, 2002): 380–92 (388).

27 Holinshed in Norton *Macbeth*, n. 9, 104.

28 William Perkins, *A Golden Chain, a Description of Theology containing the Order of the Causes of Salvation and Damnation* (1591), sig V5.

29 William Davenant, *Macbeth: A Tragedy with All the Alterations, Amendments, Additions, and New Songs* (London, 1674), as excerpted in the Norton *Macbeth*, 173.

30 Francis Talfourd, *Macbeth Travestie: A Burlesque* (Oxford, 1850), as excerpted in the Norton *Macbeth*, 185.

Chapter 5

1 These and all other quotations of Shakespeare's plays are from *The Riverside Shakespeare*, ed. G. Blakemore Evans (Boston: Houghton Mifflin, 1974).

2 Martin Luther, *Discourse on Free Will*, ed. and trans. Ernst F. Winter. (New York: Ungar, 1961), 135.

3 Milward., ed., *Shakespeare's Religious Background*, 161.

4 Charles Cannon, "'As in a Theater': *Hamlet* in the Light of Calvin's Doctrine of Predestination," *Studies in English Literature, 1500–1900* 11 (1971): 203.

5 Anthony Low, "*Hamlet* and the Ghost of Purgatory: Intimations of Killing the Father," *English Literary Renaissance* 29 (1999): 443–67; Greenblatt; Edward Oakes, Rev. of *Hamlet in Purgatory*, by Stephen Greenblatt, *Commonweal* 4 (2001): 29.

6 David Daniell, "Shakespeare and the Protestant Mind," *Shakespeare Survey* 54 (2001): 2.

7 This claim was made by Mary Ann McGrail in an interview with *New Yorker's* David Remnick in 1995.

8 Grace Tiffany, "Anti-Theatricalism and Revolutionary Desire in *Hamlet* (Or, The Play Without the Play)," *The Upstart Crow* 15 (1995): 63.

9 Daniell, "Shakespeare and the Protestant Mind," 2.

10 Ibid., 76.

11 G. M. Story, Introduction, *Lancelot Andrewes: Sermons* (Oxford: Clarendon, 1967), xv.

12 Daniell, "Shakespeare and the Protestant Mind," 6.

13 William Prynne, *Histrio-Mastix: The Player's Scourge, or Actor's Tragedy*. London, 1633, preface.

14 Bryan Crockett, *The Play of Paradox: Stage and Sermon in Renaissance England* (Philadelphia: University of Pennsylvania Press, 1995), 50.

15 Augustine, *The Confessions*, trans. Edward Pusey (New York: Norton, 2000), 36–37.

16 I have modernized Prynne's and Munday's spelling.

17 Edmund Spenser, *The Faerie Queene*, book 1, in *The Norton Anthology of English Literature*, vol. 1b, ed. M. H. Abrams, et al., 7th ed. (New York: Norton, 2000): 625.

18 Tiffany, 67.

19 Stephen Gosson, *Plays Confuted in Five Actions* (London, 1590), B4.

20 John Calvin, *Commentaries on Exodus* (Grand Rapids: Calvin Translation Society, 1948–1959), 15.9. Charles Cannon also relates this passage to *Hamlet*, arguing that the play is influenced by Calvin's vision of a holy theater.

21 Crockett, 50.

22 Quoted in ibid., 53.

23 Ibid., 55.

24 John Donne, *Sermons*, quoted in Crockett, 173, n. 22.

25 James R. Siemon, *Shakespearean Iconoclasm* (Berkeley: University of California Press, 1985), 192; Kenneth Gross, *Shakespeare's Noise* (Chicago: University of Chicago Press, 2001), 13. The New York Shakespeare Festival's 1990 production of *Hamlet*, starring and directed by Kevin Kline, physically manifested the theme of ear assault by having Hamlet kill Claudius with a retributive slash on the ear with the poisoned foil. In Franco Zeffirelli's 1990 film of the play, Claudius reacts to *The Mousetrap's* restaging of the ear-poisoning by emphatically placing his hand on his ear.

26 A similar argument is made by Walter L. Barker, "'The Heart of My Mystery': Emblematic Revelation in the *Hamlet* Play Scene," *The Upstart Crow* 15 (1995): 75–98.

27 Sophocles, *The Oedipus Cycle*, trans. Dudley Fitts and Robert Fitzgerald (New York: Harcourt Brace Javonovich, 1977), 61.

28 Martin Luther, *Werke*, quoted in Roland Mushat Frye, "Prince Hamlet and the Protestant Confessional," *Theology Today* 39 (1982): 35.

29 Anthony Munday, *A Second and Third Blast of Retrait from Plaies and Theaters* (London, 1590), 33.

30 Bryan Crockett calls attention to Playfere's sermon as a possible source of Hamlet's line (174, n. 43).

31 Ibid., 13.

32 Ibid., 82–83.

33 See *The Taming of the Shrew* (Ind.2, 134) and *A Midsummer Night's Dream* (5.1.76).

34 Andrew Gurr, *Playgoing in Shakespeare's London* (Cambridge: Cambridge University Press, 1996), 85.

35 Ibid., 86.

36 Huston Diehl, *Staging Reform, Reforming the Stage: Protestantism and Popular Theater in Early Modern England* (Ithaca: Cornell University Press, 1987), 82–83.

37 Philip Sidney, *The Defense of Poesy*, in *The Norton Anthology of English Literature*, 945.

38 Ibid., 945, n. 9.

39 Gross, 27.

40 Richard Banckes, *An Herbal* (London, 1525), 82.

41 Ben Johnson, "To My Book," (1616), p. 1393, line 2.

42 See Catharine Belsey's discussion of the idealization of the conjugal relation in Protestant Renaissance England.

43 Tiffany, 70.

44 J. Dover Wilson, *What Happens in Hamlet* (Cambridge: Cambridge University Press, 1960), 153.

45 Norman Holland avers that the dumb show is lost on Claudius because it does not reach his ear.

46 See Neil Rhodes for a discussion of the importance of *disputatio* to Hamlet's "To be or not to be" (609). Rhodes, "The Controversial Plot: Declamation and the Concept of the 'Problem Play,'" *Modern Language Review* 95 (2000): 609–22.

47 I have modernized the spelling of the *Geneva's* text.

48 Crockett, 54.

49 Ibid., 55.

50 Both Heather James and Philippa Berry have said that the importance of listening in *Hamlet* is reiterated in Dido's request that Aeneas tell her his story. See: Heather James, "Dido's Ear: Tragedy and the Politics of Response," *Shakespeare Quarterly* 52 (2001): 360–82. Philippa Berry, "Hamlet's Ear," *Shakespeare Survey* 50 (1997): 57–64.

51 Augustine, *Confessions*, 36, my emphasis.

52 Ibid., 20.

53 Louise Cary, "*Hamlet* Recycled, or The Tragical History of the Prince's Prints," *ELH* 61 (1994): 789.

Chapter 6

1 Shakespeare quotations are from *The Riverside Shakespeare*.

2 John Mahon, "Providential Visitations in Hamlet," *Hamlet Studies* 8 (1986): 40–51.

3   Daniell, *Julius Caesar*, 6.

4   Ibid., 95.

5   T. J. B. Spencer, "Shakespeare and the Elizabethan Romans," *Shakespeare Survey* 10 (1957): 29, 30.

6   Quoted in ibid., 30.

7   Richard Reynolds, *Chronicle of all the noble Emperours of the Romaines, from Julius Caesar* (London: T. Marshe, 1571).

8   Spencer, 33.

9   "Antony and Cleopatra," 5.2.120.

10 Harley Granville-Barker, *Prefaces to Shakespeare: King Lear, Cymbeline, Julius Caesar* (London: B. T. Batsford, 1958), 221, 226–27.

11 Martin Spevack, ed. *Julius Caesar* (Cambridge: Cambridge University Press, 1988), 27.

12 Robert S. Miola, *Shakespeare's Rome* (Cambridge: Cambridge University Press, 1983), 76.

13 "Antony and Cleopatra," 3.13.72.

14 René Girard, *A Theater of Envy* (New York: Oxford University Press, 1991), 223.

15 Ibid., 203.

16 Miola, *Shakespeare's Rome*, 80.

17 Naomi Liebler, " 'Thou Bleeding Piece of Earth': The Ritual Ground of *Julius Caesar*." In *New Casebooks:* Julius Caesar, ed. Richard Wilson (Houndmills, New York: Palgrave, 2002): 135.

18 Girard, *Envy*, 202.

19 Ibid.

20 René Girard, *I See Satan Fall Like Lightning*, trans. James G. Williams (Maryknoll, NY: Orbis, 2001), 98–99.

21 Maynard Mack, "The Modernity of Julius Caesar," in *Shakespeare's Early Tragedies: A Collection of Critical Essays*, ed. Mark Rose (Englewood Cliffs, NJ: Prentice Hall, 1995), 201.

22 Ibid., 208.

23 George W. Williams, "Pompey the Great," in *Renaissance Papers* (1976): 31.

24 John Velz, "Undular Structure in *Julius Caesar*," in *The Modern Language Review* 76 (1971): 21.

25 Steve Sohmer, *Shakespeare's Mystery Play: The Opening of the Globe Theater 1599* (Manchester: Manchester University Press, 1999), 268.

26 Ibid., 18.

27 Mark Rose, "Conjuring Caesar: Ceremony, History, and Authority in 1599," in *Shakespeare's Early Tragedies: A Collection of Critical Essays*, ed. Mark Rose (Englewood Cliffs, NJ: Prentice Hall, 1995), 238.

28 Ibid., 235–36.

29 *New American Bible: The Catholic Study Bible*, ed. by Donald Senior, Mary Ann Getty, et al. (New York: Oxford University Press, 1990), 101.

30 Michael Quinn, "Providence in Shakespeare's Yorkist Plays," *Shakespeare Quarterly* 10 (1959): 45.

31 Ibid., 45.

32 Ibid., 47.

33 Ibid., 50.

34 Henry A. Kelly, *Divine Providence in the England of Shakespeare's Histories* (Cambridge, Mass.: Harvard University Press, 1970), 2.

35 Ibid., 2–3.

36 Quoted in ibid., 3.

37 Quoted in ibid., 4.

38 Miola, *Shakespeare's Rome*.

39 John Andrews, ed. *Julius Caesar* (London: Dent, 1993), xxi.

40 Velz, 21

41 Daniell, *Julius Caesar*, 152–53.

42 Ibid., 60.

43 Ibid., 70.

44 Ibid., 70.

45 Ibid., 71.

46 Alexander Leggatt, *Shakespeare's Political Drama* (London: Routledge, 1992), 158.

47 Miola, *Shakespeare's Rome*, 85.

48 Ibid., 85.

49 Granville-Barker, 200.

50 T. S. Dorsch, *Julius Caesar* (London: Methuen, 1965), xlvii.

51 Derek Traversi, "*Julius Caesar*: The Roman Tragedy," in *Modern Critical Interpretations: Julius Caesar*, ed. Harold Bloom (New York: Chelsea House, 1988), 11.

52 Kenneth Burke, "Antony in Behalf of the Play," (1973) in *Shakespeare's Early Tragedies*," ed. by Mark Rose, 259, 261.

53 Jonathan Goldberg, "The Roman Actor: *Julius Caesar*," in *New Casebooks: Julius Caesar*, ed. Richard Wilson (Houndsmills, New York: Palgrave, 2002) 97.

54 Maurice Charney, *Shakespeare's Roman Plays* (Cambridge, Mass.: Harvard University Press, 1961), 57.

Chapter 7

1 William Shakespeare, *Julius Caesar*, ed. David Daniell, the Arden Shakespeare, 3rd series (Walton-on-Thames, Surrey: Thomas Nelson, 1998), 301. Citation and quotations of *Julius Caesar* are taken from this edition. Quotations of Shakespeare's works other than *Julius Caesar* are taken from *The Complete Works of Shakespeare*, ed. David Bevington, updated 4th ed. (London: Longman, 1997).

2 Sohmer, *Shakespeare's Mystery Play*, 170–71.

3   Thomas North, *Plutarch's Lives of the Noble Grecians and Romans. Englished by Sir Thomas North*, ed. W. E. Henley, The Tudor Translations, 5 vols. (London: David Nutt, 1896), 5: 68.

4   Sohmer, 120–28, 166–80.

5   Sohmer points out that "in North's *Plutarch*, Shakespeare and lettered Elizabethans would have encountered a series of uncanny parallels between the lives of Julius Caesar and Jesus Christ. Plutarch recorded that a man with the initials JC had lived at the time of the first Caesars. He was an exalted religious figure (North, 766), renowned for his piety, beloved of the poor, mistrusted by the elite (791). Certain Romans dressed him in a purple robe (975). One offered him a crown (976). Adherents hailed him by the title of king (791). One closest in his love betrayed him (793). Omens and portents surrounded his last days (797). He was martyred, but rose and was seen to walk the earth (797). Some declared him a god. He reformed the calendar (738)" (*Shakespeare's Mystery Play*, 28). See also R. E. Spakowski, "Deification and Myth-Making in the Play *Julius Caesar*," *The University Review-Kansas City* 36 (1969): 135–40.

6   Spakowski helps us understand Dante's rationale for making Brutus and Cassius archetypal "Christian" villains: "In the sense that monarchy and Caesarism intimates a universality of empire ruled by one man, likewise the principle of Christianity expresses the same connotation for the world—a universal church. In the first category, Caesar's spirit brought about the process, in the second, the spirit of Christ (139).

7   "The Soothsayer's 'ninth-hour' is a textual marker [in *Julius Caesar*]. The three synoptic gospels record that Christ died at the 'ninth hour' (Matthew 27:26, Mark 15:34, Luke 23:44)." Sohmer, 130.

8   David Kaula, "'Let Us Be Sacrificers': Religious Motifs in *Julius Caesar*," *Shakespeare Studies* 14 (1981): 197–214; Marshall Bradley, "Caska: Stoic, Cynic, 'Christian,'" *Literature and Theology* 8 (1994): 140–56; and Sohmer, 26–74, 103–80. Also see Mark Rose, "Conjuring Caesar: Ceremony, History, and Authority in 1599," *English Literary Renaissance* 19 (1989): 291–304, esp. 291–95; and Gail Kern Paster, "'In the Spirit of Man There Is No Blood': Blood as Trope of Gender in *Julius Caesar*," *Shakespeare Quarterly* 40 (1989): 284–98, esp. 294–96.

9   Bloom, *Shakespeare*, notes that in the play "[t]here may . . . be a suggestion that this Julius Caesar on some level courts martyrdom as a way both to godhead and to the permanent establishment of the empire" (105–6).

Also see Mildred O. Durham, "Drama of the Dying God in *Julius Caesar*," *Studies in Literature* 11 (1979): 49–57.

10 See *OED* v. 1B on how a cobbler clumsily mended shoes. The poor quality of cobbled shoes is reflected in Edmund Spenser's only use of a form of the word "cobbled" in *The Faerie Queen*. Concerning Avarice in the Pageant of the Seven Deadly Sins in Lucifera's House of Pride, Spenser asserts that "His life was night vnto deaths doore yuplast, / And thredbare cote, an cobled shoes he ware, / Ne scarse good morsel all his life did tast" (1.4.28.1–3), *Spenser: "The Faerie Queen,"* ed. A. C. Hamilton (1977; repr. London: Longman, 1980), 70.

11 For Heraclitus on the soul, see Bruno Snell, *The Discovery of the Mind: The Greek Origins of European Thoughts*, trans. T. G. Rosenmery (1953; repr. New York: Harper & Row, 1960), 17. For Cicero, see *De finibus bonorum et malorum*, trans. Horace Rackham, Loeb Classical Library *Cicero* 17 (1914; repr. Cambridge, Mass.: Harvard University Press, 1971), 329; and *De amicitia* in *De Senectute, De Amicitia, De Divinatione*, trans. William Armistead Falconer, Loeb Classical Library *Cicero* 20 (1923; repr., Cambridge, Mass.: Harvard University Press, 1971), 108–211, esp. 159.

12 John Skelton, *The Complete English Poems*, ed. John Scattergood (New Haven: Yale University Press, 1983), 380.

13 See A. Jonathan Bate, "The Cobbler's Awl: *Julius Caesar*, I.i.21–24," *Shakespeare Quarterly* 35 (1984): 461–62, who suggests that Shakespeare's association of "awl" and "prick" in the Cobbler's jest derives from a precedent in Dekker's *The Shoemaker's Holiday* (1599).

14 Daniell, *Julius Caesar*, 156. Analysis of the Cobbler's speeches and his role, that differ from mine, appear in R. J. Kaufman and C. J. Ronan, "Shakespeare's *Julius Caesar*: An Apollonian and Comparative Reading," *Comparative Drama* 4 (1970): 18–51, esp. 21; Marvin L. Vawter, " 'Division 'tween Our Souls': Shakespeare's Stoic Brutus," *Shakespeare Studies* 7 (1974): 173–96, esp. 183–84; William B. Toole, "The Cobbler, the Disrobed Image, and the Motif of Movement in *Julius Caesar*," *The Upstart Crow* 4 (1982): 41–55, esp. 46–47; and Sohmer, 106–7. Sohmer asserts that the Cobbler has at least two Pauline connotations: both are celibate (the Cobbler meddles with no "women's matters"); both carry an awl. "Elizabethans believed that Paul was a leatherworker, who worked with an awl" (107).

15 North, *Plutarch's Lives*, 6: 19. Italics are mine.

16 For the histrionic nature of Caesar's character in Shakespeare's play, see J. L. Simmons, "Shakespeare's *Julius Caesar*: The Roman Actor and the Man," *Tulane Studies in English* 16 (1968): 1–28, esp. 3–13. Caesar in the play is "of all the Roman actors . . . by far the greatest" (7). In this vein, also see John Drakakis, " 'Fashion it Thus': *Julius Caesar* and the Politics of Theatrical Representation," *Shakespeare Survey* 44 (1992): 65–73, esp. 69, 71. Simmons notes that "the tradition that the historical Caesar relished genuine acting was evidently widespread. Heywood, in his *Apology for Actors* (1612), mentions Caesar's delight and excellence in playing Hercules Furens" (Simmons 7, n. 19). I would assert (unlike Simmons) that, despite Caesar's thespian ability, the audience's unforeseen responses to his acting, rather than his "script" for himself and Antony, begin to dictate his role in this episode.

17 Nicholas Visser, in "Plebeian Politics in *Julius Caesar*," *Shakespeare in South Africa* 7 (1994): 22–31, esp. 28, claims that the crowd's intelligent failure to follow Antony and Caesar's script for their response by unexpectedly approving Caesar's refusal of the crown frustrates Caesar, thus indirectly causing his epileptic fit.

18 See Eric Sams, *The Real Shakespeare: Retrieving the Early Years, 1564–1594* (New Haven: Yale University Press, 1995), *passim*.

19 Richard Wilson, in " 'Is This a Holiday?' Shakespeare's Roman Carnival," *English Literary History* 54 (1987): 31–44, attributes Caesar's tendency to turn politics into theater extemporaneously to his role as Carnival King, a master of revels who knows that "authoritarian populism" demands "the true regimen of bread and circuses" (37).

20 Forms of the word "spirit" appear three times in Shakespeare's *Venus and Adonis*, in which the poet never employs the word "soul."

21 One could argue that on eight occasions in *Julius Caesar*, Shakespeare—by the word "spirit"—refers to a supernatural spirit, sometimes conjured, often referring to that of the dead (1.2.146; 1.3.69; 2.1.323; 3.1.195, 270; 4.3.280. 286; 5.3.95; 5.1.90); on five occasions to a related idea of the inner essence of a person (1.2.205; 1.3.83, 95; 2.1.168; 4.1.33); and, finally, on two occasions to the general quality of a man or a historical age (2.1.166; 3.1.163).

22 Antony's stunning artistry derives from a synthesis of rhetorical techniques presented in Thomas Wilson's *The Arte of Rhetorique* (1560), according to G. M. Pincess, "Rhetoric as Character: The Forum Speeches

in *Julius Caesar*," *The Upstart Crow* 4 (1982): 113–21, esp. 115–19. Also see Jean Fuzier, "Rhetoric versus Rhetoric: A Study of Shakespeare's *Julius Caesar*, Act III, Scene 2," *Cahiers Élisabéthains* 5 (1974): 26–65.

23 See Richard Henze, "Power and Spirit in *Julius Caesar*," *The University Review–Kansas City* 36 (1970): 307–14, esp. 312; and Jan H. Blits, "Manliness and Friendship in Shakespeare's *Julius Caesar*," *Interpretation* 9 (1981): 155–67, esp. 160.

24 Hamilton, *Spenser: "The Faerie Queen*," 84.

25 Caesar's generosity toward commoners may be associated with the fitful expression of a virtue Norman Rabkin has called Caesar's capacity for "self abnegation," which he "shows when he refuses to hear Artemidorus' suit on the grounds—not those of his prototype in Plutarch—that 'What touches us ourself shall be last served' (III.1.8)," *Shakespeare and the Common Understanding* (New York: Free Press, 1967), 112.

26 Ernest Schanzer, in *The Problem Plays of Shakespeare* (1963; repr. New York: Schocken Books, 1965), includes Caesar's reported tears for those of the poor in a listing of his virtues (32).

27 Ironically, Brutus appears blind to infirmity and disingenuousness—of his own in his accusation of Cassius: "Brutus rebukes Cassius for the manner in which he raises the money he needs to pay his legions" (Toole, 50). Also see G. Wilson Knight, *The Imperial Theme* (London: Oxford University Press, 1931), 74; and Derek Traversi, *Shakespeare: The Roman Plays* (Stanford: Stanford University Press, 1963), 64.

28 Stephen M. Buhler, "No Spectre, No Spectre: The Agon of Materialist Thought in Shakespeare's *Julius Caesar*," *English Literary Renaissance* 26 (1996): 313–32, esp. 326.

29 Ibid., 325.

30 John Roland Dove and Peter Gamble, "'Lovers in Peace': Brutus and Cassius—A Re-Examination," *English Studies* 60 (1979): 543–54, esp. 547–48.

31 Coppélia Kahn, *Roman Shakespeare: Warriors, Wounds, and Women* (London: Routledge, 1997), 95.

32 Daniell, *Julius Caesar*, 183.

33 Granville-Barker, 171.

34 *OED* sb.16; Daniell, *Julius Caesar*, 284.

35 Buhler, "No Spectre," 284.

36 Jan Blits, in the course of arguing that Cassius and Brutus's friendship is the most elaborated friendship in the play, remarks that "Brutus and Cassius call each other 'brother' as many as eight times, although Shakespeare never explains that they are brothers-in-law" (166–67). My argument demonstrates that even as Cassius abandons certain tenets of Epicureanism, so Brutus in his warm embrace of Cassius as "my dear brother" violates a principle of Stoicism. According to Marvin Vawter, in *"Julius Caesar*: Rupture in the Bond," *Journal of English and Germanic Philology* 72 (1973): 311–28, "the Stoic Wise Man sees himself as an independent entity unwilling to bind himself to any specific community. [Brutus has refused Cassius's desire that the conspirators swear an oath to assassinate Caesar.] [The Stoic's] entirely private personality and his obsession with the self-sufficiency of his virtue-reason (the essential basis of Stoic philosophy) separate him from ordinary men" (316–17). Brutus in his soul-brotherhood with Cassius thus apparently relinquishes a Stoic tenet that most likely contributed to his cold treatment of Cassius earlier in the quarrel scene. Simmons essentially agrees with Vawter in this respect (Simmons, "Shakespeare's *Julius Caesar*," 23).

37 *The Iliad of Homer*, trans. Richard Lattimore (Chicago: University of Chicago Press, 1951), 66.

38 North, *Plutarch's Lives*, 6: 216.

39 Cf., however, Thomas Pughe, "'What Should the Wars Do with These Jigging Fools?': The Poets in Shakespeare's *Julius Caesar*," *English Studies* 69 (1988): 313–22, esp. 317–18, 319–20. Pughe asserts that Shakespeare introduces the camp-poet in order to stress by contrast the absence of any saving powers of mind within Brutus: "In Brutus's case, the violent treatment of the camp-poet is an outward manifestation of his denial of imagination and intuition" (320).

40 North, *Plutarch's Lives*, 6: 230.

41 J. L. Simmons confirms that this would have been the case, in *Shakespeare's Pagan World: The Roman Tragedies* (Charlottesville: University Press of Virginia, 1973), 68, 72.

42 Rose asserts that like "the [Roman Catholic] Mass, *Julius Caesar* centers upon a sacrificial death that initiates a new era in history, the emergence of imperial Rome. Perhaps the association of Caesar to Christ is not wholly ironic" (238). Illustrating the transference of certain details of royalist policies into the rituals and designs of the Church of England, Rose concludes that "[p]robably many in Shakespeare's audience would have been prepared to see parallels between the first Emperor, as Caesar was commonly if erroneously regarded, and the great Queen [Elizabeth]. . . . Furthermore, by transforming the historical fact of the defeat of Brutus and the republican movement in Rome into a metaphysical confrontation of the inevitability of imperial greatness, Shakespeare's play implicitly confirms the legitimacy of the Tudor state" (303).

43 If a reader were to insist on considering *A Midsummer Night's Dream* a play with classical values, I would agree that the eight appearances of the word "soul" in the comedy are more casually introduced and unfocused than are the appearances of the word in *Titus* and *Errors*.

44 Miola, *Shakespeare's Rome*, 92–95. Miola states that in both Lucrece's and Brutus's cases, "[t]he inextricability of body and soul provides the basis for action. Although the action [for Brutus] aims at the destruction of a dangerous spirit, not a defiled body, the pagan Roman conscience defines the ethical problem in exactly the same terms at the same conclusion [that the Romance conscience does in *The Rape of Lucrece*]" (93).

Bibliography

Abrams, M. H., ed. *The Sixteenth Century, The Early Seventeenth Century.* Vol. 1B of *The Norton Anthology of English Literature.* New York: Norton, 2000.

Alighieri, Dante. *The Divine Comedy.* Translated by Allen Mandelbaum. 3 vols. (New York: Bantam, 1982–1986).

———. *The Divine Comedy.* Translated by C. H. Sisson. Oxford: Oxford University Press, 1998.

Allen, William. *Defence of English Catholics.* Rouen: Fr. Parsons' Press, 1584.

Andrews, John, ed. *Julius Caesar.* London: Dent, 1993.

Aquinas, Thomas. *Summa Theologia.* Translated by the Fathers of the English Dominican Province. Revised by Daniel J. Sullivan. New York: Benziger, 1947.

Aristotle. *Ethica Nicomachea.* In *Introduction to Aristotle.* Edited by Richard McKeon. New York: Modern Library, 1947.

Arnold, Matthew. *Poems.* London: Brown, Green, & Longman, 1853.

Augustine. *Confessions.* Translated by Edward Pusey. New York: Norton, 2000.

Augustine. *The Confessions, The City of God, On Christian Doctrine.* Translated by Marcus Dods and J. J. Shaw. Chicago: Encyclopedia Britannica, 1952.

Banckes, Richard. *An Herbal*. London, 1525.

Barish, Jonas. *The Anti-theatrical Prejudice*. Berkeley: University of California Press, 1981.

Barker, Walter L. "'The Heart of My Mystery': Emblematic Revelation in the *Hamlet* Play Scene." *The Upstart Crow* 15 (1995): 75–98.

Bate, A. Jonathan. "The Cobbler's Awl: *Julius Caesar*, I.i.21–24." *Shakespeare Quarterly* 35 (1984): 461–62.

Bateson, F. W., ed. *The Cambridge Bibliography of English Literature*, 5 vols. (Cambridge: Cambridge University Press, 1969).

Battenhouse, Roy W. *Shakespearean Tragedy: Its Art and Christian Premises*. Bloomington: Indiana University Press, 1969.

Becon, Thomas. *The Early Works of Thomas Becon*. Edited by John Ayre. 3 vols. Cambridge: The Parker Society, 1843–1884.

Belsey, Catherine. "The Serpent in the Garden: Shakespeare, Marriage, and Material Culture." *The Seventeenth Century* 11 (1996): 1–20.

Berry, Philippa. "Hamlet's Ear." *Shakespeare Survey* 50 (1997): 57–64.

Betteridge, Thomas. *Tudor Histories of the English Reformation 1550–1583*. Aldershot: Ashgate, 1996.

Blits, Jan M. "Manliness and Friendship in Shakespeare's *Julius Caesar*." *Interpretation* 9 (1981): 155–67.

Bloom, Harold. *Shakespeare: The Invention of the Human*. New York: Riverhead Books, 1998.

———, ed. *Shakespeare's Sonnets*. New York: Chelsea House, 1987.

Bradley, Marshall. "Caska: Stoic, Cynic, 'Christian.'" *Literature and Theology* 8 (1994): 140–56.

Buhler, Stephen M. "No Spectre, No Spectre: The Agon of Materialist Thought in Shakespeare's *Julius Caesar*." *English Literary Renaissance* 26 (1996): 313–32.

Burke, Kenneth. "Antony in Behalf of the Play." In *Shakespeare's Early Tragedies: A Collection of Critical Essays*, edited by Mark Rose, 257–65. Englewood Cliffs, N.J.; Prentice Hall, 1995.

Calderwood, James L. *Shakespearean Metadrama: The Argument of the Play in* Titus Andronicus, Lover's Labor's Lost, Romeo and Juliet, A Midsummer Night's Dream *and* Richard II. Minneapolis: University of Minnesota Press, 1971.

Calvin, John. *Commentaries on Exodus.* Grand Rapids: Calvin Translation Society, 1948–1959.

———. *The Institution of the Christian Religion.* Translated by Thomas Norton. London, 1611.

Cannon, Charles. "'As in a Theater': *Hamlet* in the Light of Calvin's Doctrine of Predestination." *Studies in English Literature, 1500–1900* 11 (1971): 203–22.

Caraman, P. *Henry Garnet, 1555–1606, and the Gunpowder Plot.* London: Longmans, 1964.

Cary, Louise. "*Hamlet* Recycled, or The Tragical History of the Prince's Prints." *English Literary History* 61 (1994): 783–805.

Charney, Maurice. *Shakespeare on Love & Lust.* New York: Columbia University Press, 2000.

———. *Shakespeare's Roman Plays.* Cambridge, Mass.: Harvard University Press, 1961.

Chaucer, Geoffrey. *The Works of Geoffrey Chaucer.* Edited F. N. Robinson. 2nd ed. Boston: Houghton Mifflin, 1957.

Chesterton, G. K. *Chaucer.* London: Faber & Faber, 1932.

———. *The Common Man.* London: Faber & Faber, 1950.

Cicero. *De Finibus Bonorum et Malorum.* Translated by Horace Rackham. Loeb Classical Library *Cicero* 17. 1914. Reprint, Cambridge, Mass.: Harvard University Press, 1971.

———. *De Senectute, De Amicitia, De Divinitate.* Translated by William Armistead Falconer. Loeb Classical Library *Cicero* 20. 1923. Reprint, Cambridge, Mass.: Harvard University Press, 1971.

Craig, W. J., ed. *The Oxford Shakespeare.* Oxford: Oxford University Press, 1954.

Crockett, Bryan. *The Play of Paradox: Stage and Sermon in Renaissance England*. Philadelphia: University of Pennsylvania Press, 1995.

Daniell, David. *The Bible in English: Its History and Influence*. New Haven: Yale University Press, 2003.

———. "Shakespeare and the Protestant Mind." *Shakespeare Survey* 54 (2001): 1–12.

Devlin, Christopher. *Hamlet's Divinity*. Carbondale: Southern Illinois University Press, 1963.

Diehl, Huston. *Staging Reform, Reforming the Stage: Protestantism and Popular Theater in Early Modern England*. Ithaca: Cornell University Press, 1987.

Donne, John. *The Complete Poetry and Selected Prose of John Donne*. Edited by Charles M. Coffin. New York: Random House, 1952.

———. *The Sermons of John Donne*. Edited by George R. Potter and Evelyn M. Simpson. 10 vols. Berkeley: University of California Press, 1953–1962.

Dove, John Roland and Peter Gamble. "'Lovers in Peace': Brutus and Cassius—A Re-Examination." *English Studies* 60 (1979): 543–54.

Downame, John. *A Treatise of Securitie*. London: Fellix Kingston & William Stansby, 1622.

Draxe, Thomas. *The Church's Security*. London: George Edd, 1608.

Drukakis, John. "'Fashion it Thus': *Julius Caesar* and the Politics of Theatrical Representation," *Shakespeare Survey* 44 (1992): 65–73.

Durham, Mildred O. "Drama of the Dying God in *Julius Caesar*." *Studies in Literature* 11 (1979): 49–57.

Edwards, Calvin R. "The Narcissus Myth in Spenser's Poetry." *Studies in Philology* 74 (1977) 63–88.

———. "Narcissus." In Hamilton et al. 496–97.

Edwards, Francis. *Guy Fawkes—The Real Story of the Gunpowder Plot?* London: Rupert Davis, 1969.

———. *Plots and Plotters in the Reign of Elizabeth I*. Dublin: Four Courts Press, 2002.

Eliot, T. S. "Hamlet," in *Selected Essays*. 2nd ed. London: Faber & Faber, 1932.

Erickson, Peter. *Patriarchal Structures in Shakespeare's Drama*. Berkeley: University of California Press, 1985.

Est, William. *The Scourge of Security*. London: Thomas Creede, 1609.

Ewbank, Inga-Stina. "The Fiend-like Queen: A Note on *Macbeth* and Seneca's *Medea*." *Shakespeare Survey* 19 (1966): 82–89.

Ferry, Anne. *The Inward Language: Sonnets of Wyatt, Sidney, Shakespeare, Donne*. Chicago: University of Chicago Press, 1994.

Fineman, Joel. *Shakespeare's Perjured Eye: The Invention of Poetic Subjectivity in the Sonnets*. Berkeley: University of California Press, 1986.

Fisher, John. *A Treatise of Prayer*. Paris, 1640.

Frye, Roland. "Prince Hamlet and the Protestant Confessional." *Theology Today* 39 (1982): 27–38.

———. *Shakespeare and Christian Doctrine*. Princeton: Princeton University Press, 1963.

Fuzier, Jean. "Rhetoric versus Rhetoric: A Study of Shakespeare's *Julius Caesar*, Act III, Scene 2." *Cahiers Élisabéthains* 5 (1974): 26–65.

Gardner, Helen. "Milton's 'Satan' and the Theme of Damnation in Elizabethan Tragedy." *English Association Essays and Studies* 1 (1948): 46–66.

———. *Religion and Literature*. Oxford: Oxford University Press, 1971.

The Geneva Bible: A Facsimile of the 1560 Edition. Madison: University of Wisconsin Press, 1969.

Gerenday, Lynn de. "The Problem of Self-Reflective Love in Book III of *The Faerie Queene*." *Literature and Psychology* 26 (1976) 37–48.

Girard, René. *A Theater of Envy*. New York, Oxford University Press, 1991.

Girard, René. *I See Satan Fall Like Lightning.* Translated by James G. Williams. Maryknoll, N.Y.: Orbis, 2001.

Goldberg, Jonathan. "The Roman Actor: *Julius Caesar.*" In R. Wilson, *New Casebooks*, 92–107.

Goldin, Frederick. *The Mirror of Narcissus in the Courtly Love Lyric.* Ithaca: Cornell University Press, 1967.

Gosson, Stephen. *Playes Confuted in Five Actions.* London, 1590.

Granville-Barker, Harley. *Prefaces to Shakespeare: King Lear, Cymbeline, Julius Caesar.* London: B. T. Batsford, 1958.

Greenblatt, Stephen. *Hamlet in Purgatory.* Princeton: Princeton University Press, 2001.

Groot, J. H. de. *The Shakespeares and "The Old Faith."* New York: Books for Libraries Press, 1946.

Gross, Kenneth. *Shakespeare's Noise.* Chicago: University of Chicago Press, 2001.

Guillory, John. "Milton, Narcissism, Gender: On the Genealogy of Male Self-Esteem." In *Critical Essays on John Milton*, edited by Christopher Kendrick, 194–233. New York: G. K. Hall, 1995.

Gurr, Andrew. *Playgoing in Shakespeare's London.* Cambridge: Cambridge University Press, 1996.

Habermann, Johann. *The Enemy of Security.* Translated by Thomas Rogers. London: R. Yardley & P. Short, 1591.

Hamilton, A. C., et al., ed. *The Spenser Encyclopedia.* Toronto: University of Toronto Press, 1990.

Harland, Paul W. " 'A True Transubstantiation': Donne, Self-Love, and the Passion." In *John Donne's Religious Imagination: Essays in Honor of John T. Shawcross*, edited by Raymond-Jean Frontain and Frances M. Malpezzi. Conway, Ark.: University of Conway Press, 1995.

Hegel, Martin. *Hegel Selections.* Edited by Jacob Loewenberg. New York: Charles Scribner's Sons, 1929.

Henze, Richard. "Power and Spirit in *Julius Caesar.*" *The University Review-Kansas City* 36 (1970): 307–14.

Hill, Robert. *The Pathway to Prayer and Piety.* 6th ed. London: William Barrett, 1615.

Holland, Norman. "The Dumb-Show Revisited." *Notes and Queries* (May 1958): 191.

Homer. *The Iliad of Homer.* Translated by Richard Lattimore. Chicago: University of Chicago Press, 1951.

Honigmann, E. A. J. *Shakespeare: The Lost Years.* Manchester: Manchester University Press, 1985.

Hooker, Richard. *Tractates and Sermon.* Edited by L. Yeandle and E. Grislis. Cambridge, Mass.: Harvard University Press, 1990.

Hume, Anthea. *Edmund Spenser: Protestant Poet.* Cambridge: Cambridge University Press, 1984.

Iwasaki Soji. *The Sword and the Word.* Tokyo: Shinszki Shorin, 1973.

James, Heather. "Dido's Ear: Tragedy and the Politics of Response." *Shakespeare Quarterly* 52 (2001): 360–82.

Jewel, John. *The Works of John Jewel, Bishop of Salisbury.* Edited by John Ayre. Cambridge: Cambridge University Press, 1845–1850.

Josephs, Lawrence. *Character Structure and the Organization of the Self.* New York: Columbia University Press, 1992.

Kahn, Coppélia. *Roman Shakespeare: Warriors, Wounds, and Women.* London: Routledge, 1997.

———. *Man's Estate: Masculine Identity in Shakespeare.* Berkeley: University of California Press, 1981.

Kaufman, R. J. and C. J. Ronan. "Shakespeare's *Julius Caesar*: An Apollonian and Comparative Reading." *Comparative Drama* 4 (1970): 18–51.

Kaula, David. "'Let Us Be Sacrificers': Religious Motifs in *Julius Caesar.*" *Shakespeare Studies* 14 (1981): 197–214.

Kelly, Henry A. *Divine Providence in the England of Shakespeare's Histories.* Cambridge, Mass.: Harvard University Press, 1970.

Kiernan, Pauline. *Shakespeare's Theory of Drama.* Cambridge: Cambridge University Press, 1996.

Kinney, Arthur. *Lies Like Truth: Shakespeare's* Macbeth *and the Cultural Moment.* Detroit: Wayne University Press, 2001.

Kirsch, Arthur. *Shakespeare and the Experience of Love.* Cambridge: Cambridge University Press, 1981.

Knight, G. Wilson. *The Imperial Theme.* London: Oxford University Press, 1931.

La Primaudaye, Pierre de. *The Second Part of The French Academie.* Paris, 1586. Reprint, London, 1618.

Lake, Peter. "Religious Identities in Shakespeare's England." In *A Companion to Shakespeare*, edited by David Scott Kastan. Oxford: Oxford University Press, 1999.

Lake, Peter and Michael Questier. *The Anti-Christ's Lewd Hat: Protestants, Papists, and Players in Post-Reformation England.* New Haven: Yale University Press, 2002.

Leggatt, Alexander. *Shakespeare's Political Drama.* London: Routledge, 1992.

Lenz, Carolyn et al. *The Woman's Part: Feminist Criticism of Shakespeare.* Urbana: University of Illinois Press, 1980.

Liebler, Naomi. "'Thou Bleeding Piece of Earth': The Ritual Ground of *Julius Caesar.*" In R. Wilson, *New Casebooks*, 128–48.

Lorris, Guillaume de and Jean de Meun. *The Romance of the Rose.* Translated by Harry W. Robbins. New York: E. P. Dutton, 1962.

Low, Anthony. "*Hamlet* and the Ghost of Purgatory: Intimations of Killing the Father." *English Literary Renaissance* 29 (1999): 443–67.

Luna, B. N. de. *Jonson's Romish Plot.* Oxford: Clarendon, 1967.

Luther, Martin. *Catechism and Lectures on Romans*. In *Luther's Works*, translated by Walter G. Tillmanns and Jacob A. O. Preus. St. Louis: Concordia, 1972.

———. *Discourse on Free Will*. Edited and translated by Ernst F. Winter. New York: Frederick Unger, 1961.

———. *The Large Catechism (1530)*. In *Triglot Concordia: The Symbolical Books of the Evangelical Lutheran Church*, edited by F. Bente and W. H. T. Dau. St. Louis: Concordia Press, 1921.

MacCary, W. Thomas. *Friends and Lovers: The Phenomenology of Desire in Shakespearean Comedy*. New York: Columbia University Press, 1985.

Mack, Maynard. "The Modernity of *Julius Caesar*." In Rose, *Shakespeare's Early Tragedies*, 199–210.

Mahon, John W. "Providential Visitations in *Hamlet*." *Hamlet Studies* 8 (1986): 40–51.

Martin, Philip. *Shakespeare's Sonnets: Self, Love, and Art*. Cambridge: Cambridge University Press, 1972.

McKeon, Richard, ed. *Introduction to Aristotle*. New York: Modern Library, 1947.

Milton, John. *Complete Poems and Major Prose*. Edited by Merritt Y. Hughes. New York: Odyssey Press, 1957.

———. *Paradise Lost*. Edited by Scott Elledge. New York: Norton, 1975.

Milward, Peter. *Biblical Influences in Shakespeare's Great Tragedies*. Bloomington: Indiana University Press, 1985.

———. *The Plays and the Exercises*. Tokyo: Renaissance Institute, Sophia University, 2002.

———. "Shakespeare and Christian Doctrine." *Shakespeare Studies* 4 (1965–1966): 36–56.

———. *Shakespeare's Meta-drama—Hamlet and Macbeth*. Tokyo: Renaissance Institute, Sophia University, 2003.

———. *Shakespeare's Other Dimension.* Tokyo: Renaissance Institute, Sophia University, 1987.

———. *Shakespeare's Religious Background.* Bloomington: Indiana University Press, 1973.

Miola, Robert S., ed. *Macbeth.* New York: Norton, 2000.

———. *Shakespeare's Rome.* Cambridge: Cambridge University Press, 1983.

Montaigne, Michel de. *The Complete Essays of Montaigne.* Translated by Donald Frame. Stanford: Stanford University Press, 1958.

Munday, Anthony. *A Second and Third Blast of Retrait from Plaies and Theaters.* London, 1590.

New American Bible (The Catholic Study Bible). Edited by Donald Senior, Mary Ann Getty, et al. New York: Oxford University Press, 1990.

Newman, John Henry. *A Grammar of Assent.* New York: Catholic Publication Society, 1870.

Noble, Richmond. *Shakespeare's Biblical Knowledge.* London: SPCK, 1935.

North, Thomas. *Plutarch's Lives of the Noble Grecians and Romans Englished by Sir Thomas North.* Edited by W. E. Henley. The Tudor Translations. 5 vols. London: David Nutt, 1896.

Norbrook, David. *Poetry and Politics in the English Renaissance.* London: Routledge, 1984.

Novy, Marianne. *Love's Argument: Gender Relations in Shakespeare.* Chapel Hill: University of North Carolina Press, 1984.

Oakes, Edward. Review of *Hamlet in Purgatory*, by Stephen Greenblatt. *Commonweal* (May 2001): 29–30.

O'Donovan, Oliver. *The Problem of Self-Love in St. Augustine.* New Haven: Yale University Press, 1980.

Ovid. *The Metamorphoses.* Translated by Horace Gregory. New York: New American Library, 1958.

Paster, Gail Kern. "'In the Spirit of Man There is No Blood': Blood as Trope of Gender in *Julius Caesar.*" *Shakespeare Quarterly* 40 (1989): 284–98.

Pendleton, Thomas A. "Hamlet's Ears." *Mid-Hudson Language Studies* 1 (1978): 51–61.

Perkins, William. *A Golden Chain, a Description of Theology containing the Order of the Causes of Salvation and Damnation.* 1591.

Pincess, G. M. "Rhetoric as Character: the Forum Speeches in *Julius Caesar.*" *The Upstart Crow* 4 (1982): 113–21.

Plato. *Laws.* Translated by R. G. Bury. London: Heinmann, 1926.

———. *Phaedrus.* Translated by W. C. Helmbold and W. G. Rabinowitz. New York: Macmillan, 1956.

Playfere, Thomas. *The Meane in Mourning, A Sermon Preached at Saint Maryes Spittle in London on Tuesday in Easter weeke, 1595.* London, 1596.

Pope, Stephen. "Expressive Individualism and True Self-Love: A Thomistic Perspective." *Journal of Religion* 71 (1991): 384–99.

Porter, Joseph A. *Shakespeare's Mercutio: His History and Drama.* Chapel Hill: University of North Carolina Press, 1989.

Prynne, William. *Histrio-Mastix: The Player's Scourge, or Actor's Tragedy.* London, 1633.

Pughe, Thomas. " 'What Should the Wars Do With Jigging Fools?': The Poets in Shakespeare's *Julius Caesar.*" *English Studies* 69 (1988): 313–22.

Quinn, Michael. "Providence in Shakespeare's Yorkist Plays." *Shakespeare Quarterly* 10 (1959): 45–52.

Rabkin, Norman. *Shakespeare and the Common Understanding.* New York: Free Press, 1967.

Rebholz, Ronald A. *The Life of Fulke Greville, First Lord Brooke.* Oxford: Clarendon, 1971.

Remnick, David. "Hamlet in Hollywood." *The New Yorker*, November 1995: 66–83.

Reynolds, Richard. *Chronicle of all the noble Emperours of the Romaines, from Julius Caesar.* London: T. Marshe, 1571.

Rhodes, Neil. "The Controversial Plot: Declamation and the Concept of the 'Problem Play'." *Modern Language Review* 95 (2000): 609–22.

Ricoeur, Paul. *Oneself as Another*. Translated by Kathleen Blamey. Chicago: Chicago University Press, 1992.

Rogers, William Elford. "Narcissus in *Amoretti* xxxv." *American Notes and Queries* 15 (1976): 18–20.

Rose, Mark. "Conjuring Caesar: Ceremony, History, and Authority in 1599." *English Literary Renaissance* 19 (1989): 291–304.

———, ed. *Shakespeare's Early Tragedies: A Collection of Critical Essays.* Englewood Cliffs, N.J.; Prentice Hall, 1995.

Rouse, W. H. D., ed. *Shakespeare's Ovid: Arthur Golding's Translation of the* Metamorphoses. New York: W. W. Norton, 1966.

Sams, Eric. *The Real Shakespeare: Retrieving the Early Years, 1564–1594.* New Haven: Yale University Press, 1995.

Sanders, E. P. and Margaret Davies, *Studying the Synoptic Gospels.* London: SCM Press, 1989.

Schanzer, Ernest. *The Problem Plays of Shakespeare.* 1963. Reprint, New York: Schocken Books, 1965.

Shaheen, Naseeb. *Biblical References in Shakespeare's Plays.* Newark: University of Delaware Press, 1999.

Shakespeare, William. *The Complete Works of Shakespeare.* Edited by David Bevington. 4th ed. New York: Longman, 1997.

———. *Hamlet.* Film. Directed by Franco Zeffirelli. Warner Brothers, 1990.

———. *Julius Caesar.* The Arden Shakespeare Series. Edited by David Daniell. Walton-on-Thames, Surrey: Nelson, 1998.

———. *Julius Caesar* (1955). Edited by T. W. Dorsch. London: Methuen, 1965.

———. *Macbeth*. Edited by Robert S. Miola. New York: Norton, 2004.

———. *The Riverside Shakespeare*. Edited by G. Blakemore Evans. Boston: Houghton Mifflin, 1974.

———. *The Works of Mr. Shakespeare*. Edited by Nicholas Rowe. London: Jacob Jonson, 1709.

Shuger, Debora K. "Subversive Faiths and Suffering Subjects: Shakespeare and Christianity." In *Religion and Politics in Post-Reformation England, 1540–1688*, edited by Donna B. Hamilton and Richard Strier, 46–69. Cambridge: Cambridge University Press, 1996.

Sidney, Sir Philip. *An Apology for Poetry*. Edited by Geoffrey Shepherd. London: Thomas Nelson, 1965.

Siemon, James. *Shakespearean Iconoclasm*. Berkeley: University of California Press, 1985.

Simmons, J. L. "Shakespeare's *Julius Caesar*: The Roman Actor and the Man." *Tulane Studies in English* 16 (1968): 1–28.

———. *Shakespeare's Pagan World: The Roman Tragedies*. Charlottesville: University Press of Virginia, 1973.

Skelton, John. *The Complete English Poems*. Edited by John Scattergood. New Haven: Yale University Press, 1983.

Smith, Bruce R. *Homosexual Desire in Shakespeare's England*. Chicago: Chicago University Press, 1991.

Smith, John. *A Pattern of True Prayer*, 1605.

Snell, Bruno. *The Discovery of the Mind: The Greek Origins of European Thoughts*. Translated by T. G. Rosenmery. 1953. Reprint, New York: Harper & Row, 1960.

Sohmer, Steve. *Shakespeare's Mystery Play: The Opening of the Globe Theatre 1599*. Manchester: Manchester University Press, 1999.

Sophocles. *The Oedipus Cycle*. Translated by Dudley Fitts and Robert Fitzgerald. New York: Harcourt Brace Jovanovich, 1977.

Spakowski, R. E. "Deification and Myth-Making in the Play *Julius Caesar*." *The University Review-Kansas City* 36 (1969): 135–40.

Spencer, T. J. B. "Shakespeare and the Elizabethan Romans." *Shakespeare Survey* 10 (1957): 27–38.

Spenser, Edmund. *The Complete Poetical Works of Spenser*. Edited by R. E. Neil Dodge. Boston: Houghton Mifflin, 1908. Reprint, 1936.

———. *The Faerie Queene*. Edited by J. C. Smith. 2 vols. Oxford: Clarendon, 1909.

———. "*The Fairie Queene*." Edited by A. C. Hamilton. 1977. Reprint, London: Longman, 1980.

———. *Minor Poems*. Edited by Ernest de Sélincourt and J. C. Smith. Oxford: Oxford University Press, 1970.

———. *Poetical Works*. Edited by J. C. Smith and Ernest de Sélincourt. Oxford: Oxford University Press, 1912. Reprint, 1935, 1960.

———. *Selections from the Minor Poems and "The Faerie Queene*." Edited by Frank Kermode. London: Oxford University Press, 1965.

Spevack, Marvin, ed. *Julius Caesar*. Cambridge: Cambridge University Press, 1988.

Stachniewski, John. "Calvinist Psychology in *Macbeth*." *Shakespeare Studies* 20 (1988): 169–89.

Stockholder, Kay. *Dream Works: Lovers and Families in Shakespeare's Plays*. Toronto: University of Toronto Press, 1987.

Stockwood, John. *A Very Faithful and Necessary Sermon*. London: Thomas Dawson, 1584.

Story, G. M. "Introduction." *Lancelot Andrewes: Sermons*. Oxford: Clarendon, 1967. xi–xlviii.

Strickland, Agnes. *The Life of Queen Elizabeth*. New York: George H. Doran, n.d.

———. *The Lives of the Queens of England.* Philadelphia: Lea & Blanchard, 1848.

Tiffany, Grace. "Anti-theatricalism and Revolutionary Desire in *Hamlet* (Or, The Play Without the Play)." *The Upstart Crow* 15 (1995): 61–74.

Toole, William B. "The Cobbler, the Disrobed Image, and the Motif of Movement in *Julius Caesar.*" *The Upstart Crow* 4 (1982): 41–55.

Traub, Valerie. *Desire and Anxiety: Circulations of Sexuality in Shakespearean Drama.* London: Routledge, 1992.

———. "Desire and the Differences It Makes." In *The Matter of Difference: Materialist Feminist Criticism of Shakespeare*, edited by Valerie Wayne. Ithaca: Cornell University Press, 1991.

Traversi, Derek. "*Julius Caesar*: The Roman Tragedy." In *Modern Critical Interpretations:* Julius Caesar, edited by Harold Bloom, 5–27. New York: Chelsea House, 1988.

———. *Shakespeare: The Roman Plays.* Stanford: Stanford University Press, 1963.

Tuve, Rosemond. *Allegorical Imagery.* Princeton: Princeton University Press, 1966.

Tyndale's New Testament. New Haven: Yale University Press, 1989.

Vawter, Marvin L. "'Division 'tween our Souls': Shakespeare's Stoic Brutus." *Shakespeare Studies* 7 (1974): 173–96.

———. "*Julius Caesar*: Rupture in the Bond." *Journal of English and Germanic Philology* 72 (1973): 311–28.

Velz, John. "Undular Structure in *Julius Caesar.*" *The Modern Language Review* 76 (1971): 21–30.

Vendler, Helen. *The Art of Shakespeare's Sonnets.* Cambridge, Mass.: Harvard University Press, 1997.

Vinge, Louise. *The Narcissus Theme in Western European Literature up to the Early Nineteenth Century.* Translated by Robert Dewsnap. Lund, Sweden: University of Lund, 1967.

Visser, Nicholas. "Plebian Politics in *Julius Caesar*." *Shakespeare in South Africa* 7 (1994): 22–31.

Vyvyan, John. *The Shakespearian Ethic*. London: Chatton & Windus, 1959.

Waddington, Raymond. "Lutheran Hamlet." *English Literary Notes* 27, no. 2 (1989): 27–42.

Walsham, Alexandra. *Providence in Early Modern England*. Oxford: Oxford University Press, 1999.

Watt, Tessa. *Cheap Print and Popular Piety, 1550–1640*. Cambridge: Cambridge University Press, 1991.

The Westminster Shorter Catechism. Phillipsburg, N.J.: P & R Publishing, 2003.

Williams, George W. "Pompey the Great." In *Renaissance Papers* (1976): 31–36.

Wilson, J. Dover. *What Happens in Hamlet*. Cambridge: Cambridge University Press, 1960.

Wilson, Richard. " 'Is This a Holiday?': Shakespeare's Roman Carnival." *English Literary History* 54 (1987): 31–44.

———, ed. *New Casebooks:* Julius Caesar. Houndmills, New York: Palgrave, 2002.

Wiltenburg, Robert. *Ben Jonson and Self-Love: The Subtlest Maze of All*. Columbia: University of Missouri Press, 1990.

Wordsworth, William. *The Prelude*, Book III (London: E. Moxon, 1805).

Zweig, Paul. *The Heresy of Self-Love: A Study of Subversive Individualism*. New York: Basic Books, 1968. Reprint, Princeton: Princeton University Press, 1980.

Contributors

Beatrice Batson, professor emerita of English at Wheaton College, holds the B.A., M.A., and Ph.D. degrees. She served as chair of the department of English for thirteen years and taught courses in Shakespeare for thirty-three years. Professor Batson is the author (or editor) of eight books—including editor of *Selected Comedies and Late Romances of Shakespeare from a Christian Perspective*, and the author of numerous chapters in edited volumes. She has also written many articles for journals and magazines, and scores of book reviews. During her teaching career, she was a frequent lecturer on college and university campuses in the United States and Canada. At present, Professor Batson is the coordinator of the Shakespeare Special Collection on Shakespeare and the Christian Tradition at Wheaton College.

David Daniell is professor emeritus of English at University College, London, and honorary fellow of Hertford and St. Catherine Colleges, Oxford. He is the author of numerous articles and books, including the Arden edition of *Julius Caesar*. For Penguin Classics, he edited William Tyndale's *Obedience of a Christian Man*. Yale University Press published his editions of *Tyndale's New Testament*, *Tyndale's Old Testament*, his critically acclaimed *William Tyndale: A Biography*, and *The Bible in English*. Forthcoming is his book on Shakespeare and Christianity.

Maurice Hunt (Ph.D. University of California, Berkeley) joined the Baylor faculty in 1981 where he currently serves as department chair. His teaching and research interests include Shakespeare; sixteenth-century English poetry and drama, especially the works of Edmund Spenser and Sir Philip Sidney; and the plays of Ben Jonson. Professor Hunt has published numerous articles for scholarly journals and essays for edited books; many of his writings focus on the works of William Shakespeare, including *Shakespeare's Romance of the Word* (1990), *Shakespeare's Labored Art* (1995), *"The Winter's Tale": Critical Essays* (1995) and *Shakespeare's Religious Allusiveness: Its Play and Tolerance* (2003). At present, he is editing Shakespeare's *Cymbeline* for the MLA New Variorum Series.

John W. Mahon, professor of English at Iona in New Rochelle, New York, is coeditor of *The Shakespeare Newsletter*, which Iona acquired from Louis Marder in 1991, through Mahon's initiative. He teaches Shakespeare and Irish literature, and has published in various journals, including *Hamlet Studies* and *The Shakespeare Newsletter*. He has contributed essays to several collections including those he has coedited *"Fanned and Winnowed Opinions": Shakespearean Essays Presented to Harold Jenkins* (1987) as well as *"The Merchant of Venice": New Critical Essays* (2002). For Shakespeare Association of America 2003 in Victoria, British Columbia, he and another Shakespearean directed a seminar on "Two Problem Plays of Shakespeare."

Peter Milward, SJ, was born in London, educated at Oxford. He went to Japan in 1954, studied Japanese, then theology at St. Mary's College, Tokyo, and was ordained a priest in 1960. He was on the faculty of theology before he began teaching in the department of English Literature at Sophia University in 1962 where his field of study was Shakespearean drama. He is the author of more than three hundred books, many of these on the Christian dimension of Shakespeare's works. Among his publications on Shakespeare are *Christian Themes in English Literature, Shakespeare's Religious Background,*

Religious Controversies of the Elizabethan Age, Biblical Influences in the Great Tragedies and *Biblical Themes in Shakespeare: Centering on "King Lear."* Professor Milward has also contributed essays to numerous edited volumes. Equally impressive is his output of articles, numbering approximately two hundred. In addition to being vice-chair of the Renaissance Institute of Sophia University, he is editor of Renaissance Monographs. He is also a frequent lecturer on Shakespeare in various countries.

Robert S. Miola (Ph.D. Rochester) is the Gerard Manley Hopkins Professor of English and professor of classics at Loyola College, Maryland. His research interests include Shakespeare, Renaissance drama and poetry, and the classical backgrounds of English literature. He is the author of *Shakespeare's Reading*; *Shakespeare's Rome*; *Shakespeare and Classical Tragedy: The Influence of Plautus and Terence*; *Shakespeare and Classical Tragedy: The Influence of Seneca*, as well as of numerous articles. At present, he is working on a new book, *The Catholic Renaissance: An Anthology of Primary Sources*, to be published by Oxford University Press.

Robert L. Reid, educated at Yale and Virginia, is the author of the recently published book, *Shakespeare's Tragic Form: Spirit in the Wheel*. He teaches at Emory & Henry College, where he is the Henry Carter Stuart Professor of English and English department chair. He has published articles on Shakespeare, Spenser, and Renaissance psychology in *Modern Philology, Studies in Philology, Renaissance Papers, Comparative Drama, The Upstart Crow, Hamlet Studies*, and *The Spenser Encyclopedia*. Professor Reid has lectured widely on Shakespeare and served as Shakespeare lecturer for the Virginia Foundation for the Humanities in 1988–1989.

Grace Tiffany is professor of English at Western Michigan University. Prior to coming to Western Michigan, she taught at Fordham and the University of New Orleans. She is the author of *Erotic Beasts and Social Monsters: Shakespeare, Jonson and Comic Androgyny,* and the editor of *Reformation, Religion, Rulership, and the Renaissance Stages*. Her articles on Shakespeare have appeared in *Shakespeare Studies, The Upstart Crow, Comparative Drama, Renaissance Quarterly* and others. Her novels include *The Turquoise Ring, Will, My Father Had a Daughter* and *Ariel*.

www.ingramcontent.com/pod-product-compliance
Lightning Source LLC
Chambersburg PA
CBHW030624230426
43661CB00053B/2137